America First!

America First!

Its History, Culture, and Politics

Bill Kauffman

Prometheus Books

59 John Glenn Drive
Amherst, New York 14228

Published 2016 by Prometheus Books

Inquiries should be addressed to

Prometheus Books
59 John Glenn Drive
Amherst, New York 14228
VOICE: 716–691–0133
FAX: 716–691–0137
WWW.PROMETHEUSBOOKS.COM

20 19 18 17 16   5 4 3 2 1

Library of Congress Cataloging-in-Publication Data Pending

978-1-63388-309-3 (pbk)
978-1-63388-310-9 (ebook)

Printed in the United States of America

So let us think about the people who lost.

—William Appleman Williams

Contents

Preface

Rereading a book one wrote in his salad days is not exactly like remasticating a twenty-plus-year-old salad, but it is a strange experience nonetheless.

One approaches the text with a measure of trepidation. *Did I really say that? My, what an intemperate young man!*

Nah, not really. Like Edward Abbey, I have become more radical as I grow older, but radical in the sense of "cutting away the overgrowth and getting back to the roots," as Allen Tate said.[1] Having roots, being anchored to a place, makes one at once radical *and* reactionary.

I wrote much of this book in the wake of the 1992 presidential election—the most interesting and significant of my lifetime, at least until 2016, and in neither case is a candidate surnamed Clinton or Bush at all germane to that significance. I will expatiate upon this in the epilogue—don't skip ahead!—and only say now that Donald Trump, in his crude and bombastic and sometimes-offensive but other times refreshingly provocative way, is a twenty-first-century amalgam of that earlier election's Pat Buchanan and Ross Perot, though without the former's intellectual acuity and the latter's Boy Scout patriotism. To continue the psephological parallel, Bernie Sanders is Jerry Brown, substituting Judaism for Jesuitism, and theoretical socialism reified in practical Vermont politics for disillusioned post–New Dealism delivered with New Age effervescence.

America First! (where in hell that exclamation point came from I

i

never did figure out) is a young writer's (late twenties, early thirties) attempt to construct his own pantheon after several years' immersion in regional and local color novels, Beat poetry and punk rock, libertarian and populist political history, and a homecoming about which I later wrote in *Dispatches from the Muckdog Gazette* (2003). Oh, and also my experience as a legislative assistant to Senator Pat Moynihan (D–NY)—"a transformative game changer!" in contemporary Babbitt-speak—for which I am forever grateful and from which I emerged a more or less pacific anarchist.

America First! is informed by a capacious and often-sentimental sympathy for "the people who lost," as the epigraph from the Iowa-bred New Left historian William Appleman Williams suggests.[2] Benjamin Schwarz, in the *Atlantic*, called *America First!* "as much a cultural polemic as a political one," and he had a point.[3] An efflorescence of North Dakota prose is ultimately more significant than any election could ever be.

Much of my subsequent career, if we can dignify (or cheapen) my literary wobble through American history with that dreary planning-for-retirement word, consists of variations upon that Williamsian theme. I have written since a biography (*Forgotten Founder, Drunken Prophet*) of Luther Martin, the most voluble (and maybe valuable) of the Anti-Federalists, those prescient critics of the US Constitution as the blueprint of empire; a discursive history of conservative and Middle American foes of expansion and militarism and war (*Ain't My America*); a film about an Upstate New York farmer, an old Jefferson-Jackson Democrat, who objected to the War between the States and paid the dissenter's price (*Copperhead*); and numerous essays and book chapters on the Loco Focos and populists and agrarians and isolationists and anarchists and Main Street patriots—Dorothy Day, Wendell Berry, Gene McCarthy, Carolyn Chute, Norman Mailer, Grant Wood—in whose lives and work we find the heart and soul of an America worthy of our love . . . a country of the Kiwanis Club and runaway slaves, Johnny Cash and Crazy Horse, Walt Whitman and the Daughters of the American Revolution.

Have I changed my mind about anything in the quarter century since I wrote this book? Of course; haven't you?

But while I've modified—no, let's say *refined*—certain opinions or historical judgments, I disavow nothing.

I've resisted the temptation to emend. I would rewrite some passages if I could, but I can't any more than I can time travel.

Two items do beg for revision.

First, I would no longer use the term "Americanist." True American culture (as opposed to the factitious corporate egesta spewing from the TV and the Web) is the fruitful sum and blend of ten thousand local cultures. It exists only insofar as Butte and Binghamton hum their own (distinctive) tunes. (I've written about this at length in *Dispatches from the Muckdog Gazette* and *Look Homeward, America*.)

Second, while I still believe that the failure to free the slaves by means other than a civil war that claimed 700,000 lives and put northern industrial capitalism into the driver's seat was the towering and tragic mistake of American history, I have developed a considerably higher opinion of certain 1850s Republicans and a correspondingly lower opinion of the generality of that decade's Democrats, most of whom were expansionists. And boy, did those chickens ever come home to roost.

The final third of the book, in which the Old Right and the anti-FDR Progressives of the 1930s give way to the 1990s insurgencies of left, right, and radical middle, limns themes that have not faded. To the contrary, they have intensified in this latest electoral cycle, given voice by the raucous campaigns of Donald Trump and Senator Bernie Sanders. The question of the hour is whether Trump, in particular, is an anomaly or a harbinger. The entirety of the Republican and conservative establishment hopes desperately that he is the former, and that after his defeat in November (for which they burn offerings to Baal, Bill Kristol, and both new and classic Kochs) he will disappear as thoroughly as Comet Hale-Bopp. GOP status quo ante will be restored, and an endless succession of Bushes and Bush epigoni (if such a thing be possible!) will stand for election on a platform of more war, more surveillance, more immigration, more trade deals, and lower taxes on those who fund their campaigns.

Then the *New York Times*, Yahoo! News, and our conformist clerisy will have the kind of opposition they prefer, which is to say no opposition at all. If, however, Trump and Sanders are foretokens— bellwethers of the Middle American populist revolt sketched in this book's final chapters, and adumbrated, in various ways, by the Perot, Buchanan, and Brown campaigns herein discussed—well, then the revolution's here. (That's a tip of the cap to Thunderclap Newman, not a call to violence: the American Empire, which over the last fifteen years has killed perhaps half a million Iraqis and Afghans and sacrificed almost ten thousand American soldiers and civilians to Moloch, has a monopoly on *that*.[4])

What else?

Mr. M and Henry W. Clune, whom we meet in the introduction, are dead. So is my friend and foreword writer Gore Vidal, a great American patriot whose maxim "I hate the American empire, and I love the old Republic" remains lapidary wisdom.[5] Gore, whose favorite politician was the populist-isolationist Huey Long, the Kingfish who was revered by the plain people and despised by the *New York Times* and all those who think only Approved Thoughts, would have loved the 2016 election.

John McClaughry, whom we meet in chapter 10, never did figure out a way to market Jeffersonianism for the age of the Kardashians and Twitter, though his Vermont begat the most refreshingly radical political eruption of the early twenty-first century: the small-is-beautiful Second Vermont Republic, which advocates seceding from the colossus. I wrote about these Green Mountain patriots and other decentralist movements in *Bye Bye, Miss American Empire* (2010). McClaughry disparages them as feckless hippies.[6] But then we love him for his curmudgeonliness.

I offer no excuse for the desultory nature of the endnotes, except to say that I had conceived this as an essayistic exercise in literary, cultural, and political history à la Edmund Wilson's magisterial *Patriotic Gore* and then realized, too late, that I really ought to tack on a few citations. (The bibliography is much better.)

The reader deserves to know my own biases. As I wrote in *Look Homeward, America*, "my politics are localist, decentralist, Jeffersonian. I am an American rebel, a Main Street bohemian, a rural Christian pacifist. I have strong libertarian and traditionalist conservative streaks." I am for peace, the Bill of Rights, and the local. Voting behavior is an unreliable, if not downright poor, index of anything beyond momentary caprice, but I cast my ballot for Bernie Sanders in April 2016. I've no idea what I'll do in November. Over the years I have voted, in primary and general presidential elections, for Ralph Nader, Pat Buchanan, Ross Perot, Jesse Jackson, Ron Paul, Barack Obama, and Gary Johnson. The peace candidates.

The single most consequential and dispiriting change in American political culture since this book's publication has been the virtual disappearance of a widespread commitment, even if only rhetorical, to freedom of speech.

When I was a boy, we used what seemed a hackneyed phrase to justify contrary opinions or actions: "It's a free country."

No one says that anymore. Because it's not true.

The uncompromising defenders of free, robust, even profane speech who made me a teenaged liberal—William O. Douglas, Lenny Bruce, Roger Baldwin, Allen Ginsberg—are heirless. The narrowing bounds of acceptable opinion are now patrolled not by FBI agents or scolding Mrs. Grundys but by nasty and humorless "social-justice" ideologues with the desiccated souls of concentration-camp guards. They are, to use a phrase that would set off enough trigger warnings to close Oberlin College for good, *un-American*.

America, like the good gray poet of Camden, who counseled "Resist much, obey little," contains multitudes, is self-contradictory, unruly, tolerant in a way that the hall monitors and tattletales of mandatory "tolerance" can never understand. It embraces the prickly; it listens to the cacophonous. It may hector and holler and heckle, but it will not shut you up. That's what Nazis and Trotskyites do. Alas, these censorious thugs have found in anti-social media their true métier.

"America First," as a tendency or allegiance, must stem from a love of one's own country, not the disparagement of others. If I love my own place, its history and cuisine and topography and music and even its foibles and its sins, then I must understand, and respect, others who love their own places. This is what I find most troubling about Trump: not his hyperbole, which is in the amusing tradition of American blowhard braggadocio, or his pugnacious refusal to bow to the false idols of political correctness, which is stirring and admirable, but his animadversions upon Mexico and its people. Raillery, yes; rivalry, okay; rancor—not for a patriot.

The only thing that really matters is love. "There is no truth excepting it is from love," as William Saroyan wrote in the novel that almost got him court-martialed.[7] Hate and war are the modus operandi of the ruling class and its shills. But at the end of all our exploring, love wins. Doesn't it?

NOTES

1. Allen Tate, "Remarks on the Southern Religion," in *I'll Take My Stand: The South and the Agrarian Tradition*, by Twelve Southerners (Baton Rouge: LSU Press, 1977/1930), p. 175.

2. William Appleman Williams, *Empire as a Way of Life: An Essay on the Causes and Character of America's Present Predicament along with a Few Thoughts about an Alternative* (New York: Oxford University Press, 1980), p. 212.

3. Benjamin Schwarz, "The Lost Crusade," *Atlantic* (April 2005).

4. "Casualties in Iraq," antiwar.com (accessed July 19, 2016); www.justforeignpolicy.org.

5. Charles Glass, "Gore, Poddy and Midge," *Spectator* (September 20, 1986): 13.

6. Bill Kauffman, *Bye Bye, Miss American Empire* (White River Junction, VT: Chelsea Green, 2010), p. 233.

7. William Saroyan, *The Adventures of Wesley Jackson* (New York: Harcourt, Brace, 1946), p. 247.

Foreword

Gore Vidal

In the mindless babble that passes for political debate in the United States nothing means what it appears to mean, particularly those key words "liberal" and "conservative." For political purposes the latter seems to have demonized the former. But has this really happened? Americans tend to be divided by race, religion, and class. The idea of a political idea is alien to our passionate folk and that is why Karl Marx and his admirers could never get through to so thoughtless a polity while neither Tom Paine nor Tom Jefferson made much impact. So-called liberals—always for some mysterious reason called "so-called" by conservatives; does this mean that conservatives want to be thought of as *true* liberals?—want to extend democracy as well as see to it that the Bill of Rights applies to everyone and that the Declaration of Independence, a truly radical liberal document, be heeded so that life, liberty, and the pursuit of happiness can be made available to each American, even William Safire.

I would have thought that all of this was fairly simple but now, thanks to television and to a myriad of religious and political demagogues, our average citizen is demonstrably the most ignorant in the First World, knuckles heavily calloused from too close a contact with the greensward as he lurches from error to error, all the while hating niggers and fags and uppity women and whatever else was put in his trough that week. Currently Americans are roughly divided between reactionaries and fascists (admittedly the latter involves a degree of thought and might be too difficult for TV-calloused brains). Officially, what passes for conservatism at this time is, at best, a liking for the status quo if the citizen has money and, at worst, a hatred of minorities if he doesn't—*they* are always the reason why he is income-challenged.

For years Bill Kauffman, the sage of Batavia, has been trying to make sense of our political scene. He has labored long in the Augean stable and, though he is no Hercules, he has cleaned out an interesting corner or two. By studying our history—something that is not allowed in Academe, say, while the media is pastless—he has latched on to some interesting facts (as opposed to opinions) that turn completely inside out the tedious liberal versus conservative debate, or grunting contest. He has discovered that from Jefferson to the Party of the People at the end of the last century (members known, for short, as populists) the strain of liberalism was a powerful one in our affairs. Extending the democracy, the literal meaning of liberalism, was very much a populist ideal despite the racism and sexism endemic to the Southern and Southwestern poor farmers and other mechanicals who followed the likes of William Jennings Bryan. The conservatives of the Atlantic seaboard were status quo types, quite happy to own the banks that collected the interest on farm mortgages. The rise of Bryan terrified them. Revolution was at hand. They fought back and, as one wrote to another in 1898, "A small war might take the people's mind off our economic problems."

Kauffman is at his best when he illuminates that most insidious word "isolationism." The people, in those days, were very much aware of their own true interests. They wanted access to cheap money. They wanted to be allowed to live their own lives without interference from government. They wanted no part

of the foreign wars that the moneyed conservative Eastern class
so much enjoyed and benefited from. The people knew that
they were the ones who would do the dying while the friends
of Theodore and Franklin Roosevelt, Woodrow Wilson, and
the last half dozen Oval Ones (oddities to a man) made the
money. The people at large took seriously George Washington's
warning against foreign entanglements. Mind our own business
which is business was his advice and so remains the centerpiece
of the true liberal doctrine.

With Franklin Roosevelt, the words "liberal" and "conservative" were reversed. Because, during the short-term New Deal,
he had made some liberal reforms (Social Security), he was
thought to be liberal, but at heart he was a traditional Eastern
conservative, with a love of foreign wars inherited from his first
employer, Woodrow Wilson, and from his cousin Theodore
before that. The people, instinctively liberal in these matters, and
their tribunes wanted no part of either the First or the Second
World Wars. So the conservative media, generally Anglophile,
painted the liberal majority of the country as racist dullards who
would not take part in profitable foreign adventures for fear
of being killed. The word "isolationist" became synonymous with
Southern racism and rural backwardness. The conservative
minority defeated the liberal majority, as we all know. Two deadly
wars were fought. From the first we got, aside from the dead
and wounded, fifteen years of the prohibition of alcohol, which
turned the whole country lawless, as well as an all-out assault
on the Bill of Rights that has continued, with occasional truces
(the Warren Court), until this morning.

From the Second War we got a permanently militarized
economy which, to date, has given us four trillion dollars worth
of debt and a worn-out infrastructure which can no longer be
repaired unless the economy is demilitarized, something our
conservative rulers don't want to do and the liberal majority
doesn't know how to do. An essential part of the militarized
economy is the enormously profitable "war" on drugs which must

always be fought but never, ever won. There would be no problem, of course, if the prohibition of drugs were repealed, a liberal notion, of course.

So we end up with all the key political words turned inside-out. Once that happens, as Confucius wisely noted, no state is governable since the people cannot understand their rulers and the rulers cannot understand themselves much less the people. Meanwhile, we must preserve the free world (actually un-free; we have elections but no politics) from—let's see, Kim Il Sung's son and his atomic armada; and then there is Haiti where we must restore order and justice and freedom as we did when Franklin Roosevelt invaded the island (he was in the Navy Department at the time, and one of the bizarre lies that he liked to tell ever after was how he, personally, had written the excellent constitution of Haiti). Perhaps Gulf War II might be useful, to justify the military budget and the taxes that now go almost entirely for "Defense" (Social Security income and outgo are separate from the budget, a fact that is kept permanently secret from the taxpayers who are supposed to respond in a Pavlovian way to "wasteful people programs").

Let us hope that Kauffman's ideas start to penetrate and that the potential mind-our-own-business liberal majority will come to its senses and convert a military to a peacetime economy before we end up with a glamorous Brazilian economy and political system as well as, to be fair, a Brazilian-class soccer team.

Introduction

I stood with Mr. M, my parents' 94-year-old neighbor, in the garden he has cultivated since before the Flood. He cut some rhubarb stalks and remembered his twentieth birthday, Armistice Day 1918. He was not enthusiastic about the First World War.

"That was one maybe we shoulda stayed out of," I offered.

"We shoulda stayed out of them all," said Mr. M, a rock-ribbed Republican and Scots-American and Methodist, in roughly that order. Mr. M ran the YMCA for many years; befitting his position, he was a stalwart of the local GOP. A gymnasium and a Sunday School class are named for him.

"I'm worried about this thing in Bosnia," he said, wiping the sweat from his brow. (He'd been weeding for two hours under a springtime sun before I came along.) "We always get into these wars. None of our business. Why don't we just stay over here and let them take care of over there. Don't send 'em money, nothing."

Mr. M volunteered that he'd voted for George Bush in 1992 but regretted it; he was eager to vote for "this guy Perot" next time, when he will be ninety-seven, a year older than the century.

The novelist Henry W. Clune, who, at 103, is Mr. M's senior, was similarly vexed by the war drums when I saw him the next day.

"It's stupidity," he said, sipping his martini. "I'm like Fred Allen: I'd resign from the human race if I could get my membership fee refunded. We're trying to police the world when we can't even police our own streets."

Henry is a Main Street Republican born during the administration of President Benjamin Harrison, whose only memorable utterance is a Clune-ish "we have no commission from God to police the world." Henry cast his first vote for William Howard Taft in 1912. He became disaffected in the 1960s, when he denounced the Vietnam War as an "obscene enterprise" in his Gannett newspaper column. He was for normalcy in 1920 and America First in 1940 and peace in 1966. (Henry does remember, as an eight-year-old, pinning a "Remember the *Maine*" button to his chest. He was hawkish on the Spanish-American War, but we can forgive him this youthful indiscretion.)

Henry is the remarkable incarnation of Students for a Democratic Society (SDS) President Carl Oglesby's contention that "the Old Right and the New Left are morally and politically coordinate."[1] (Henry's one unpublished novel, *Retreat,* which he wrote in his late seventies, was sympathetic toward a Vietnam-era draft-dodger.)

The Republican party of Mr. M and Henry W. Clune no longer exists. Nor does the Democratic party of William Jennings Bryan and Huey Long and Senator Burton K. Wheeler. We are afflicted with belligerent intellectuals every bit as eager to entangle us in wars that Middle America does not want as the Schlesingers, the Achesons, and the Rusks were. But there is no Robert Marion La Follette, no William Edgar Borah, no Robert A. Taft to represent what Sinclair Lewis called the Mind Your Own Business party. And it is my contention that the dearth of America First leadership in the political arena is the consequence of the fading of what I call "Americanist" culture. Only by reviving this culture will the provincial and particularistic patriotism that was among our noblest tendencies flower once more.

No, we haven't a Republican party to speak for Main Street. Nor have we a national Democrat in the anti-imperialist grain. We are blessed, however, with a remnant of extraordinary men—Mr. M and Henry W. Clune, for instance—who remember what America used to be, because they built it, they grew it, they wrote it, and for them, at least, it will never die.

And for us?

The American Republic is deader than "Fighting Bob" La Follette. But unlike the good senator, the Republic can be revivified. The most controversial political movement of our day seeks to do just that. This book is about America Firsters, past and present. It is about the world that Messrs. M and Clune knew. And one that we can still know.

First, let's define these hobgoblin terms *populism* and *isolationism*. American populism in its various guises has been distinguished by three basic beliefs: (1) concentrated wealth and power are pernicious; widespread distribution is the proper condition; (2) war and militarism are ruinous to the republic and to the character (not to mention physical health) of the populace; and (3) ordinary people can be trusted to make their own decisions. This trio of values has been mangled beyond recognition in establishment historiography. Richard Hofstadter, the laureled historian who, in *The Paranoid Style in American Politics,* ascribed all dissent from the Cold War consensus to mental illness, sneeringly put it in his *The Age of Reform* (a 1955 Pulitzer Prize winner): "Populist thought often carries one into a world in which the simple virtues and unmitigated villainies of a rural melodrama have been projected on a national and even international scale."[2] The excrescences of populist thought include "such tendencies in American life as isolationism and the extreme nationalism that usually goes with it; hatred of Europe and Europeans; racial, religious, and nativist phobias; resentment of big business, trade-unionism, intellectuals, the Eastern seaboard and its culture."[3]

This is topsy-turvyism at its most tendentious: it was the populists, after all, who in both world wars *opposed* exporting bombs and bayonets to massacre "Europe and Europeans." Above all, populism is the raw and honest voice of Middle America: it speaks for the Kansas farmer against the Wall Street financier, for the tattered hired hand against the cosmopolitan, for the hardscrabble against the money pit, for us against them. It has been slandered and mauled and buried more times than we can count. In its recurring forms it has never been tolerated in the way that fringe movements sometimes are, because there is nothing fringe about it: American populism is patriotic and incendiary. When John Lydon of the punk rock group the Sex Pistols snarled, "We mean it, man," his remark encapsulated what makes populism so dangerous.

Central to the populist faith was the maintenance of the isolationist foreign policy of the Founding Fathers. To a man they abjured war and imperialism and the fatiguing phantom of the white man's burden.

"Isolationist" is meant to be an invidious word. Created to smear opponents of war, the term has been rejected by most of its purported exemplars. Nevertheless, the latest generation of "isolationists" is by and large comfortable with this quondam pejorative. I prefer the word to "noninterventionist" because it connotes a belief in American exceptionalism (though there are isolationists, for instance some doctrinaire libertarians, whose devotion to the "where liberty dwells, there is my country" principle precludes any attachment to this land beyond the theoretical).

I shall use "isolationist" to indicate those Americans who believe that the defense policy of these United States ought to be just that—defense against direct or immediate threats to our territory. This means, in practice, an opposition to (1) imperialism (which is to say, we should not have acquired such spoils of the Spanish-American War as Puerto Rico or the Philippines); (2) wars or interventions on behalf of internationalist principles (such as World War I, which was to "make the world safe for democracy") or at the behest of global political entities (e.g., U.S. participation in United Nations police actions in Somalia, Bosnia, and Lebanon); and (3) institutions or treaties that transfer U.S. sovereignty to international or multinational bodies (the League of Nations, the North American Free Trade Agreement, and possibly the United Nations).

Isolationists have, in the main, opposed U.S. involvement in the Spanish-American War, the First and Second World Wars, the Korea and Vietnam conflicts, the Gulf War, and the various petty invasions (of the Dominican Republic, Nicaragua, Grenada, Haiti, and Panama) that have become a staple of twentieth-century American statecraft. Isolationists are a vigorous, contentious, spirited lot, averse to orthodoxy and witchhunts; there has never been a party line, and various personages have supported the odd war or treaty. In contemporary politics, I apply the term to such disparate figures as Ross Perot, Gore Vidal, and Patrick J. Buchanan, who among them have enough rifts and ruptures to cleave and sink the entire state of California.

The classic expression of American isolationism was George Washington's farewell address of September 17, 1796, a statement partly ghosted by Alexander Hamilton. The president counseled, "The great rule of conduct for us in regard to foreign nations is, in extending our commercial relations to have with them as little *political* connection as possible. . . . It is our true policy to steer clear of permanent alliances with any portion of the world" (original italics). With foresight Washington saw that "excessive partiality for one foreign nation and excessive dislike of another" would lead to a disastrous situation wherein "real patriots who may resist the intrigues of the favorite are liable to become suspected and odious."

President Washington also warned against "overgrown military establishments which, under any form of government, are inauspicious to liberty." A century and a half later these "military establishments" had evolved into the huge "military-industrial complex" against which President Eisenhower cautioned in his own farewell address. The current combined military and foreign assistance budget runs in excess of three hundred billion dollars a year, and we are committed to defending more than forty nations.

The last stand of American isolationism—before its remarkable revival in the 1990s—was made by the America First Committee (AFC) in 1940–41.

The AFC has received such uniformly bad press for half a century that today it exists, in the public mind, as a ragbag of foaming primitives and goose-stepping German-American beerhall bullies, sprinkled with a pinch of high-toned Mayflower descendants who barred Jews from country clubs.

This is a victor's history, complete with demonization of the vanquished foe, and it is absurd. America First was born in September 1940 and died at Pearl Harbor. Dedicated to the proposition that "American democracy can be preserved only by keeping out of the European war," the AFC attracted 850,000 card-carrying members and millions more sympathizers, mostly in the Midwest. Its rallies and newsletters amplified antiwar cries of all strains and accents, from Socialist Norman Thomas to progressive stalwarts Senator Gerald P. Nye and journalist John T. Flynn to the greatest American hero, aviator Charles Lindbergh. It was populist and patrician, Main Street and windswept prairie, Exeter and Sauk Centre. Financial backers included meatpacking mogul Jay C. Hormel and Sterling Morton of the salt company; e.e. cummings was a card-carrying member, as was Sinclair Lewis. Young America Firsters included John F. Kennedy and Sargent Shriver, as well as Gerald R. Ford, who, however, resigned when he feared that his activities might cost him his job as assistant football coach at Yale.

America First agreed with the radical essayist Randolph Bourne, who had said, apropos of America's entry into World War I, that "war is the health of the state." Traditional American liberties—the freedoms of speech, assembly, petition, association, and trade—were endangered by the culture and economy of militarism. Oswald Garrison Villard, columnist and former editor of the *Nation,* retired from that journal when in 1940 the magazine renounced its venerable near-pacifism and whooped it up for a war that Villard predicted "will inevitably end all social and political progress, lower still further the standard of living, enslave labor, and, if persisted in, impose a dictatorship and turn us into a totalitarian state." The old liberal marveled "that a Hitler beyond seas could so have swept the greatest republic from its moorings."[4] (The *Nation*'s editor, the noxious Stalinist Freda Kirchwey, countered that Villard's was "exactly the policy for America that Nazi propaganda in this country supports"—a neat example of the way in which the smear techniques used against isolationists in 1940 prefigured those used against peace activists barely a decade later. Senator Joseph McCarthy said nothing that hadn't already come from the mouth of Kirchwey or FDR's hatchet man Harold Ickes.)

The America Firsters were in no wise pro-Hitler or even vaguely fascist. Indeed, the creed of most members—the nineteenth-century liberal standard of equal rights under law, limited and decentralized government, strict adherence to the Bill of Rights, and the maintenance of an army whose sole purpose was the protection of American soil—was the antithesis of fascism, with its emphasis on a planned economy, the transfer of power from the provinces to the capital, a huge government workforce, and bloodletting expansionist crusades. It was those elements that prosper under fascism which underwrote and oversaw the U.S. drive toward war. As Senator Robert Taft asserted on the eve of Pearl Harbor:

> The most conservative members of the party—the Wall Street bankers, the society group, nine-tenths of the plutocratic newspapers, and most of the party's financial contributors—are the ones who favor intervention in Europe. . . . The war party is made up of the business community of the cities, the newspaper

and magazine writers, the radio and movie commentators, the Communists, and the university intelligentsia.[5]

Ah, but we are lectured, America First can never expiate its original sin, that of anti-Semitism. The leading historian of the America First Committee, Wayne S. Cole, finds this defamation groundless. The AFC included a number of Jewish pacifists, radicals, and Middle American conservatives. (Sidney Hertzberg, the AFC's publicity director, was one of several Jews in prominent positions within the organization.) The committee refused any cooperation—indeed, any acknowledgment of common ground—with such pro-Nazi or Germanophile groups as the German-American Bund. Nevertheless, the charge rankled, and in the subsequent fifty years America First—the largest antiwar organization in our history—has been tainted largely because of one speech delivered by one man: Charles Lindbergh in Des Moines, Iowa, on September 11, 1941. The aviator's theme was as follows:

> The three most important groups who have been pressing this country toward war are the British, the Jewish, and the Roosevelt Administration. Behind these groups, but of lesser importance, are a number of capitalists, anglophiles, and intellectuals. . . .[6]

The only member of this bellicose trio for whom Lindbergh offered sympathetic exculpation was American Jewry. In three paragraphs—what Cole calls "Lindbergh's only public reference to the Jews"—America First's reputation was forever sullied:

> It is not difficult to understand why Jewish people desire the overthrow of Nazi Germany. The persecution they suffered in Germany would be sufficient to make bitter enemies of any race. No person with a sense of the dignity of mankind can condone the persecution of the Jewish race in Germany. But no person of honesty and vision can look on their pro-war policy here

today without seeing the dangers involved in such a policy, both for us and for them.

Instead of agitating for war, the Jewish groups in this country should be opposing it in every possible way, for they will be among the first to feel its consequences. Tolerance is a virtue that depends upon peace and strength. History shows that it cannot survive war and devastation. A few far-sighted Jewish people realize this, and stand opposed to intervention. But the majority still do not. Their greatest danger to this country lies in their large ownership and influence in our motion pictures, our press, our radio, and our Government.

I am not attacking either the Jewish or the British people. Both races, I admire. But I am saying that the leaders of both the British and the Jewish races, for reasons which are as understandable from their viewpoint as they are inadvisable from ours, for reasons which are not American, wish to involve us in the war. We cannot blame them for looking out for what they believe to be their own interests, but we also must look out for ours. We cannot allow the natural passions and prejudices of other peoples to lead our country to destruction.[7]

Just how these remarks qualify as anti-Semitic rhetoric remains a mystery. One may strongly disagree with Lindbergh's argument but it contains nothing repellent or even incontestably untrue. I shall deal in chapter 3 with Lindbergh's (and Senator Nye's) assertion that "Jewish influence" was producing motion pictures frothing with warlust: I find the charge overstated and misguided—in fact, wrong—but it is certainly a defensible position. In any event, the blot of anti-Semitism will stain the reputations of several of the men discussed in this volume— often unfairly.

It is strange that the antiwar movements of the 1960s to the 1990s pay no homage to America First, which was broader, more inclusive, and far more populist than the admirable but often one-note opposition to the Vietnam, Central American, and Gulf wars. Polls taken in the late fall of 1941 found the vast majority of Americans—as much as 80 percent—against our entering the European war as combatants, even though there was substantial support for the *ignis fatuus* of "aid short of war."

Then came that December day in Hawaii (whose annexation the populists and isolationists of the 1890s had bitterly opposed: how the fates play their little jokes). America First sentiment would endure at the grassroots level but would go unrepresented in national discourse for fifty years. To the horror of both political parties and seemingly every academic and journalist and talking head in our land, America First has returned. Where did it come from? Where is it going? Glad you asked.

I am deeply grateful to Allan Carlson and Thomas Fleming of the Rockford Institute and Antony Sullivan of the Earhart Foundation for keeping the creditors—well, most of them—at bay while I wrote this book. Tom and Allan are the grand young men of the resurgent Old Right (or right-wing Newer Left?) and their thumbprints can be seen all over the more sensible parts of this book. My effusive thanks, too, to Gore Vidal for his counsel, his foreword, and his example.

For help, encouragement, and suggestions at various times, I also thank Wayne S. Cole; Arthur A. Ekrich, Jr.; the late Murray N. Rothbard; Justus Doenecke; Leonard Liggio; Ralph Raico; Bill and Martha Treichler; Kate Dalton; Charles Augello; Henry W. and Peter H. Clune; Robert Koch; Paul Gordon and Jay Pascucci; Bill Bradford; Joseph Peden; Laura Main; Maria Andonian; Paul M. Buhle; Carl Oglesby; the late Phil Fixler; Jesse Walker; Greg Kaza; Thomas O. Melia; Karl Zinsmeister; Louis Mario Nanni; Father Ian Boyd; Kelly Ross; Mike Kauffman; Eric Marti; Andres Leetmaa; Lucy and Lindsay Aspergren; Marty Zupan; Bob Poole; Chaz Ruffino; George and Ann Gray; John Groom; Paula Meyer; Martin Wooster; Ted Carpenter; Jane Kauffman; Dorothy Coughlin; Barry Gifford; John Montgomery; Frank Annunziata; Mark Shephard; Lew Rockwell; the staffs of the Richmond Memorial, Genesee Community College, and University of Rochester libraries—and Lucine Kauffman, of course.

NOTES

1. Carl Oglesby, "Vietnamese Crucible," in Carl Oglesby and Richard Schaull, *Containment and Change* (New York: Macmillan, 1967), p. 67.

2. Richard Hofstadter, *The Age of Reform* (New York: Vintage, 1955), p. 73.

3. Ibid., p. 20.

4. Oswald Garrison Villard, "Issues and Men," *The Nation,* June 29, 1940, p. 782.

5. Quoted in Murray N. Rothbard, "The Foreign Policy of the Old Right," *Journal of Libertarian Studies* (Winter 1978): 88.

6. Quoted in Wayne S. Cole, *Charles A. Lindbergh and the Battle against American Intervention in World War II* (New York: Harcourt Brace Jovanovich, 1979), p. 161.

7. Ibid., pp. 171–72.

Part One

The Evolution of
Populist Antiwar Sentiment

1

Ham 'n' Amos: The Populist and Patrician Roots of America First

"The patriot never under any circumstances boasts of the largeness of his country, but always, and of necessity, boasts of the smallness of it."
— G. K. Chesterton, *The Napoleon of Notting Hill* (1904)

Thomas Fleming, the editor of *Chronicles*—and perhaps the only man ever to listen reverently to both the Tennessee agrarian novelist Andrew Lytle and the avant-garde rock-and-roll band the Velvet Underground—has called the incipient Middle American revolt of the 1990s a battle of "Nebraska against New York." This powerful populist metaphor has yet to be concretized: no two glamorous senators are closer than Omaha's Bob Kerrey and Pat Moynihan of New York's Hell's Kitchen (or, as the waggish ex-Mayor Ed Koch put it, "Hell's Condominium"); the prairie schooners of revolt in North Platte and Hastings are not leading war parties against Manhattan.

Still, Fleming's trope is a brilliant one, for the roots of the present rebellion against the American Empire can be found in the midland states of a century ago. And no better guide exists than the self-proclaimed "son of the middle border," Hamlin

27

Garland, whose fury and scattershot lit the skies of an age in which Nebraska, in the person of the sweating "missionary isolationist" William Jennings Bryan, really did wage war against the New York of J. P. Morgan and Theodore Roosevelt and the dragon Wall Street.

HANNIBAL HAMLIN GARLAND

Hannibal Hamlin Garland, named for Lincoln's first vice president, was born in 1860 in Green's Coulee, Wisconsin, "a delightful place for boys." His father, Richard, had been a Maine carpenter who spent a lifetime moving west, ever optimistic that the cornucopia lay over the next meadow. The Garlands moved to Minnesota, and then to Iowa, where Richard took a town job as buyer for the Grange, the farmers' cooperative which acted as seedbed for the coming agrarian revolt. Hamlin went to school at the Cedar Valley Seminary, where he developed a wicked sinker ball. After a period of wanderlust and a teaching stint, Hamlin rejoined his family in the Dakota Territory, where Richard and his wife, Isabel, were struggling to be like novelist Ole Rölvaag's giants in the earth. Hamlin staked his own claim, with an eye toward turning a profit; but a winter spent "in a pine-board shanty on a Dakota plain with only buffalo bones for fuel" made him "eager to escape the terror and the loneliness of the treeless sod."[1] So with the brash and engaging heedlessness of his pioneer father, Hamlin set off for Boston to make his mark.

"No Jason ever sought a Golden Fleece with less knowledge of the seas before him," Garland later recalled. He was a brown-bearded rube in a "Prince Albert frock of purplish color"; Stephen Crane, whom he would befriend, said he looked "like a nice Jesus Christ." Garland rented a room on Boylston Place, "a dismal blind alley" near the public library, which he haunted for ten hours a day, taking time out for the fifteen-cent lunch of bread and meat which sustained the penurious pilgrim. Discouraged that he was not permitted to check out books without an endorsement, Garland worked up the nerve to pay a visit to Edward Everett Hale, whom he remembered as a name on a card from the "Authors" game he had played as a boy on rainy days. Hale kindly assisted the rough-hewn mendicant, and Garland was on his way.

"Outwardly seedy, hungry, pale and lonely, I inhabited palaces and spoke with kings," Garland later recalled. He read with desperate avidity, mindful of the inexorable dwindling of his $140 stake. He read Herbert Spencer, Walt Whitman, and the economist Henry George. This unlikely triad nurtured in Garland a confluence of sentiments that made him a walking, talking, fire-snorting omnibus of American populism. He was a romantic individualist whose pulse raced with what Thomas Wolfe would call "the richness, fabulousness, exultancy and wonderful life of America." Yet he saw clearly the bleakness and desolation of life on the pitiless frontier: "no beauty, no music, no art, no joy—just a dull and hopeless round of toil. What is it all worth?" Garland asked after a trip home in 1887. He was a staunch Jeffersonian, a believer in widespread distribution of private property, a decentralized and minimal state, and "individual liberty as opposed to the socialistic ideal." Yet Garland parted company with the Sage of Monticello on one critical issue: while he detested paternalistic government he preached Henry George's doctrine of common land ownership.

As a lecturer, a book reviewer, and then a short story writer, Hamlin Garland conquered literary Boston—at least its non-Brahmin precincts. William Dean Howells, dean of American letters, was taken with the nervy young outlander who interrupted him at dinner to expound his theory that "American literature, in order to be great, must be national, and in order to be national must deal with conditions peculiar to our own land and climate. Every sincere writer must write of the life he knows best and for which he cares most."

Garland found a patron in Benjamin O. Flower, publisher of the quirky monthly *The Arena*. Flower played Maecenas to a stable of bards, visionaries, and kooks. While one critic called him "an egregious fellow, ready and willing to swallow any proposed reform without the slightest preliminary examination,"[2] Flower's enthusiasm and generosity fueled Garland's determination to play the unheard music: "I was feeling my way toward a delineation of life in Iowa and Dakota, a field in which I had no predecessor."

Joseph Kirkland, whose *Zury: Meanest Man in Spring County* (1887) was Illinois's best-known work of local color, encouraged Garland with all the hyperbolic rhetoric of friendship: "You are the first actual farmer in literature. Tolstoy is a make-believe. You are the real thing."

Garland was young and green enough to buy it. Benjamin Flower brought out Garland's first book, a collection of six stories titled *Main-Travelled Roads* (1891), whose tone was set in the dedication and epigraph. The book was for "my father and mother," Garland wrote, "whose half-century pilgrimage on the main-travelled road of life has brought them only toil and deprivation." (Isabel thanked her son for this curiously condescending inscription; the proud Richard said nothing.) The main-traveled road, claimed the author, was "long and wearyful, and has a dull little town at one end and a home of toil at the other." The stories depict farmers and their wives beaten by the elements, dumb luck, and a rigged system into slack-jawed hebetude. Though Garland was later to sing, "Youth and love are able to transform a bleak prairie town into a poem, and to make of a barbed-wire lane a highway of romance," the transmutative properties of love are absent here. Even a weary Union private coming home to his "beautiful valley" in Wisconsin "is looking down upon his own grave." Fellow feeling and kindness, the currencies that were to circulate so freely in the Friendship Village stories of another Wisconsin writer, Zona Gale, rarely obtrude, though one farmer does allow, "When I see a man down, an' things on top of 'm, I jest like t' kick 'em off an' help 'm up. That's the kind of religion I got, an' it's about the *only* kind." (Deliverance, according to the story "Under the Lion's Paw," was simple: adopt Georgist libertarianism!)

William Dean Howells spoke of the book in glowing terms: "If any one is still at a loss to account for that uprising of farmers in the West which is the translation of the Peasant's War into modern and republican terms, let him read *Main-Travelled Roads.*" Angry, credentialed, and itching for a fight, the young radical took his place on the front lines of agrarian revolt.

On *The Arena*'s money, Garland spent 1891–92 riding the rails—some 30,000 miles worth, he estimated—"meeting all the leading advocates of revolt in the South and West." The author claimed, "I'm going west to listen mainly," but he wrote, too: in 1892 alone Garland published four books, three of them (*Jason Edwards, A Member of the Third House,* and *A Spoil of Office*) fervent propaganda novels on behalf of the People's, or Populist, party.

In Hamlin Garland, the most prolific Populist novelist and an accomplished speechifier, too—he crisscrossed Iowa in 1891 and 1892 stumping for the party—we find a populism that is both ardent and thoughtful, measured and radical, sanguine and morose. Garland was committed to populism by both blood and intellect. The Grange, the agrarian cooperative for which his father worked briefly, served—together with the more militant Farmers' Alliance—as kindling for the Populist brushfire. Richard was a county officer of the People's party in South Dakota; like most American fathers of writers he dismissed his son's vocation as sissified, though he wept with pride when at the Omaha People's party convention of 1892 Hamlin read "Under the Lion's Paw" to a thunderous ovation.

The convention cheered madly for the platform preamble, which was drafted and delivered by silver-tongued Ignatius Donnelly, the ex-congressman from Minnesota:

We meet in the midst of a nation brought to the verge of moral, political and material ruin. Corruption dominates the ballot-box, the legislature, the Congress. . . . The people are demoralized. . . . The newspapers are largely subsidized or muzzled, public opinion silenced, business prostrated, our homes covered with mortgages, labor impoverished, and the land concentrating in the hands of the capitalists. The urban workmen are denied the right of organization for self-protection, imported pauperized labor beats down their wages, [and] a hireling standing army, unrecognized by our laws, is established to shoot them down. . . . The fruits of the toil of millions are boldly stolen to build up colossal fortunes for a few unprecedented in the history of mankind, and the possessors of these, in turn, despise the republic and endanger liberty. From the same prolific womb of governmental injustice we breed the two great classes—tramps and millionaires.[3]

Solutions were plentiful, pullulating like mushrooms after a shower. While Populists generally shared a Jeffersonian bias toward the small producer, the family farmer, and the skilled workman, their remedies ranged from the free coinage of silver to widespread use of initiative and referendum to a Georgist land-tax to discourage speculation. (This final scheme was written into the platform by Garland and his ally, the great Kansas crusader Sockless Jerry Simpson.)

Conforming to Richard Hofstadter's caricature, Garland's political novels do feature villains waxing mustaches as well as coquettish damsels virginal beyond belief. But though suffused with the didacticism of the evangelist—"my grandiose plan for a panoramic novel of agricultural unrest degenerated into a partisan plea for a stertorous People's Party," Garland later admitted of *A Spoil of Office*—they teem with ideas, often pungently expressed.

No soapbox is safe when Garland takes pen in hand. In a typical passage from *A Spoil of Office* his alter ego Radbourn, a Populist journalist, catechizes: "Every year the army of useless clerks increases; every year the numbers of useless buildings increases. The whole thing is appalling, and yet the people are getting apparently more helpless to reform it. Laws pile upon laws, when the real reform is to abolish laws. Wipe out grants and special privileges. We ought to be legislating toward equality of opportunity in the world. . . ." (A venerable judge in the novel criticizes the Grangers for demanding "class legislation" rather than "equal rights for all, special privileges for none.")

Garland the saturnine plowboy was also an indignant moralist. In *A Member of the Third House* lobbyists are "a body of corrupt men who stand between the people and legislation." Venality flourishes "in the fumes of whiskey and tobacco." Garland remained a staunch prohibitionist right up to the repeal of the Eighteenth Amendment. This is difficult to square with his passion for individual liberty; William Jennings Bryan, himself a teetotaler, perhaps had it better when he defended the legal sale and consumption of alcohol on the grounds of personal freedom.

In *The Arena* Garland explained the Populist creed: "We are individualists, mainly, let that be understood at the start. We stand unalterably opposed to the paternal idea in government. We believe in fewer laws and the juster interpretation thereof." As president of the Boston Anti-Poverty League he strenuously opposed government ownership of railroads, arguing that "we are advancing along the line of absolute freedom, and it is not freedom to put into governmental hands . . . the running of trains." Garland's antimonopolism carried him so far as to bemoan the absence of competition in mail delivery.

"Free trade, free land, free men!" declared the pamphlets he often enclosed with his correspondence, to the irritation of such conservative friends as the novelist Mary E. Wilkins. ("Free love," on the other hand, was never a hobbyhorse: although his novel *Rose of Dutcher's Coolly* was denounced by bluenoses for hinting that farmgirls know whence babies come, Garland was in reality a prude who could be made apoplectic by a single cinematic glimpse of Clara Bow's gams.)

While some Populists urged socialist measures—usually nationalization of the railroads and utilities, industries that had battened on government subsidies and were now quite beyond the discipline of the market—most remained tenacious Jeffersonians. C. Vann Woodward has written of the populists of the 1890s:

> Individualistic and middle-class in tradition and aspiration, they accepted the basic capitalist system. [Georgia Populist Thomas] Watson summed up their objectives: "Keep the avenues of honor free. Close no entrance to the poorest, the weakest, the humblest. Say to ambition everywhere, 'the field is clear, the contest fair; come, and win your share if you can!' "[4]

Even Benjamin Flower, lover of the outré, communer with the dead, follower of barefoot prophets, declared Populism to be "a revolt of the millions against the assumption of paternal authority on the part of the general government, and the prostitution of this authority or power for the enriching of a favored few."

The old Populists, unlike their America First heirs, welcomed free trade; they held with John Taylor of Caroline, the farmer-theorist of early nineteenth-century Virginia, that tariffs create "a capitalist interest, which instantly seizes upon the bounty taken by law from agriculture; and instead of doing any good to the actual workers in wood, metals, cotton or other substances, it helps to rear up an aristocratical order, at the expense of the workers in the earth." The tariff is mother to the trust, went the shibboleth, and on this matter the children of Whitman and George and Herbert Spencer agreed.

But not all populists urged the wholesale repeal of laws. Platform author Donnelly, lovingly known as the "Prince of Cranks," had been a Minnesota congressman and indefatigable gadfly who mixed speculative books on Atlantis and Bacon's authorship of Shakespeare's plays with an almost frighteningly intense agrarian radicalism.* In his dystopian novel *Caesar's Column* (1890), Donnelly envisions an America of 1988 in which the government owns all the guns; "newspapers are simply the hired mouthpieces of power"; and a stunted, mongrelized workforce toils for multinational megacorporations until the peons commit suicide "by the pleasantest means possible" and their corpses are burned in the huge furnaces that rage all through the night. "We are a republic in name, free only in forms," shouts one radical. Yet the author asserted, "We have but to expand the powers of government to solve the enigma of the world": certainly a Garlandian libertarianism did not constitute the whole of agrarian populism.

In Donnelly's novel—still a fast and exciting read, by the way, similar to Jack London's *The Iron Heel*—we see in stark outline the populist bogeys: overweening and meddlesome government determined to stamp out dissent; corporate media that are handmaidens to the state; large rootless financial interests that profit from war; the defenselessness of farmers, laborers, and small businessmen; and the alloying of the American population through immigration and annexation. Unfortunately, in Donnelly's nightmare "the aristocracy of the world is now almost altogether of Hebrew origin." This suspicion about Jews as clannish and not entirely trustworthy Americans, though repudiated by many populists and subsequent generations of America Firsters, was to become an albatross around their necks. Time

---

*A case can be made for the Populists as the most literary of American political parties. The Omaha convention also hosted a contingent of "Nationalists" who dreamed of the regimented heaven described in Edward Bellamy's 1887 sensation *Looking Backward.* A Mississippi Valley variation on Bellamy's theme by an Iowa reformer was Henry Olerich's bizarre and suggestively titled 1893 novel *A Cityless and Countryless World.* Olerich's dystopia is a sterile planet in which all particularistic loyalties—to country, town, neighbor, family, even children—have been extirpated. One thousand atomistic individuals live in identical eight-story high dwellings spaced at regular intervals. They are what Aldous Huxley, in his preface to *Brave New World,* called "slaves who do not have to be coerced, because they love their servitude." Helots have always been with us, even in so refractory a lot as the Populist party.

and again we will see populist isolationists calumnied as anti-Semites—a baseless charge, in most cases.

When in 1898 the United States waged against Spain what John Hay called a "splendid little war," U.S. imperialism stretched far across the seas. President McKinley's decision not to grant independence to the Philippine Islands, which we had acquired from the defeated Spanish, created an opposition that was at once populist and patrician, very much like the America First Committee of 1940–41. Anti-imperialists included William Jennings Bryan and Massachusetts Senator George Frisbee Hoar, Mark Twain and Henry Adams, Henry James and Hamlin Garland. (This last pairing is not as queer as it appears. James had praised Garland for his "saturation" in the life of his region; he dubbed the author "the soaked sponge of Wisconsin.")

"Everybody but myself seems to be thirsting for blood," Garland fretted in April 1898. We had "stumbled and sinned in the dark," the poet William Vaughn Moody memorably put it. Populist Tom Watson spoke for his party on the Spanish-American War:

> The privileged classes will profit by this war. It takes the attention of the people off economic issues, and perpetuates the unjust system they have put upon us. Politicians profit by this war. It buries issues they dare not meet. What do the people get out of this war? The fighting and the taxes. What are we going to get out of this war as a nation? Endless trouble, complications, expense. Republics cannot go into the conquering business and remain republics. Militarism leads to military domination, military despotism. Imperialism smooths the way for the emperor.[5]

(In the First World War Watson's hatred of conscription, which he regarded as enslavement, was so fierce that this avowed racist defended, in the pages of the *Jeffersonian,* two Georgia Negroes who had resisted registration. Shortly thereafter the *Jeffersonian,* along with other native American radical antiwar publications, was barred from the U.S. mails by the Wilson administration.)

Racial themes run through anti-imperialist literature. James T. Du Bois, in the poem "Expansion" (1900), has his narrator encounter a variety of exotics who, when asked where they're from, reply "Puerto Rico, U.S.A.," "Santiago, U.S.A.," "Manila, U.S.A.," and so on. Exasperated, he huffs:

> "Hully gee," says I, "I never heard o'
> These here cannibals before.
> Air these heathens yere all voters?
> Will we stan' fur enny more?
> Nex' you know you'll ask a feller
> Whur he's from, he'll up an' say
> With a lordly kind o' flourish,
> 'All creation, U.S.A.' "[6]

This belief in a pure America for Americans, unsullied by foreign strains or influences, was given stirring treatment in Garland's 1894 manifesto *Crumbling Idols*. Seven years earlier, he had asked of his native Midwest, "Why has this land no story-tellers like those who have made Massachusetts and New Hampshire illustrious?"

The void was to be filled by what Garland termed "veritism," or a politicized form of the local color school of fiction. The twelve essays in *Crumbling Idols* exhort hinterland Americans to ignore "Eastern comment" and old world decadence to create five, ten, one thousand regional literatures. "Each locality must produce its own literary record," Garland insisted. Of his own case, he said:

> I am a Western man; my hopes and ambitions for the West arise from absolute knowledge of its possibilities. I want to see its prairies, its river banks and coules, its matchless skies, put upon canvas. I want to see its young writers writing better books, its young artists painting pictures that are true to the life they

live and the life they know. I want to see the West supporting
its own painters and musicians and novelists; . . . the Western
writer must, above all other things, be true to himself and to
his time. To imitate is fatal. *Provincialism (that is to say, localism)
is no ban to a national literature.*[7] (Original italics)

"Be true to your own land," is the counsel that recurs throughout *Crumbling Idols*; it is the cultural complement to the isolationist view that America must tend its own house, right its own
wrongs, and serve as example to the world, not be master of it.

"I assert it is the most natural thing in the world for a
man to love his native land . . . the nearest-at-hand things are
the dearest and sweetest after all." Garland's was more than the
sentimental patriotism of the exile; in any event, in 1893 he had
removed to Chicago and bought his toil-weary parents a home
in West Salem, Wisconsin, where the author was to summer
in subsequent years. Garland's enlightened parochialism—his
awareness that love, if it is to be enriching, must be directed
rather than diffused—is essential to the Americanist worldview.

Just as wealth and power ought to be dispersed, so must
the cultural life of the nation. Garland called it "decentralization
together with . . . unification," and he did his part by setting
up shop in Chicago, despite his distate for the slaughterhouse
city as "an ugly, smoky, muddy town built largely of wood and
without a single beautiful structure."[8]

Provincialism, after all, was the precondition for a national
political and literary revival. It was no coincidence that the
insurgent inland populism paralleled the explosion of regional
fiction whose paladins included Sarah Orne Jewett of Maine,
Mary E. Wilkins of Massachusetts, E. W. Howe of Kansas,
Harold Frederic of upstate New York, Edward Eggleston of
Indiana, and many others. Garland envisioned such cities as St.
Paul, St. Louis, Cincinnati, and Denver as literary centers that
would surpass New York and Boston, just as he hoped that
populism would restore a Jeffersonian Arcadia. With Whitman-

esque flourish, he predicted that this efflorescence "will be born of the mingling seas of men in the vast interior of America, because there the problem of the perpetuity of our democracy, the question of the liberty as well as the nationality of our art, will be fought out."[9] Garland may have been wrong in his prophecy, but his dream was neither silly nor ignoble. (In "Democratic Vistas," Whitman, whose individualist politics were similar to Garland's, had identified as "our fundamental want" of 1870s America "native authors [and] literatures.")

Harold Ross, founder of *The New Yorker,* liked to boast that his magazine was not for the little old lady in Dubuque, but Garland knew that freshwater readers "possess a broader Americanism and a more intimate knowledge of American life than the aristocrat who prides himself on never having been farther west than Buffalo."

When Garland got cranking, no one was immune to his enthusiasms. He visited Henry James at Rye in 1899 and marveled that his host "had no understanding of the midland America. Chicago was almost as alien to him as a landscape on Mars." A few minutes of Ham's feverish panegyrics were all it took— at least in Garland's retelling—to convert the expatriate to Americanism. James allegedly confided, "If I were to live my life over again, I would be an American. I would steep myself in America, I would know no other land. I would study its beautiful side. The mixture of Europe and America which you see in me has proved disastrous. It has made of me a man who is neither American nor European."[10] (Garland's acuity is open to question. He once confidently wrote of Will Rogers, "He does not drink or smoke.")

Hamlin Garland was a nativist; he looked with suspicion on the polyglot and multiethnic "turbulent millions" who crowded into New York City, and he wondered whether they carried the germ that would destroy his country. "Millions of these people have never been west of the Hudson River. What can they know of America? What do they care of America?"

Garland's distaste for immigration, at least in his early years, owed less to any feeling of racial superiority than to his belief that newcomers, whether German or Italian or Polish, transplanted Old World cultural forms onto native soil when what was needed was an autochthonous American flowering. He quoted with approval his friend, the composer Edward MacDowell: "If a composer is sincerely American at heart, his music will be American. Almost any hack composer can imitate the Persian, Chinese, or any other racial music, but the spirit is not caught. The weakness of our music is in its borrowing."[11]

Echoing the dark suspicions of Ignatius Donnelly, Garland scribbled in his diary in 1926: "The Jews are gaining possession of courts, the law business, publishing, theater, moving pictures and by the weight of their numbers and wealth they will soon control the expression of opinion here. And as the whole nation gets a large part of its information from here, that information is un-American at its very source." (In his defense, Garland championed author Israel Zangwill and other Jewish writers; his grievance was with Jewish immigrants who were not, in his view, willing to become assimilated Americans.)

"People of my kind are dying out," Garland lamented. "We are already submerged. These floods of peasants from southeastern Europe and from Russia and Poland are sweeping away all that Whitman and Emerson stood for." In an October 1915 speech to a teachers' convention in Albany he stated: "It is no longer a question of rooms filled with German and Scandinavian children taught by an American teacher; it is a question of foreign teachers and foreign pupils. What becomes of the American tradition in such schools? You may say it is well to abandon American traditions, but I cannot do so."[12]

Garland did, however, abandon the Middle Border, in part because he felt that it had abandoned him. His pique at Midwestern critics who execrated him as "a bird willing to foul his own nest" combined with his aborning love of the Rocky Mountain West and his discouragement over the People's party's ebbing to lead him to write a series of profitable romances about High Country life that fattened his bank account and eroded his reputation. Garland wrote of the Hopi, the Ute, Cripple Creek miners; but he wrote as a tourist, an act of effrontery he had warned against in *Crumbling Idols.*

Garland remained a Jeffersonian and an American isolationist: he voted for Bryan in 1900 despite the fact that running for vice president on the Republican ticket was his bosom pal, Theodore Roosevelt, "frien[d] and fellow enthusias[t] for the West and Western literature"[13]—and a pro at flattering those, like Garland, who could be ensorcelled by a wink from the mighty. Garland would oppose the United States' entrance into the First World War, and he was furious at President Wilson in 1916 for picking a fight with Mexico: "I would be willing to help defend our border but I don't believe in subjugating these small brown men. . . . The War Spirit is aflame and I fear we are entering upon a long period of militarism."[14]

Garland went over to the enemy, at least on the surface, by taking up residence in Manhattan in 1916. He busied himself with family biography (*A Daughter of the Middle Border* won the Pulitzer Prize for 1921, always a bad sign) and the doings of the American Academy of Arts and Letters, the Elks Club of American litterateurs. He confessed to feeling "the disease for social advancement," and when taunted by young enthusiasts for his capitulation he replied, "thirty-five years is a long while to carry a mood." The hustle and bustle of modern life repelled him, and in his blacker fits of spleen he doubted the system of "American enterprise" itself, as "sons were deserting their work-worn fathers, daughters were forgetting their tired mothers. Families everywhere were breaking up. Ambitious young men and unsuccessful old men were in restless motion. . . ."[15]

Garland left New York in 1931 for Los Angeles, where he inveighed against a decadent Hollywood while sniffing the lotuses. (Bathing suit ads in the *Los Angeles Times* were a particular bugbear.) After an Iowa Society dinner in Los Angeles,

Garland wrote in his diary that the six hundred expatriate attendees were "nonliterary, nonaesthetic and utterly outside the dinner coat zone"—the haughty remark of a bitter dotard cut off from that which had nourished him. He was equal parts odd duck and old fogey: he busied himself attending séances and supervising an award for diction on the radio (an invasive invention he hated) and composing four volumes of a tedious "literary log," which measures its subjects (from Howells to the novelist Irving Bacheller) by the grandeur of their houses and the robustness of their bank accounts. Their "sumptuous desks and easy chairs" trump his "meager income." The title of one volume, *My Friendly Contemporaries,* suggests the work's general insipidity.

There is a pathetic quality to these final books. Hamlin Garland the midlands bohemian is revealed to be Hannibal H. Garland, an envious and insecure West Salem burgher who marvels that Henry Ford "did not appear to despise me for my failure to make money." He sedulously courted those of higher social station and was grateful when these rich ninnies didn't patronize or dismiss him, as Garland believed they had every right to do. He grew old and lonely and crestfallen, convinced that he would be forgotten by a decaying America. The writer whom H. L. Mencken had crowned a "stranger on Parnassus" had become a stranger in his own land.

"I have not the faith I once had in the future of the Republic. The far future is now a stormy shadow!" Garland exclaimed in 1930. In the New Deal he saw profligacy and the whip. In 1938 he wrote, "The reckless spending of money by our Congress, dictated by the President, the war threat in the old world and the lowering of standards in human conduct appall me. . . . [M]y children and my grandchildren . . . may be regimented by a dictator and his aides. They may be rationed by heads of bureaus. They may cease to be free agents."[16]

When Hamlin Garland died in 1940, few mourned his passing, for he was recalled as some kind of hazy populist, a relic in an age of consolidation and bigness. As for his most original contribution, *Crumbling Idols,* well, that was cultural America Firstism run amok, and in 1940 Americanism, at least of Garland's kidney, was quite beyond the pale in an America primed for war.

The Garland with dirt under his fingernails deserves better. So does the fiery young polemicist playing catch with Stephen Crane, arguing over the fine points of "inshoots" and "outdrops" (curves and sliders) and talking revolution.

William Allen White, the Emporia, Kansas, newspaper editor and novelist, recalls in his autobiography that upon meeting Garland "his passion for his cause disturbed me." Even after the acquaintance blossomed into friendship, White found Garland "always serious, always a rebuke to our ribaldry." (In his diaries, Garland calls White "fat boy.")

But in the end, the stern lad from the Middle Border kept the faith while the jocose pudgy Kansan sold out. In 1940, the year Hamlin Garland died, William Allen White chaired the Committee to Defend America by Aiding the Allies, the chief antagonist of the isolationist America First Committee. As his son admitted, White's name was valued by the Eastern seaboard-dominated committee because his name "savored . . . of the traditionally isolationist Midwest." Like Arthur Vandenberg, Harry Truman, and other heartland opportunists who converted from antiwar provincialism to belligerent internationalism, White is honored in death while those who remained truer to their region's temperament and traditions repose in obscurity or disgrace. The most-traveled road of all remains that of the recreant.

AMOS R. E. PINCHOT

Wealth gains fools the entree to power, but once in the door, house rules apply. The fool may be silly or sordid, gushingly liberal or brutally social darwinist, but ironclad decorum dictates that he never, ever question the system that swept him up into such lofty surroundings.

By 1904 the populist moment had passed. The idols stood intact. The presidential contest pitted Hamlin Garland's admirer (and ideological opposite) Theodore Roosevelt against Wall Street lawyer Alton Parker—"two drinks from the same jug," sneered Populist standard-bearer Tom Watson, who tallied barely 100,000 votes. Salons and ladies' leagues and reform clubs were spawning the movement known as progressivism, which was urban, technocratic, distrustful of the hoi polloi, and eager to vest unelected— ergo, pure—civil servants with unthinkably broad powers. Progressivism foisted upon the American people the First World War and the city manager system, conscription and Prohibition. It was everything populism was not, but within progressivism's genteel hurly-burly a brooding and athletic young dandy materialized to grab the Garlandian baton and carry it, eventually, all the way into the America First Committee.

Amos R. E. Pinchot helped bankroll ex-President Theodore Roosevelt's antic Bull Moose campaign of 1912. This was, Pinchot later realized, a catastrophically stupid decision, an act of naivete born of class solidarity and guilelessness. He did not make the same mistake twice.

Amos Pinchot is known today, if at all, merely as the younger brother of Gifford Pinchot, the Pennsylvania leader of the conservation movement. Gifford fit snugly into the Rooseveltian camp: he cherished Hamiltonian notions of state power and had a zealot's belief in the malleability of man; he remained an ardent prohibitionist well after everyone this side of Bishop Cannon (and Hamlin Garland) had written the noble experiment off as a colossal blunder. Amos, on the other hand, extolled liberty, which in the twentieth century has not been a wise career move.

By virtue of birth and his famous brother, Amos was usually Among Those Present, but he was always joining futile insurgencies or impossible rebellions; he is a footnote in histories of the era, his name often appearing midway through a list of feckless plotters. His influence was scant. Amos Pinchot had audiences with presidents, he corresponded with Theodore and Franklin Roosevelt, he wrote for most of the major liberal journals of his day, but no one listened; the maps he drew for the captains of state he knew wound up in every important trash can in America. Yet as a thinker, a polemicist, and an activist he is a critical link in the America First chain to such postwar avatars as Gore Vidal and Edmund Wilson, whom we shall take up in later chapters.

Amos Richards Eno Pinchot was born in Paris in 1873 to a wallpaper import baron who resided in Gramercy Park, New York, and summered in Milford, Pennsylvania. The Pinchot home in Milford, a French-style chateau known as Grey Towers, is now administered by the Forest Service. High atop a hill overlooking Milford and the Delaware River, it sits in shady isolation, a home suitable, perhaps, for a wealthy anchorite but not for a little boy. Landscaping later done under the supervision of Amos's sister-in-law Cornelia features Lucullan touches—including an oval wading pool at which visitors took lunch, passing lavish dishes in wooden vessels through the water—which may go a long way toward explaining why Cornelia lost several races for the House of Representatives.

Amos was Skull and Bones at Yale and, after serving as a private in the Spanish-American War and practicing law briefly, he devoted all his time to managing the family money while Gifford trod the muddy path of political ambition. Amos, a "society swell," whiled away the hours counting the Pinchot fortune and parting with a fraction of it through what he termed "civic dissipations"—throwing alms to the poor, the confined, and the insane, not to mention parties for the usual cultural charities.

Chief Forester Gifford Pinchot's run-in with President Taft in the once-famous Ballinger case (involving improprieties in the leasing of Alaskan lands to mining interests) lured Amos into the public arena. Filial affection embroiled him in politics, and though H. L. Mencken once jibed that politics is as fatal to a gentleman as a bordello is to a virgin, Amos tested the water and found it fine. He penned a long tedious screed for the September 1910 *McClures* magazine, "Two Revolts against Oligarchy," in which he drew an unconvincing parallel between the Republicans upholding the freeman's banner during the Doughface-dominated 1850s* and the progressives fighting the good fight in the Taft years. "The Insurgents are the true Republican party," he claimed; the modern slaveowners were the railroads, industrial trusts, and high-tariff men. The article made an inexplicable splash, and Amos was off on a thirty-year career as a publicist dedicated to the proposition that "wealth is merely another name for power over every phase and function of society."

As charter members of the National Progressive Republican League, formed in 1911 to promote an alternative to President William Howard Taft, Amos and Gifford Pinchot pumped twenty thousand dollars into the incipient campaign of Senator Robert La Follette before abandoning "Fighting Bob." At first they tried to persuade the mulish La Follette that his talents were best suited to being number-two man on a ticket topped by the inimitable Teddy Roosevelt. Their efforts at persuasion proving fruitless, the Pinchots simply dumped La Follette as they would an unneeded servant, using as a pretext the senator's rambling, denunciatory, semicoherent address to newspaper publishers on February 2, 1912. (La Follette claimed exhaustion accounted for his dismal performance; enemies hinted at neurasthenia, drunkenness, or sheer lunacy. La Follette's intended point—that newspapers had become mouthpieces of the

---

*The flaw in Pinchot's analysis is that the Doughfaces, those Northern Democrats (and Whigs such as Millard Fillmore) solicitous of the slave interests of the South, were generally strict constructionists, while the Republican party of John C. Fremont and Abraham Lincoln sought to expand the powers of the central government. The protectionists and barons of industry against whom Amos Pinchot railed would have been far more comfortable with Abe Lincoln than with Stephen Douglas.

great fortunes and the most puissant interests—may have led
some of his audience to exaggerate his level of incoherence.)

The betrayal of La Follette was a disastrous gambit by Amos,
if not by Gifford, whose paternalistic instincts were much closer
to Roosevelt's New Nationalism than the La Follette brand of
shopkeeper-farmer populism. "Roosevelt has always been able
to pull the wool over [Gifford's] eyes,"[17] Amos said to La Follette,
whose anger was assuaged when a contrite Amos later subsidized
his antiwar research.

How could Pinchot have miscalculated so badly? In 1911
Teddy Roosevelt recognized the dichotomous nature of progressivism:

> Half of [us] are really representative of a kind of rural toryism,
> which wishes to attempt the impossible task of returning to the
> economic conditions that obtained sixty years ago. The other
> half wishes to go forward along the proper lines, that is, to
> recognize the inevitableness and the necessity of combinations
> in business, and meet it by a corresponding increase in gov-
> ernmental power over big business; but at the same time these
> real progressives are hampered by being obliged continually to
> pay lip loyalty to their colleagues, who, at bottom, are not
> progressive at all, but retrogressive.[18]

Rooseveltian progressivism found its house theorist in
Herbert Croly, founder of the *New Republic,* the weekly that,
with its clarion calls for war—whether in Europe, Korea, or
the Middle East—has grimly performed its job as sexton, burying
the old republic. In his *The Promise of American Life* (1909),
Croly set out to "emancipate American democracy from its Jeffersonian bondage." The republic requires "more rather than less
centralization," Croly stated; he reserved his hosannas not for
the boy at the plow or one of Whitman's strong-bodied mechanics,
but for "the huge corporations [which] have contributed to
American economic efficiency." Oversized corporations were not
only efficient but inevitable, and the small independent business-

man, a relic of the "individualist and provincial democracy" of our forbears, had better get big or get out.

By contrast, the La Follette-Amos Pinchot retroprogressives "preferred an individualistic, rural, small-town social structure, with wide distribution of property and power,"[19] writes Wayne S. Cole, the grand old historian of Midwestern progressivism. While Amos Pinchot was at social poles from the angry patrons of husbandry and the merchants of Gopher Prairie, his bias toward dispersive Jeffersonianism bridged the cultural gap. He never shed his Gramercy Park snobbishness: he dismissed Iowa Senator Smith W. Brookhart, whom he deemed an imbecile, as "a typical product of the Middle West," and the insult was understood. But of course one can defend the liberties of The People without desiring to sit down and break bread with them.

Failing to wrest the GOP nomination from Taft, Roosevelt and his acolytes and sugar daddies (including the brothers Pinchot) hastily cobbled together a Progressive party, popularly known as the Bull Moose. Though the jerrybuilt party's social base was drawn from the Newport tans of Ward McAllister's 400 and other social registries, the Progressives were so riven by sectarianism as to make American socialism seem like an extended von Trapp family. And at the center of the infighting, on the nation's front pages for the only time in his life, was Amos R. E. Pinchot.

George W. Perkins, the Morgan partner and organizer of the Harvester trust, whom Alice Roosevelt Longworth called "the Dough Moose," served as chairman of the national executive board of the Progressive party. Perkins bore the Herbert Croly stripe: he sincerely believed that bigger was better, and that a return to a nation of small farmers and independent artisans living in autonomous communities was impracticable and, moreover, contrary to economic law.

There is no reason to believe that Perkins did anything but represent the biases of the Bull Moose himself; the financier was, as his biographer, John A. Garraty, writes, "a brilliant com-

petitor who eschewed competition" and assumed the inevitable
triumph of "large business units." Any insurgency led by a
Morganite was bound to be tame and utterly unthreatening; the
irony is that Wilson *and* Taft were each much closer to Amos
Pinchot's politics than was his consolidationist hero, Roosevelt.

In the confusion of the slapdash Progressive convention held
in Chicago in the summer of 1912, George Perkins gutted the
antitrust plank, expunging favorable mention of the Sherman
Act, and Pinchot went into orbit—although he delayed making
this internecine battle public until after Roosevelt had gone down
to defeat with only eighty-eight electoral votes.

The ex-president had good-naturedly accepted Pinchot's
unsolicited advice for several years—"a Cassandra to the Colonel"
is how Pinchot saw himself—but the colonel's forbearance went
only so far. Pinchot dashed off a letter to "My dear Colonel
Roosevelt" on December 3, 1912, urging that Perkins be removed
as "titular" head of the party because this "director of the Steel
and Harvester trusts" had "emasculated our platform in the
interest of big business."

His "dear Colonel" was tolerant of Pinchot's reproving mis-
sive—at least once he cooled off. He counseled his intemperate friend not "to alienate the moderate men": "My dear
Amos . . . remember that the ability to think and act independ-
ently is no more essential than the ability to get on with others
in work for a common cause. . . . [Y]ou impair the power of
your future usefulness if you give the impression that you never
can work with any people for an achievable end."[20]

Pinchot remained unpropitiated. In the best aristocratic
tradition, he was anything but tongue-tied in the presence of
mere politicians. ("Hang it, there's only a month left; let us be
vulgar and have some fun—let us invite the President," said Mr.
Bonnycastle in Henry James's story "Pandora.") In May 1914
Pinchot sent a circular to the members of the Progressive party
national committee demanding that Perkins be removed from
his chairmanship:

> To talk against monopoly, to place the words "Social and
> Industrial Justice" upon our banner, and then to hand over this
> banner to a man who has been monopoly's ardent supporter
> and one of the most distinguished opponents of social and
> industrial justice that our generation has produced, is, in my
> opinion, a handicap to the party, and a fraud on the public.
> It is also highly and destructively ridiculous.[21]

The dispute was now in the open—Amos R. E. Pinchot
in one corner, George W. Perkins and J. P. Morgan in the other—
and every malefactor and editorial writer in New York jumped
on the innocent blueblood. The *New York Times* huffed, "To
drop [Perkins] at the cry of the wild and restless spirits in the
movement would be to serve notice that devotion to the cause
is of no value unless it is leavened with insanity." With inadvertent
shrewdness, the *New York World* stated, "Amos Pinchot cannot
read George W. Perkins out of the Progressive party without
reading Theodore Roosevelt out, too."

Roosevelt had had his fill. "Amos has not enough capacity
for coherent thought to make him a Socialist; he is a kind of
parlor anarchist or amateur I.W.W. [Industrial Workers of the
World] follower," he complained to a fellow Progressive in
November 1914. "He is utterly impotent as a foe and the only
damage he can do is as a treacherous friend and he should never
be allowed inside the ranks again."[22]

The occasional references to Pinchot in Roosevelt's letters
grow more splenetic: he is one of the "restless, mischievous
creatures" who associate with anarchistic Wobblies and pacifists
and suchlike riffraff. "We dignify Amos Pinchot needlessly by
giving the slightest heed to his antics," Roosevelt curtly put it
in November 1914. The vascular colonel's followers, taking a
cue from his bullying demeanor, clenched fists and growled:
imperialist Senator Albert Beveridge, in a letter he wrote but
never sent to Pinchot, threatened, "I only wish you were here
and that I had the physical strength to thrash you."

Pinchot was an irritant, a nuisance. He was rash and headstrong, and he paid for it. In a 1916 speech he referred to his old Colonel as "the bell hop of Wall Street"; Roosevelt, on hearing about this, broke off relations with this brusque note of November 3, 1916:

> Sir: When I spoke of the Progressive party as having a lunatic fringe, I specifically had you in mind. On the supposition that you are of entire sound mind, I should be obliged to say that you are absolutely dishonorable and untruthful. I prefer to accept the former alternative.[23]

For pulling back the curtain on the Progressive Oz, Amos Pinchot was dispatched not to Kansas but to Coventry. Yet, in hindsight, his case against Perkins is airtight. Amos did not, after all, accuse the financier of malfeasance or venality but rather of excessive fealty to big business, a loyalty Perkins made manifest every day of his adult life. (Of J. P. Morgan, Sr., Perkins said in 1915, "There was never a man in a place of big responsibility toward labor who was a better friend of the working man. "[24])

Support for Amos Pinchot's position slowly emerged. Bull Moose vice-presidential candidate Hiram Johnson, the blustering Californian with whom Hamlin Garland had taken to the hustings in 1912, blamed Perkins for subverting the party. And Bull Mooser Harold Ickes, in his reminiscence published in *American Historical Review* (January 1941), "Who Killed the Progressive Party?" likewise fingered Perkins as the homicide. (Ickes never mentions Pinchot, who by then dwelt in discredited obscurity.)

Being right, as we shall see time and again, is no defense in American political life. Excommunicated, Pinchot joined the "unhung traitors," in Roosevelt's pungent curse, who wanted to steer clear of the European madness. Pinchot endorsed Wilson in 1916 because "he kept us out of war," and he served as chairman of the American Union Against Militarism and testified before Congress against the suppression of antiwar publications. ("He is always right," said Wilson advisor Colonel Edward House—"at the wrong time.")

Pinchot's radicalism sharpened. He was an angel (in the financial sense) and contributor to the socialist *The Masses*. He championed the Wobblies and, indeed, all strikers. He was a founder of the National Civil Liberties Bureau, which later became the American Civil Liberties Union, upon whose executive committee he sat until his death. He honed his prose style until it actually became readable, spiking his fact-laden attacks on monopolies with the free-swinging wit of a man who knows he's a fanatic and can't help it. He wrote for the *New York Times* and *Anthracite Labor News*, *The New Republic* and *The Masses*—whoever would publish him. (It helps, of course, when you're signing the checks that pay the editors.) Pinchot subsidized Senator La Follette's wartime research (thus healing, with green sutures, the rupture of 1912), and in December 1919 he helped found the Committee of 48, an organization of old-fashioned liberals seeking to create a third party incorruptible by a Perkins and immune to the heart-swelling thump of war drums. He blenched from the socialists who overran the group's July 1920 convention in Chicago that was to nominate Parley P. Christensen for president; he and his confrere George Record walked out when what was to be a red, white, and blue convention discarded the latter two colors. Pinchot supported La Follette and Wheeler in 1924, Al Smith in 1928, and in 1932 he pronounced the Hyde Park Roosevelt "by all odds the best man nominated by either party since Woodrow Wilson"—although within five years he was badgering FDR that "if a leader pursues the path of bureau—cratic regimentation of industry and agriculture, he must go forward into dictatorship, whether he wants to or not."[25] FDR dismissed Amos, who kept pestering him with captious letters, as a mere crank, too insignificant to work up a lather over.

What, exactly, did Amos Pinchot want? What strange obsession impelled him virtually to will himself into a pariah?

Like all good obstreperous Americans, Pinchot hated coercion. He was a voluntarist, not a socialist, and he understood monopoly and imperialism to be twin menaces to the republic. As a Jeffersonian, he idealized human-scale competitive enterprise and the widespread distribution of wealth and political power. He hated bigness of any sort; as Otis L. Graham, Jr., wrote in his excellent study *The Old Progressives and the New Deal,* Amos Pinchot was "a courageous individualist for whom reform meant a battle against size."

In his several roles—as a libertarian, a eulogist of small-scale democracy, a foe of militarism, and a critic of a governing class that he believed had become very nearly an occupying army—Amos R. E. Pinchot was the compleat and prototypical America Firster.

"Better than anyone, except perhaps A. J. Nock in our time, he was a precursor of the libertarian movement," writes historian Arthur A. Ekirch.[26] The libertarian pedigree is obvious in Amos's defense of *The Masses'* right to publish, his cofounding of the ACLU, and his conviction that the New Deal carried the seeds of dictatorship; it is seemingly eclipsed, however, by his advocacy of government ownership of railroads and utilities.

Even at his most unlibertarian, in calling for public ownership of the railroads, Pinchot invoked his favorite professor, individualist sociologist "Billy Sumner," and said that he was only trying to keep "equal chance alive." The largest financial interests were using the Iron Horse "to destroy free competitive industry"; the "industro-financial baronage" that controlled transportation was fixing prices and driving out competitors. The railroads, with their massive land grants and subsidies, had largely been a creation of the Gilded Age; the resultant octopus "concentrates wealth, concentrates power, and results in the defeat of democratic theory."[27] Only the untried expedient of public ownership could restore the premonopoly competitive economy that had built America. "We must make transportation and raw materials . . . accessible to all on even terms," Pinchot argued. "That

is why I advocate government ownership of railroads and . . .
natural resources."[28]

He saw as the challenge of the day "to break the power
of the monopolistic groups, reestablish competitive industrial life
and restore in production, distribution, and politics . . . the 'equal
chance.' " To this end Pinchot urged Teddy Roosevelt (unsuccessfully) to advocate steep reductions in tariffs.

Theodore Roosevelt "frequently took me to task for my
unorthodoxy on the trust question," Pinchot recalled years later,
"remarking that men like Brandeis and myself would never be
happy until the steel industry had been reduced to the blacksmith
shop, and the railroads to the eighteenth-century stagecoach."[29]

This is the standard tactic used on twentieth-century Jeffersonians: to admit to the emotional appeal of their vision but
to scoff at its hopelessly backward-looking romanticism. In fact
there never was anything inevitable about the triumph of
gigantism; as economic historians ranging from Marxist Gabriel
Kolko to free marketeer Murray N. Rothbard have shown, the
largest corporations grew fat precisely because the level playing
field Pinchot demanded had been tilted by the array of subsidies,
licensing arrangements, tariffs, import quotas, and tax advantages
that stock the monopolists' armory.

Like his mentor Sumner, Pinchot was a thoroughgoing anti-
imperialist. His American Union Against Militarism failed to
keep the United States out of the First World War, and, as
with so many radicals of his vintage, he always feared a replay.
The "radical" position of Pinchot and the leading congressional
isolationist, Senator La Follette, included opposition to the
Conscription Act, the Sedition Act, and the Espionage Act. For
upholding the frayed American banner of free men and free
speech, they suffered every calumny and were nearly driven out
of public life.*

---

*A novel proposal supported by Pinchot, La Follette, William Jennings Bryan,
and a populist-radical liberal coalition called for a public referendum on any
congressional declaration of war. Retired Rear Admiral Samuel McGowan added

"War," lectured Pinchot on behalf of another peace group, the Committee for Democratic Control,

> means the turning of labor from the creating of food to the making of munitions. . . . War means the suppression of civil liberties here, or at the very mildest, the domination of the military element. . . . War would mean the risk of putting our domestic liberties at the mercy of the most reactionary groups. And if our concern is not for our own liberties but for the liberty of the world, let us ask ourselves what democratic contribution could be made to the world after the war by an America in the grip of its most illiberal forces.[30]

Pinchot was dismissed as an isolationist; but like such political compadres as Senators William E. Borah (R-Idaho) and James Reed (D-Missouri), he rejected drawbridge protectionism. These men were not pacifists, yet they consistently denounced U.S. meddling in Nicaragua and our potential involvement in such international tribunals as the World Court, which, as Senator Gerald Nye (R-North Dakota) charged, "is being forced upon our Nation, not by the people who would provide against future wars, but by men who are the makers of war, the international bankers."[31]

Pinchot denied that his brand of isolationism was the cartoonist's ostrich-in-the-sand indifference to world affairs. Like the colorful Marine General Smedley Butler, Pinchot was a "military isolationist" who was in favor of "having all sorts of friendly contacts with all other nations on earth."[32] Isolationism simply meant keeping our military forces "within our own boundaries"; militarism, war, and the preparation for war ought not to distract the nation from pressing domestic problems.

---

the ingeniously mischievous proviso that those voting yes be drafted and assigned to combat posts. *The Nation*'s Oswald Garrison Villard claimed that No War Without Referendum was the most popular plank in La Follette's 1924 Progressive party presidential platform. This experiment in direct democracy, later known as the Ludlow Amendment, is examined in chapter 12.

"The American dollar away from home is on its own and must take its chances," Pinchot wrote in 1927 in opposition to Calvin Coolidge's saber-rattling in Mexico. "We should abandon" the "war-breeding doctrine" that the U.S. military is the guarantor of American investments in foreign lands.*

Pinchot the cultivated maverick cut a dashing figure while condemning the "privileged governing class"—composed, as it happened, largely of his peers and friends—which he believed ran America. He sneered at "a nation gone serenely Babbitt," though in the rarefied sphere in which he floated it is unlikely Amos Pinchot ever bumped into the likes of a George Babbitt. (Fact is, they'd have agreed on quite a few things, rococo architecture and the poetry of Chum Frink aside.)

In various ways, Pinchot resembles Gore Vidal. His analysis in 1931 of why Herbert Hoover had sidled up to the utilities industry sounds very Vidalian:

Every aspiring politician knows that barring a great national issue or some accident such as happened in the cases of Theodore Roosevelt and Woodrow Wilson, he can never land in the White House unless, so to speak, shoved from behind by at least one strong industro-financial interest. For the man who sets his cap for the Presidency, the strategy, therefore, is predetermined. It is to win the backing of the best-organized and, politically speaking, most aggressive big-business group available.

Curtained off from the somewhat shoddy, inconsequential, but relatively open game we call politics, there goes on forever a game of another sort which, luckily for his peace of mind, the sovereign citizen is rarely allowed to glimpse—much less to sit in on. It is here, in the invisible game of grand politics, that things really happen. Here Presidents are chosen. Here history is made—also money in exceedingly large quantities. And as a means to these high ends, small men with large ambitions

---

*A clever theatrical version of Pinchotism is provided by the 1927 George S. Brooks-Walter B. Lister play *Spread Eagle*, with its farcical U.S. war against Mexico to protect the vast holdings of a mineral magnate.

are transformed by the magic of propaganda into perfectly serviceable demigods, later, when occasion arises, to be flipped into office to the shouts of the happy multitude.[33]*

Remoter than ever from the corridors of power, Pinchot came to regret his earlier advocacy of public ownership, seeing in it the virus of rampaging statism. Hooverian corporatism, he charged in the *Nation,* had "warred on individualism, equal opportunity, and competition." Roosevelt's New Deal was carrying the battle further, into realms heretofore wholly private, and the republic might never break free of the quicksand. The New Deal was a sham revolution, a political postiche, and no matter how many verses Archibald MacLeish scribbled about FDR the redeemer the owners of the country still held title. As Pinchot's ally, Wisconsin Governor Philip La Follette (who organized a short-lived National Progressive party in the late 1930s) grumbled in 1938: "Roosevelt has no more real interest in the common man than a Wall Street broker. He was playing the same kind of game as Big Business, only he sought, got, and intended to keep *Power,* rather than money" (original italics).[34]

Amos Pinchot's loathing of the New Deal was by no means of a piece with the royalist critique. Like most radical liberals of integrity, he shunned the DuPont-controlled Liberty League, though he did join other anti-FDR organizations such as the Sound Money League and the National Committee to Uphold Constitutional Government.

Pinchot thought the Republican response to the Depression

---

*The late revisionist historian William Appleman Williams and his students have striven manfully to resuscitate Hoover's reputation as a somewhat dour prophet of a "corporatist decentralism" that is, arguably, cousin-german to Pinchot's philosophy. See Joan Hoff Wilson's *Herbert Hoover: Forgotten Progressive,* and ponder Williams's comment: "Hoover, in the depths of the hell of 1931, said that 'what this country needs is a great poem. Something to lift people out of fear and selfishness.' If you kill a Quaker engineer who came to understand that—and to believe in and to commit himself to that—then you have murdered yourself."

ridiculously inadequate. Only "the farm bloc" had anything to offer, he wrote in the *Nation*; Eastern Republicans were bidding "for the support of those august financial powers who alone can throw into the fight the motley army of mercenaries and propagandists which, like hired janissaries, will bring victory to the longest purse." (Although he marched with the Western progressives, Pinchot upbraided them for their porcine demand "that the West be allowed to stick its snout in the hog trough in common with the Eastern hogs.")

Amos endorsed federal relief in the form of road building. Indeed, every progressive isolationist in the Senate in the mid-1930s supported the establishment of both Social Security and the Works Progress Administration. With a nod to Emerson's line about a foolish consistency and hobgoblins, ideological consistency *is* boring and often more reflexive than reflective. What counts is backbone, and this Pinchot had. As Ezra Pound wrote him in 1936, "You are an old man, but you have not been a coward. . . . But I suspect the *whole* of your generation in the USA was fed on second-rate English slop" (original italics).[35]

The self-styled liberals of the late 1930s, Pinchot lamented, "stand for concentration of power in the executive, destruction of power in the legislative branch of the government, coercion, and various things that heretofore have been correctly assigned to reaction."[36] Similarly, John T. Flynn, the *New Republic's* watchdog with a taste for plutocrat blood, complained that FDR had

> adopted a plan borrowed from the corporative state of Italy and sold it to all the liberals as a great liberal revolutionary triumph. And, curiously, every American liberal who had fought monopoly, who had demanded the enforcement of the anti-trust laws, who had denied the right of organized business groups, combinations and trade associations to rule our economic life, was branded a tory and a reactionary if he continued to believe these things.[37]

The Schumacherian revival of "small is beautiful" lay far beyond the horizon. Meanwhile, the cult of bigness was cutting its destructive swath across America, and leading New Deal policy intellectuals from Rexford Tugwell to Frances Perkins derided as nostalgic folly the Jeffersonian ideal of a nation of small farmers and shopkeepers. Paul Douglas, the New Deal economist and later senator from Illinois, thought it "both ridiculous and humiliating to have Senator La Follette dictate to the Cleveland convention which nominated him in 1924 a program which was almost entirely based upon the vanished days of small and independent business. "[38]

The dilemma of Pinchot's coevals had been summed up by lawyer-reformer Lawson Purdy in the fascinating *Survey* symposium of February 1926, "Where Are the Pre-War Radicals?" "The radicals of my generation," stated Purdy, "believed that a man has a right to do all he wills so long as he does not infringe the equal freedom of others. . . . The modern radical appears to be willing to impose any kind of restraints upon people and any kind of burdens on them but he does not appear to be willing to take away the privileges they enjoy. "[39]

William Hard, columnist for the *Nation,* was similarly disquieted. "Liberty is what we're for," he announced in 1924. "That's why we're progressive. . . . We hate the modern increases of governmental powers and functions. We do not want government big. We want it small. That's why we're conservative. A true progressive must at this time often be a conservative."[40]

So, too, for Pinchot, the radical individualist progressive, the left-wing conservative. As Graham notes, his "deeply conservative reformism easily . . . passed for a very radical variety."[41] If he has seldom been adequately classified, let alone studied, the fault lies with his unimaginative progeny, who cannot conceive ideological alternatives to the prison whose wardens are Arthur Schlesinger, Jr., and Ronald Reagan.

Although by the 1930s he was calling himself one of many "misguided nobodies," Pinchot remained on the field, albeit somewhat beyond the foul lines. In March 1932, as Pinchot was on the verge of passing seamlessly from "left" to "right," he declared,

> In spite of their present low ebb, the difficulty with our political system—that is, democracy—and our economic system—that is, capitalism—is not . . . that they are unsound systems, or out-worn, or unworkable. It is that we have allowed interested parties to inject into them a large amount of unfair advantage, privilege, and favoritism, which has bent and clogged their mechanism—badly, it is true, but by no means beyond repair. If our liberal leaders would unite and make a determined effort to get rid of this foreign matter, they would probably find that our political and business institutions, imperfect as they are, would serve our needs well enough.[42]

In the December 1937 *North American Review* Pinchot staked out what he vainly insisted was "the liberal position"—an eminently worthy set of maxims that ran counter to the regnant New Deal liberalism. One imagines Pinchot penning these by lamplight, diligent and yet hopeless; perfectly aware of the futility of it all, yet unable to hold back. He had come to such vision the hard way, weathering opprobrium and scorn. In his despair Pinchot had gained clarity of vision. His creed is as follows:

1. Managed economy will prove undesirable. It should be abandoned. It requires a degree of discipline and control which must turn it into fascism. It is restrictive and sterile. It devitalizes production and reduces the incentive for creating wealth.

2. Managed economy, because it is economically impotent and conducive to underproduction, tyranny, and unhappiness, leads to militarism and war.

3. A government cannot efficiently produce wealth. By wealth we mean the goods and services people need. Governments are not properly organized for industry. But, by statutes of wide

and general application, governments can lay down and enforce the rules that shall govern the industrial game. And, when this has been done, if a government is wise and mindful of its people's good, it will make itself as scarce as possible.

4. Labor and other groups cannot effectively be protected by subsidies and government-given privileges. These paralyze production and impoverish all classes.

5. Labor should be unionized for its own sake, and for industry's sake, as well. And there should be responsible bargaining on both sides. But labor's main reliance for good wages and conditions of employment, and for employment itself, is the vitality and resourcefulness of industry conducted for profit.

6. Machine industry, while it brings temporary unemployment, has the long-range effect of increasing employment, provided monopoly does not intervene to raise prices and reduce consumption. Dislocation of labor, on account of technological advance, is a problem that can be taken care of by private and public insurance and by work on government projects.

7. Monopoly can be prevented. And the line of attack should be that of separating the monopolist from the privilege, or privileges which give him his power to destroy competition and fix prices.

8. It is probable that good monetary control can greatly reduce the chance of major depressions, if not prevent them. The flow of money and credit should be controlled centrally. But the agencies of control should be responsible to Congress and not to the president.

9. A government controlled by the discretion of a ruler, or a group, is probably the ugliest and most costly phenomenon to be found in society. On the other hand, a government democratically controlled, and functioning through common council and law, is the highest and most hopeful achievement of man.[43]

The aversion to militarism led Pinchot into his final losing battle, the struggle to keep his United States out of the Second World War. Pinchot became president of the New York chapter of the America First Committee. Intervention in the European war, he wrote Hiram Johnson, would "serve Mr. Roosevelt as an excuse for breaking the anti-third term tradition and expanding the already immense powers of the President to the point of dictatorship." Just as Hoover had bartered his soul to big business, FDR was selling the country out to "a small, close corporation of internationally minded and exceedingly powerful men," among them John Maynard Keynes, Ernest Bevin, and Harold Laski.

President Roosevelt found it necessary to propitiate the retro-progressive isolationists with the occasional witness for peace. In his memorable August 14, 1936, speech in Chautauqua, New York—in diction redolent of the king of the Chautauqua circuit, William Jennings Bryan—FDR declared: "We are not isolationists except insofar as we seek to isolate ourselves completely from war. . . . I have seen war. . . . I have seen blood running from the wounded. I have seen men coughing out their gassed lungs. I have seen the dead in the mud. I have seen cities destroyed. . . . I hate war."[44]

This was flatly untrue, as anyone knows who has seen the Roosevelt home at Hyde Park, with its collection of prints of naval scenes and battles. War is soul-stirring, at least for those who push the pieces around the Risk board and can keep their children out of harm's way.

The America that Hamlin Garland and Amos Pinchot had known could not survive four years of a draft and its consequent mass displacement; the rationing of meat and foodstuffs; an economy which in its degree of central planning came to resemble that of the Soviet Union; the curtailment of domestic dissent; and, by war's end, the establishment of American hegemony over vast portions of the globe.

The sine qua non of any functioning republic—a vocal opposition—was now deemed dishonorable; bipartisanship poisoned the air, and such converts as Arthur Vandenberg and Harry Truman were lionized. As Jefferson had written during President Adams's saber-rattling against France in 1798: "At this moment all the passions are boiling over, and one who keeps himself cool and clear of the contagion is so far below the point of ordinary conversation that he finds himself insulated in every society."[45]

Still, isolationist strays and stragglers kept at it for a few years. Senator Robert A. Taft, the respected "Mr. Republican" whose skepticism about the Second World War and the Cold War kept him from getting what was rightfully his, a Republican presidential nomination between 1940 and 1952, warned his Cold Warrior colleagues: "We simply cannot keep the country in readiness to fight an all-out war unless we are willing to turn our country into a garrison state and abandon all the ideals of freedom upon which this nation has been erected."[46]

The scarecrow of internationalism, of the smirching of American exceptionalism, could still be conjured. Colonel Robert McCormick's *Chicago Tribune,* fearing U.S. immersion in the United Nations, editorialized in 1945:

> To American patriots the glory of this country has been that here, on a continent separated by wide oceans from the strife of the old world, men of all races and countries have learned to live together in peace, developing their land, their institutions and the possibilities of their own spirits. . . . If we are taken into a world league, we shall never be quite the same as we have been. The corrosive agencies of Europe will have set to work on the American amalgam.[47]

But the consolidationist, homogenizing tendencies in American life were too strong. The crotchety independent newspaper publisher disappeared, swallowed up by the capacious gullet of the chains. The new medium of television rapidly fell under the control of just three New York-based networks. The farm population dwindled apace. The political leaders of America First were defeated for re-election (Nye in 1944, Wheeler in 1946) or died (Taft in 1953). Isolationist magazines such as *Scribner's Commentator* vanished, and the new flagship of the Right was *National Review,* a militantly anti-Communist journal run largely by ex-Communists and Catholic internationalists.

One of the last of the retroprogressive isolationists, Senator Robert La Follette, Jr., though less able than his father, kept the faith, and for his constancy was repaid with a defeat in the 1946 Wisconsin Republican primary to an interventionist named Joseph R. McCarthy. (See chapter 11.) Even *Life* magazine, celebrant of a mushy nationalism, perceived that young Bob's was "a far purer and more consistent body of radical doctrine than was the New Deal, being built not only on social welfare, but on a deep faith in small business, equal opportunity and individual freedom. It is a peculiarly American kind of radicalism, free from taint of all 'foreign ideologies.' "[48]

The junior La Follette was soon to be a suicide; his brand of homegrown radicalism was to sleep with anger for many years. These despairing lines by Oswald Garrison Villard, written in 1941, might serve as an epitaph for the isolationist:

> He grew old in an age he condemned
> Felt the dissolving throes
> Of a social order he loved
> And like the Theban Seer
> Died in his enemies' day.[49]

And what of poor Amos Pinchot? Widely regarded as a crackpot, he wanted no part of the new republic. Pinchot slashed his wrists in a relative's bathroom in August 1942. He survived, unlike his first daughter, the actress Rosamund, who had inhaled carbon monoxide in a Long Island garage four years earlier. It was a theatrical family, with a flair for the grand gesture. (I am told that the slapstick comedic actor Bronson Pinchot is not a descendant.)

Pinchot died at last in 1944 at a sanitarium in the Bronx. He was, at the end, a broken old aristocrat convinced that his country had gone to hell. If antimonopolism and anti-imperialism were relics, Pinchot was the bereaved relict.

A year after his death, Pinchot's daughter Mary wed Cord Meyer, Jr., the moody golden boy who was to become president of United World Federalists and later a top official in the Central Intelligence Agency—two organizations Amos Pinchot would have loathed with all his heart. Mary was a beautiful and talented woman, a painter and reporter who, after divorcing her husband, became a mistress of President Kennedy.

Mary Eno Pinchot was murdered in broad daylight along the towpath in Georgetown in October 1964. Within minutes of the discovery of Mary's body, CIA agent James Jesus Angleton broke into her home; he stole and then destroyed her diary and other material in order to "protect the presidency." A vagrant was arrested for the crime, tried, and acquitted; the murder was never solved. (Mary's sad case was dredged up in 1993 by *New York Times* columnist William Safire as he searched for precedents to the apparent suicide of Clinton confidant Vince Foster.)[50]

Thus ended Pinchotism—for the time being.

NOTES

1. Hamlin Garland, *A Son of the Middle Border* (New York: Grosset & Dunlap, 1917), pp. 309–12.

2. Quoted in David H. Dickason, "Benjamin Orange Flower, Patron of the Realists," *American Literature* 14 (1942): 148.

3. John D. Hicks, *The Populist Revolt* (Lincoln: University of Nebraska Press, 1961/1931), p. 436.

4. C. Vann Woodward, *Tom Watson: Agrarian Rebel* (New York: Oxford University Press, 1972/1938), p. 217.

5. Ibid., pp. 334–35.

6. *Liberty Poems: Inspired by the Crisis of 1898–1900* (Boston: James H. West, 1900), p. 83.

7. Hamlin Garland, *Crumbling Idols* (Cambridge: Harvard University Press, 1960/1894), pp. 30–31.

8. Hamlin Garland, *Roadside Meetings* (New York: Macmillan, 1930), p. 262.

9. Garland, *Crumbling Idols,* p. 143.

10. Garland, *Roadside Meetings,* p. 461.

11. Ibid., pp. 322–23.

12. Hamlin Garland, *My Friendly Contemporaries* (New York: Macmillan, 1932), p. 73.

13. Garland, *Roadside Meetings,* p. 333.

14. *Hamlin Garland's Diaries,* edited by Donald Pizer (San Marino, Calif.: Huntington Library, 1968), p. 236.

15. Garland, *A Son of the Middle Border,* p. 440.

16. *Hamlin Garland's Diaries,* p. 259.

17. Robert M. La Follette, *A Personal Narrative of Political Experience* (Madison, Wis.: Blied Printing, 1911), p. 593.

18. Quoted in Spencer C. Olin, Jr., *California's Prodigal Sons* (Berkeley and Los Angeles: University of California Press, 1968), p. 67.

19. Wayne S. Cole, *Roosevelt and the Isolationists (1932–45)* (Lincoln: University of Nebraska Press, 1983), p. 37.

20. *The Letters of Theodore Roosevelt,* edited by Elting E. Morison (Cambridge: Harvard University Press, 1954), 7: 669–70.

21. Amos E. Pinchot, *History of the Progressive Party,* edited by Helene Maxwell Hooker (New York: New York University Press, 1958), p. 262.

22. *The Letters of Theodore Roosevelt,* 7: 550.

23. Ibid., 8: 1122.

24. Quoted in George E. Mowry, *Theodore Roosevelt and the Progressive Movement* (New York: Hill & Wang, 1946), p. 296.

25. Quoted in Otis L. Graham, Jr., *The Old Progressives and the New Deal* (New York: Oxford University Press, 1967), p. 49.

26. In a letter to the author, April 25, 1993.

27. Amos Pinchot, "A Fair Deal for the Public," *The Forum,* February 1924, p. 204.

28. Pinchot, *History of the Progressive Party,* p. 41.

29. Ibid., pp. 124–25.

30. Quoted in Ernest C. Bolt, Jr., *Ballots before Bullets* (Charlottesville: University Press of Virginia, 1977), p. 30.

31. Quoted in Wayne S. Cole, *Senator Gerald P. Nye and American Foreign Policy* (Minneapolis: University of Minnesota Press, 1962).

32. Quoted in Hans Schmidt, *Maverick Marine* (Lexington: University of Kentucky Press, 1987), p. 241.

33. Amos Pinchot, "Hoover and Power," *The Nation,* August 5, 1931, p. 125.

34. Quoted in Cole, *Roosevelt and the Isolationists,* p. 292.

35. Quoted in Graham, *The Old Progressives and the New Deal,* p. 177.

36. Quoted in Ronald Radosh, *Prophets on the Right* (New York: Free Life, 1978/1975), p. 324.

37. John T. Flynn, *Country Squire in the White House* (Garden City, N.Y.: Doubleday, Doran, 1940), p. 83.

38. Quoted in R. Alan Lawson, *The Failure of Independent Liberalism* (New York: Putnam's, 1971), p. 40.

39. "Where Are the Pre-War Radicals?" *Survey,* February 1, 1926, p. 562.

40. William Hard, "In Bad All Around," *The Nation,* December 3, 1924, p. 599.

41. Graham, *The Old Progressives and the New Deal,* p. 74.

42. Amos Pinchot, "Captain Hoover Afloat in a Sieve," *The Nation,* March 23, 1932, p. 338.

43. Amos Pinchot, "The Liberal Position," *North American Review,* December 1937, pp. 386–88.

44. Quoted in Cole, *Senator Gerald P. Nye and American Foreign Policy,* p. 137.

45. Quoted in Norman Risjord, *Old Republicans: Southern Conservatism in the Age of Jefferson* (New York: Columbia University Press, 1965), p. 12.

46. Quoted in Garet Garrett, *The People's Pottage* (Caldwell, Idaho: Caxton), p. 114.

47. Quoted in Ted Galen Carpenter, "The Dissenters: American Isolationists and Foreign Policy, 1945–1954." (Ph.D. dissertation, University of Texas at Austin, 1980), p. 64.

48. Quoted in Edward N. Doan, *The La Follettes and the Wisconsin Idea* (New York: Rinehart, 1947), p. 160.

49. Quoted in Graham, *The Old Progressives and the New Deal,* p. 185.

50. William Safire, "Foster Death Was Mishandled," Rochester, N.Y., *Democrat and Chronicle,* August 3, 1993, editorial page.

2

There Are Left the Mountains: American Writers and the Perishing Republic

"Everything before the war is out."
—John P. Marquand, *B.F.'s Daughter* (1946)

The poet Archibald MacLeish—"macarchibald maclapdog macleish," e. e. cummings dubbed him—wondered, from his sinecure as Librarian of Congress in 1940, why "the writers of our generation in America" had such a provincial indifference to the war in Europe.[1] They seemed, in Bernard de Voto's phrase, more interested in Paris, Illinois, than Paris, France.

The reaction to MacLeish's question—indeed, the fact that it was asked at all—tells us much about the lost America of prewar days. MacLeish was jeered by his peers and taken to task by his more talented and "acutely isolationist" coeval Edmund Wilson, who observed that MacLeish "has a good deal to say about liberty . . . but he makes it perfectly plain that he believes that, as a matter of policy, certain kinds of dissentient writers should be discouraged from expressing their ideas."[2]

This has ever been true, but in Wilson's day the "dissentients" still had moxie enough to protest. I am reminded of a reporter who traveled recently to Wilson's hometown of Talcottville, New

69

York. The visitor asked the locals for their recollections of the great man; typical was the woman who remembered, as a girl, walking home from school past Wilson's Old Stone House every day, and every day a stout, stuttering, scarlet-faced drunk would emerge onto the porch to holler, "G-g-g-get the hell out of here!"

This is the ne plus ultra of curmudgeonliness, but the proprietary principle underlying Wilson's bile is valuable: the lawn (and this country) belonged to him, and he would not allow interlopers to defile it.

Edmund Wilson had plenty of company, although we as a nation have accepted the myth that American writers—make that all persons of intelligence and worth—had rallied behind the banner of Mars by 1940. Oh, there were exceptions, we know—for instance the sanitarium-bound, Jew-baiting fascist Ezra Pound or the Germanophile poet George Sylvester Viereck—but they merely proved the rule.

In fact, the MacLeishes were outnumbered (and outwritten) by the Wilsons: for every Edna St. Vincent Millay versifying the magnificence of mass slaughter there was a Robinson Jeffers issuing dark warnings that war carried the seed of the empire that would replace our perishing republic. Indeed, we might compare Jeffers, Wilson, and company to the men fighting to stay human in Don Siegel's classic movie *Invasion of the Body Snatchers*. If they are sometimes hysterical, so was Wilson's brother-in-law Kevin McCarthy, whose idyllic Santa Mira was remade as thoroughly as our America.

American writers were once citizens of the republic first and foremost, and they participated in the nation's governance as such. The best were by and large Jeffersonians: figures as disparate as Nathaniel Hawthorne, Herman Melville, and Walt Whitman called themselves "Loco Focos."*

---

*The Loco Focos were the radical libertarians of the Jacksonian coalition of the 1830s. Journalist William Leggett was their chief polemicist. See *Democratick Editorials,* edited by Lawrence H. White (Indianapolis: Liberty Press, 1984), for a Leggett sampler.

The dominant political coloring of American writers has been "petty-bourgeois anarchist," in science-fiction novelist Ursula Le Guin's self-evaluation. You can trace a straight line from Emerson ("Massachusetts, in its heroic day, had no government—was an anarchy. Every man stood on his own feet, was his own governor; and there was no breach of peace from Cape Cod to Mount Hoosac") to Hemingway ("I hate tyranny and, I suppose, government. . . . No larger unit than the village can exist without things being impossible").

When in 1898 a confused William McKinley ignored the sound Ohio advice of his front-porch advisors Mark Hanna and William Rufus "Good" Day and plunged us into war with Spain, a wide variety of men of letters opposed our splendid little misadventure, among them William Dean Howells, Mark Twain, *The Atlantic*'s Thomas Bailey Aldrich, Hamlin Garland, and William Graham Sumner. They were a politically diverse lot, ranging from the mild Ohio socialism of Howells to Professor Sumner's Yale laissez-faire capitalism. Far from being "unhung traitors," they were true patriots who despaired at "seeing the America of my youthful dreams vanish from my sight," in the plaintive words of E. L. Godkin, editor and founder of *The Nation.*

Four decades after McKinley the imperial reveries of the Roosevelt of Oyster Bay were materializing under his fifth cousin from Hyde Park. This time, even more American writers joined the opposition: Sherwood Anderson, e.e. cummings, Kathleen Norris, Theodore Dreiser, William Saroyan, Louise Bogan, Edgar Lee Masters, Henry Miller, Henry W. Clune, Sinclair Lewis, Samuel Hopkins Adams, and Dwight Macdonald, among others. How perfect that Lewis, Anderson, and Masters, the Midwestern trio that led what was (mistakenly) termed "the revolt from the village"—in fact each sought to *revive* the village—were isolationist defenders of the old America.

Masters, the crotchety elder of the bunch, could have told

them what was in store for those who object to a holy war. The Spoon River poet had had a picturesque Illinois childhood that endowed him with a confident Americanism. As a boy, Masters had known Lincoln's law partner William Herndon and John McNamar, the man who dumped young Ann Rutledge into melancholy Abe's lap. Fiercely independent, Masters became a vituperative critic of Lincoln and a poetic champion of his state's less favored son, Stephen Douglas. Masters's hostile *Lincoln, the Man* (1931) provoked harsh reactions; his reputation, already tarnished by his uneven work since *Spoon River Anthology* in 1915, sank to the level of the poetaster Edgar Guest.

Masters could be sour and splenetic, but he was also a sentimental Jeffersonian who, as a young man, loathed the Spanish-American War and insisted that his hero William Jennings Bryan "hold America to its noble path, its primal vision." Forty years later the primal vision was dimming, and Masters slipped into old age bitter over the recurring leitmotif of American history, that of the good guys—Douglas and Bryan and Masters himself— losing time after time and getting clobbered by the history books in the bargain.

Not all these writers who fought and mourned the republic's demise were of a high order. Samuel Hopkins Adams, for instance, the feisty muckraker of Lake Owasco, fits Vernon Parrington's assessment of William Cullen Bryant: "He may not have been a great poet, but he was a great American."[3]

Such a description applies also to Kathleen Norris, the prolific ladies' novelist who spoke frequently at America First gatherings. Mrs. Norris spent her girlhood among the redwoods in Mill Valley, California, where, as she describes in her charming auto-biographical sketch, *Noon* (1924), her father "read us the Declaration of Independence and the Gettysburg Address, and talked to us of the glories of our own nation."

Indeed, it was *our* nation, these writers knew, and they were not afraid to raise their voices when the political leadership acted foolishly or malevolently. Sinclair Lewis would have scoffed at

Norris's claim that "the happiest life in the world" was "the life of American women in a small American town," but that is because he seriously believed that Gopher Prairie, which he loved beyond measure, should be an American Athens.

The decentralist populism implicit in Mrs. Norris's formulation provided the only real alternative to the New Deal. Its political expression was articulated by such men as Senators Burton K. Wheeler, Gerald P. Nye, and Hiram Johnson; it looked to the plains towns and tidy villages, to the shopowners and farmers and artisans and anyone else who, like Edmund Wilson, "thinks up his own notions and signs his own name."

The mighty cities were falling, and the dream had taken to the hinterlands. From Carmel, California, Robinson Jeffers wrote:

> But for my children, I would have them keep their
>   distance from the thickening center; corruption
> Never has been compulsory, when the cities lie at the
>   monster's feet there are left the mountains.[4]

The specter of bureaucracy and regimentation bothered even the more perceptive interventionists. Playwright Maxwell Anderson, a reluctant hawk, warned that "participation in a modern war means dictatorship, even for us, and the abrogation of our liberties. Dictatorships are hard to get rid of, liberties are hard to win back."[5]

Anderson was an ornery Pennsylvanian. His Pulitzer Prize-winning play *Both Your Houses* (1933) featured a fresh young congressman so naive that he makes Frank Capra's Mr. Smith look like Dan Rostenkowski. The honest tyro quickly learns that "the sole business of government is graft, special privilege and corruption."[6] Despite his rough baptism he remains an optimist, convinced that sooner or later The People will revolt; but a wiser hack delivers a prescient postscript: "They're just learning to pay taxes," he says of the suckers beyond the Potomac.

"In a few more years you'll really give 'em taxes to pay."[7]

Anderson was a peculiarly American sort of crank who refused to fill out his Social Security application on the grounds that it infringed upon his rights as a free man. (Governments are "run by pimps who get kicked out of hothouses for picking the customers' pockets," a rebel soldier says in the playwright's superb 1934 verse drama, *Valley Forge*).

Maxwell Anderson learned firsthand the narrowing limits of dissent in the brave new republic. His original script for *Knickerbocker Holiday* (1938), a collaboration with Kurt Weill, contained numerous pungent references to FDR until his fellow members of The Playwrights Company—rugged recusants all, they'd tell you, carefree bohemian seekers of the truth—pressured him to soften the satire. So toothless was Anderson's revised script that the president himself heartily enjoyed a Washington, D.C., production of the play. Anderson did, however, refuse to attend a cast party at the White House—the ultimate humiliation for a proudly heterodox man.

Anderson-like submission was never an option for an obstreperous Armenian boy from Fresno named William Saroyan. As a youngster he was a dreamy foe of nationalism; his early story "Antranik of Armenia" rages against the futility of war: "It is always people, not nations, because it is all one nation, the living, so why . . . kill one another?"

Yet he was also a proud son of the diaspora. Carol Marcus, the former debutante who married Saroyan twice, wrote, "You could not spend more than five minutes with Bill without knowing not only that he was Armenian, but that he was *the* Armenian. You learned in a half hour the entire history of the Armenian people and even a few words of their language."[8] Saroyan was a patriot in the Mark Twain sense of "loyalty to one's country, not to its institutions or its office-holders."

Carol, the model for Truman Capote's Holly Golightly, recalls that Saroyan's fire was damped when he was drafted in 1942. Rejecting her comforting thought that things would soon return to normal, he said, "It will never be the same." Carol adds, "And he wasn't. He never got over the war. It ruined his life."[9]

William Saroyan was not killed or maimed in combat; he never so much as sliced his finger doing KP duty. He was ruined because he was a gregarious anarchist, a free Armenian-American spirit at a time when the country had been taken over by men like MacLeish, who had "the soul of a meat axe and the mind of a commissar," to borrow Clare Booth Luce's description of Harold Ickes.

Terrible at soldiering, miserable in his London billet, Saroyan struck a deal with Kentucky agrarian-turned-superhawk Herbert Agar in the Office of War Information. He would churn out a patriotic novel in exchange for a month-long furlough in New York with Carol and his infant son.

The novel, *The Adventures of Wesley Jackson* (1946), may well be the best thing Saroyan ever wrote. It's a charming tale of a shy nineteen-year-old draftee from San Francisco with a Saroyanesque kind heart who comes to feel that "our own Army was the enemy."

Wesley Jackson chooses loyalty to his drunken father, waiflike wife, and shambling pals over obedience to the authorities. "There is no truth excepting it is from love," Jackson learns, and this knowledge fills him with contempt for the liars and poltroons who run his country. Attached to a unit of writers and directors making training films, Wesley comes to detest these intellectuals who are

> full of the lust to kill, full of hate for the dirty little yellow-belly Japs or the cowardly Germans, and full of a most astonishing and superhuman courage in the face of death. But they always drove out to the country in the evening, and when everybody else got shipped overseas they were still writing scenarios for films encouraging everybody else to face death like a scenario writer.[10]

We may imagine Commissar Herbert Agar's face as he read this manuscript, ostensibly a propaganda job, which ends, "Human beings must not murder one another. They must wait for God to take them in His own good time." Agar and his fellow censors were furious. They rejected the novel, canceled the leave, and even threatened the author with court-martial.

When the book was finally published in 1946, Saroyan began earning his time on the cross. "He uses fantasy and sentimentality for a dangerous and sinful purpose—to discredit the causes in which we fought and the men who did the fighting," fumed Irwin Shaw in his review in the *New York Times*. Actually, the "men who did the fighting" come off quite well, as ordinary people always do in Saroyan's works.

No matter. Overnight, the immensely popular Saroyan went into one of those eclipses that we later profess to be inexplicable but whose causes are in fact plain even to the purblind. Saroyan's new country had become unrecognizable, so he retreated, in spirit, to the old. He grew a walrus mustache and played the part of Armen Armenian to perfection. His only outlets were the small and experimental presses, and even the worthy episodic memoirs he gave us in his final years attracted little notice. The daring young man had fallen from the trapeze, and to a scornful clerisy he was just a bloated Armenian elder sipping arrack in the taverns of Fresno.

Saroyan became a bitter old man beside whom Edmund Wilson seemed a mellow, cuddly teddy bear. He wrote a brilliant obituary for Carl Sandburg, observing that the People, Yes! poet "had no failure or frustration, had never been accused of treason, never committed to a hospital for the insane, never been hated, despised, held in contempt, abandoned, hounded, misunderstood, misinterpreted, scorned, belittled, dishonored."[11]

Like Maxwell Anderson, Saroyan committed lèse-majesté. He loved later to boast that he and James Thurber, alone among a throng of artists being wined and dined at Hyde Park by the first family, refused to shake FDR's hand. Petty and ungentlemanly or a defiant act of conscience—you make the call.

William Saroyan stood as resolute and upright as he could while the arrows whizzed by his head. Against the *New York Times* and the U.S. Army, a bibulous, garrulous Armenian anarchist hadn't a chance.

Nor did Robinson Jeffers, however popular his poetry, however impregnable was Tor House, the stone cottage he built with his own hands. Jeffers had seen "the dance of the Dreamled masses down the dark mountain" a quarter-century before, and like other American republicans he feared a replay.

Jeffers suffered the indignity of a publisher's disclaimer prefacing his volume *The Double Axe* (1948). Affixed by Bennett Cerf, it stated, "Random House feels compelled to go on record with its disagreement over some of the political views pronounced by the poet." Cerf congratulated himself for recognizing "the writer's freedom to express his convictions boldly and forthrightly," but refrained from mentioning that ten poems had been expurgated from the book. (One of the suppressed poems had FDR meeting Woodrow Wilson in Hell; another envisioned bombers dropping "wreaths of roses" upon a cheerful village whose boys "hang Hitler and Roosevelt in one tree, painlessly, in effigy." No one could accuse Jeffers of being oblique.)

The poet—"an old-fashioned Jeffersonian republican . . . defender of the spartan and honest American commonweal against the thickening of the empire," in Jeffers scholar Robert Hass's phrase—had prescience, which we often confuse with pessimism. As early as 1943 Jeffers predicted:

> Two bloody summers from now (I suppose) we shall have
>   to take up the corrupting burden and curse of victory.
> We shall have to hold half the earth; we shall be sick
>   with self-disgust,
> And hated by friend and foe, and hold half the earth—
>   or let it go, and go down with it. Here is a burden

We are not fit for. We are not like Romans and
  Britons—natural world-rulers,
Bullies by instinct—but we have to bear it. Who has
  kissed Fate on the mouth, and blown out the lamp—
  must lie with her.[12]

For his clear vision and his refusal to jettison his anachronistic beliefs, Jeffers "put his signature on a death warrant," critic William Everson has written. Critics who one year earlier had lauded Jeffers's adaptation of *Medea* as a major achievement in American drama now spat upon the pariah. A "necrophilic nightmare!" *Time* magazine called *The Double Axe*. Jeffers's eclipse was as complete as Saroyan's—though, happily, a later generation of naturalists would revive the man who loved the feathered hawks and loathed the human kind.

The antiwar writers were not, in the main, pacifists. They were, rather, American patriots who understood that war and the resultant empire would bury the American republic and corrupt the American people. This was true even of the pedigreed conscientious objector Robert Lowell. This great descendant of a prominent literary family had an endearing New England proprietary patriotism. Like a true Brahmin, Lowell sent President Roosevelt a "Declaration of Personal Responsibility" which explained that "in 1943 we are collaborating with the most unscrupulous and powerful of totalitarian dictators to destroy law, freedom, democracy, and above all, our continued national sovereignty."[13] A Massachusetts eccentric and hater of cant, Lowell would have no part of a crusade-in-arms with Stalin. The poet won a stint behind the metal of honor (i.e., went to jail) for his resistance.

(Twenty-five years later Lowell accompanied one of the last of the American republicans, Senator Eugene McCarthy, on his suicidal challenge to the Democratic establishment. The painfully earnest young liberals who surrounded McCarthy regarded

Lowell as a debilitating distraction: in Lowell's company, the candidate would joke and drink and compose irreverent doggerel, and act altogether human and unworthy of the support of Americans for Democratic Action.)

Despite the widespread anti-FDR sentiment one finds among American writers, disappointingly few novelists wrote explicitly political books about the ways in which the New Deal and the Good War were changing America. John Dos Passos contributed a diffuse novel, *The Grand Design* (1949), which follows two well-meaning mid-level New Dealers from the first 100 days to the onset of war as they try "to make America over from Portland, Oregon, to Brownsville on the Rio Grande."

Halfway through the novel Dos Passos abandons his story and runs off to scrawl placards denouncing manipulative Communists who dupe lonely single career gals into spilling state secrets. If only Dos Passos had been indifferent to the Spanish Civil War, as most good Americans were, he would not have cluttered his books with such urgent sloganeering, and we'd be more convinced when Dos Passos concludes *The Grand Design* with this adjuration:

> we must learn
> to found again
> in freedom
> our republic.

Dos Passos's friend Edmund Wilson thought *The Grand Design* a decent novel that was poorly received because it "shocked people as blasphemy against the Great White Father."[14] Dos Passos was a good amateur historian who understood what was up in his changing country, and this knowledge accounts for the funk into which his midcentury fiction fell. Wilson, too, understood our predicament, which is why he, almost alone among major critics, paid respectful attention to Dos Passos's "right-wing" novels.

The amiable dispute between these two old pals tells us much about the crazy skew of American politics. They agreed on almost all the big issues: but for the lack of italicized prose poetry, Wilson's *The Cold War and the Income Tax* (1964) could be taken for a terser Dos Passos in a foul mood. Alas, the din of the Left versus Right katzenjammer deafened them to the harmony of their views, and they quarreled over trifling matters such as Dos Passos's ardor for Barry Goldwater, which Wilson called "too girlish for words."[15]

More effective than Dos Passos at delineating the ways in which America had been remade was the novelist John P. Marquand, who by 1941 had adopted a public pose of political ambiguity, thus avoiding—partly—the calumny heaped upon more forthright isolationists.

Mrs. Adelaide Marquand was an active America Firster, and while her husband was sympathetic he didn't need a weatherman to tell him which way the wind blew. Marquand told a friend in 1939 that the monies raised at his Harvard class reunion should be put to "keeping America out of the European war," but a year later he was throwing up his hands: "I find myself in the uncomfortable position of not being able to decide what the United States ought to do in this war." Marquand permitted the America First Committee to hold dinners at his apartment, where he hobnobbed with Norman Thomas and Charles Lindbergh, at the same time assuring his interventionist friends, "Don't bother about Adelaide's America First stuff— an activity with which I have never been wholly in sympathy, and less now than ever before."

Marquand straddled the fence, a good Republican, a "non-New Dealer" who insisted, "There has never been any isolationist sentiment to speak of . . . among those who are in the New England tradition."[16]

But his skillful novels make plain the author's sympathies. *So Little Time,* published in 1943, is a requiem for the old America, fast disappearing in the smoke and clangor of wartime. *B.F.'s*

Daughter (1946), which the author called "a novel of manners" drawn from his wartime service in Washington, contains a satiric portrait of a New Deal speechwriter, Tom Brett, demotic on the surface but walking evidence that "all liberals were turning into self-righteous, complacent social snobs." Tom marries the daughter of a headstrong but honest titan of industry who, as one fatuous radio warmonger puts it, "represented a way of life and a mechanism of life that is completely gone. . . . It's gone, and I don't know where it went, and what's more, I can't entirely remember what it was, although we all lived in it. We're like fish being moved from one aquarium to another."[17]

This idea of loss and uprootedness recurs throughout the novel. The war is changing America: indeed, "nothing matters that happened before the war." A new order is at hand, drab and grey and conformist. "No one seems to be an individual anymore," one spirited lady complains, even as the air is thick with platitudes about the Four Freedoms and the coming More Abundant Life.

"Personally, I thought the world we used to live in, cockeyed though it was, was better," says another of Marquand's gentlemen.

So did many Americans.

By the 1950s it was all over: America was remade, from sea to shining sea. Although the Beats noticed this and raised a fuss ("America was invested with wild self-believing individuality and this had begun to disappear around the end of World War II with so many great guys dead," fretted Jack Kerouac[18]), they were ridiculed and condemned as barbarians and then honored for all the wrong reasons; finally these holy fools were dealt the *coup de grâce* of postwar America: they got tenure and won NEA grants.

By 1963 Edmund Wilson, despairing that "our country has become today a huge blundering power unit controlled more and more by bureaucracies whose rule is making it more and more difficult to carry on the tradition of American individualism," had concluded that "this country, whether or not I continue to live in it, is no longer any place for me."[19]

Wilson stayed, though no one much cared, and in his final years he retreated to Talcottville, as secluded a fastness as any Jeffers stone tower. He died deeply in debt to the IRS.

Wilson was one of the lucky ones. He was treated indulgently, as a kind of national village crank, but even the Presidential Medal of Freedom that his fellow America Firster John F. Kennedy awarded him could not keep Wilson from falling—with Masters and Saroyan and the rest—into the slough of despond. The republic had perished, and these men were quite unable to revive it. They left us only road maps, soiled upon issue and now yellowed from years of neglect, but readable just the same.

NOTES

1. Archibald MacLeish, "The Irresponsibles," *The Nation*, May 18, 1940, p. 618.

2. Quoted in Paul Fussell, *Wartime* (New York: Oxford University Press, 1989), p. 173.

3. Vernon Parrington, *Main Currents in American Thought*, Book II (New York: Harcourt, Brace, 1930), p. 246.

4. Robinson Jeffers, "Shine, Perishing Republic," in *Rock and Hawk*, edited by Robert Hass (New York: Random House, 1987), p. 14.

5. Quoted in Alfred S. Shivers, *The Life of Maxwell Anderson* (New York: Stein and Day, 1983), p. 182.

6. Maxwell Anderson, *Both Your Houses* (New York: Samuel French, 1933), p. 103.

7. Ibid., p. 179.

8. Carol Matthau, *Among the Porcupines* (New York: Turtle Bay, 1992), p. 34.

9. Ibid., p. 30.

10. William Saroyan, *The Adventures of Wesley Jackson* (New York: Harcourt, Brace, 1946), p. 113.

11. William Saroyan, "Carl Sandburg," in *The New Saroyan Reader* (Creative Arts, 1984), p. 248.

12. Robinson Jeffers, "Historical Choice," in *Rock and Hawk,* p. 235.

13. Ian Hamilton, *Robert Lowell* (New York: Random House, 1982), p. 89.

14. Quoted in Townsend Ludington, *John Dos Passos: A Twentieth-Century Odyssey* (New York: Dutton, 1980), p. 444.

15. Ibid., p. 492.

16. Quoted in Millicent Bell, *Marquand* (Boston: Little, Brown, 1979), pp. 295–98.

17. John P. Marquand, *B.F.'s Daughter* (Boston: Little, Brown, 1946), p. 75.

18. Jack Kerouac, "The Origins of the Beat Generation," *Playboy* (June 1959).

19. Edmund Wilson, *The Cold War and the Income Tax* (New York: Signet, 1964), p. 125.

3

The Merchants of Death
of Sunset Boulevard

"If movies can win a war, I guess they can avoid one too."
—William Saroyan, *The Adventures of Wesley Jackson* (1946)

Playwright Robert E. Sherwood, the six-foot-seven weather vane of midcentury liberalism, once complained, "The trouble with me is that I start off with a big message and end with nothing but good entertainment."[1]

That's no trouble at all, as the writer-director Preston Sturges insisted in his wonderful film *Sullivan's Travels* (1942), but then Sherwood was unduly modest. On back lots and in ginny writers' conferences, he and others in Hollywood's prewar "creative community" connived to turn the parochial mind-your-own-business citizens of America into battle-primed belligerents. Our shell-shocked nation has never recovered.

Adolf Hitler said of Sergei Eisenstein's *Battleship Potemkin,* "This is a film which could turn anyone into a Bolshevik."[2] Beginning in 1939, the spectacle of our stateside Eisensteins, many of them foreign-bred, urging American natives to sacrifice their sons for Winston Churchill, provoked a brief, sad, and futile protest by the pugnacious guardians of the Old Republic.

Under the influence of European-born moguls, immigrant directors, and British actors, "movies have ceased to be instruments of entertainment," charged North Dakota Senator Gerald P. Nye. "They have become the most gigantic engines of propaganda in existence to rouse the war fever in America and plunge this Nation to her destruction."[3]

Nye, an agrarian populist and legendary scourge of the masters of war, was his chamber's champion muckraker. Between 1934 and 1936 he led a Senate investigation exposing the "merchants of death": those "great American and European bankers and the powerful international munitions makers" who had suckered us into the First World War, or so Nye believed. He dedicated the rest of his career to preventing a replay.

Alas for poor Nye, Hollywood had retaliatory powers beyond J. P. Morgan and Company's wildest dreams.

Nye made his case in an August 1, 1941, nationwide radio address. "Before we plow a million boys under the dust and mud of Africa, Indochina, France, and faraway Russia," the senator declared, we ought to examine why "movie companies have been operating as war propaganda machines almost as if they were being directed from a single central bureau."[4]

Nye named several films—among them *That Hamilton Woman, Man Hunt,* and *Sergeant York*—that "whip up the warrior spirit in young men, glorify war, glorify militarism," and altogether ignore Sam Goldwyn's sly dictum, "If you have a message, send it Western Union."

Nye's target was clear. He was an Anglophobe, like so many Middle-American populists, and he had no desire to sacrifice Dakota farmboys in order to pull the British Empire's chestnuts out of the fire. (In 1933 the North Dakota Senate had debated whether to secede from the Union, in part to extricate the state from the tentacular grip of the Wall Street-British octopus.)

"Go to Hollywood," Nye urged his radio audience. "The place swarms with refugees. It also swarms with British actors."

This charming Anglophobia, though jarring to modern ears, acted as a brake on the Wise Men. It has, regrettably, gone the way of the Anti-Masonry movement of the 1830s and the free coinage of silver. When we hear maledictions against Hollywood today we sniff for anti-Semitism; Nye, unfortunately, played down to our expectations by stating: "There are eight major film companies. The men who dominate policy in these companies—own or direct them—are well known to you."[5] They included Louis B. Mayer, Harry and Jack Cohn, Adolph Zukor, Joseph Schenk, Arthur Loew, and Sam Goldwyn. Exotic names, none too American-sounding. Most were Jewish.

The reaction was fierce and immediate. "This was deliberately cooked up for the double purpose of terrorizing the Jews on the one hand to keep them from active participation in the anti-isolationist fight and on the other to arouse public prejudice against the interventionist cause on the Jew angle," fumed the hawkish (and prolix) newspaper columnist Robert S. Allen.[6]

Braving a hailstorm of vilification, Nye and his senatorial confrere Burton K. Wheeler arranged subcommittee hearings in 1941 to investigate the propaganda activities of the motion picture and radio industries. Nye, a scrapper, kicked things off by asserting that the film industry was run by men "born abroad and animated by the persecutions and hatreds of the Old World."[7] Many directors "come from Russia, Hungary, Germany, and the Balkan countries."[8] This was true, by the way, if veracity matters.

Nye applied to anti-Semitism his most stinging epithet— "un-American"—but he insisted that "those primarily responsible for the propaganda pictures are born abroad. They came to our land and took citizenship here entertaining violent animosities toward certain causes abroad. . . . If they lose sight of what some Americans might call the first interests of America in times like these, I can excuse them. But their prejudices by no means necessitate our closing our eyes to these interests and refraining from undertaking to correct their error."[9]

Nye's economic determinism led him to look at the export market for films. "If Britain loses, seven of the eight leading companies will be wiped out." The question, then, was this: "Are you ready to send your boys to bleed and die in Europe to make the world safe for this industry and its financial backers?"[10] The imputation here is too harsh, but again, Nye is at least arguably correct. *Variety* reported that in 1939, the foreign market—with England leading the way—accounted for one-third of American film company revenues.

The motion picture industry paid out $100,000 to its counsel, Wendell Willkie, whose 1940 Republican presidential nomination was largely engineered by House of Morgan henchman Thomas Lamont.* Willkie called Senator Nye's testimony "divisive," which meant, then as now, that his shovel was digging a little too close to the buried corpse for comfort.

The best witness was John T. Flynn, recently fired from *The New Republic,* a left-wing antimonopolist and author of the best-selling *Country Squire in the White House.* Flynn disclaimed any interest in censorship. What he decried was "monopoly control" by the major studios, many with ties to England. Unlike Nye, who was no cineast, Flynn actually went to the movies.

Flynn took a particular scunner to the Laurence Olivier-Vivien Leigh melodrama *That Hamilton Woman* (1941), a romantic account of the affair between Lord Horatio Nelson and Lady Emma Hamilton. The film glorified decadent Old World adulterers and pushed a pro-interventionist line with such clumsy earnestness that American moviegoers must have exited theaters all afire to have their republic declare war on Napoleon.

---

*Lamont's sidekick, Dwight Morrow, had a beautiful daughter named Anne, who fell in love with the pilot of the *Spirit of St. Louis.* This handsome public face of the America First movement, Charles Lindbergh, disliked his in-laws and, indeed, all "anglophile bankers."

(Gore Vidal has discussed, with customary wit and insight, the peculiar charms of *That Hamilton Woman* in his *Screening History*.)

Flynn pointed out that the film's director, Alexander Korda, was a British subject, as was Charles Chaplin, a major stockholder in United Artists, which had produced the film. Counsel Willkie laughed at the foolish nativist; the next day's *New York Times* dripped with venomous scorn for Flynn the gutsy liberal-turned-crazy xenophobe.

Years later it was revealed—by his nephew Michael, among others—that Korda had been Churchill's man in Hollywood. Sir Winston himself penned one of Lord Nelson's overwrought speeches. Korda was an agent of British intelligence; his New York and Los Angeles offices served as fronts for his country's espionage operations. Flynn, though mocked, had been right all along: Korda should have been deported as a spy.[11]

At the hearings witness Flynn was marvelous: he spoke with acuity, asperity, and passion. "Why is it that no picture is produced depicting the tyrannies and oppressions in India where at the moment there are 20,000 Indian patriots in jail?" he asked. "No, what we get are pictures . . . glorifying the magnificence, humanity, and democracy of the British Empire"[12]—usually made by subjects of that empire.

Willkie ridiculed Flynn's obsession with "the old monopoly humbug." Within the decade, the Department of Justice would find that humbug to be quite real, and order the studios to divest themselves of their thousands of theaters. But see how the ground was shifting under Flynn's feet: a Wall Street flunky was defending monopoly and war and foreign spies, and the liberals cheered.

Where Flynn and Nye went off the rails was in pinning the blame on foreign-born directors. Their anticipation of auteur theory is commendable, but far more culpable were the screenwriters who were, as a group, solidly prowar—and mostly American-born.

It is a curiously forgotten fact that before Pearl Harbor most "real" writers—novelists and poets and essayists—were antiwar. Yet nearly all the top Hollywood scenarists were rabid for war, and the exceptions—Donald Ogden Stewart, for instance—were often Communist party foot soldiers who became rabid war hawks once Hitler had betrayed Stalin. (Lillian Gish, the most outspoken Hollywood opponent of U.S. involvement in the war, was virtually blacklisted for her pacifist heresy.)

The dour Robert Sherwood, whom Noël Coward dubbed "this nine-foot tower of gloom," was typical. A native-born graduate of Milton and Harvard, Sherwood wrote a series of pacifist-flavored works culminating with *Idiot's Delight,* winner of the 1936 Pulitzer Prize. The play is something of a screwball antiwar comedy. A motley crew—vaudevillians, newlyweds, a doctor seeking a cure for cancer, a fake White Russian countess, and others—is detained at a mountain resort on the Italian-Swiss border as the next world war breaks out. Bombers are taking off from an adjacent runway; the detainees are desperate to make it into neutral Switzerland. Among those present is Achille Weber, a munitions manufacturer whom an idealistic young Frenchman denounces as a "merchant of death" who has armed belligerents on all sides. At one point in the play (although not, signally, in the film version) we are told that England instigated this new war to preserve her empire.

The play contains raw, brutal descriptions of war's carnage. Irene, the phony countess, imagines a pregnant woman in a bombed-out cellar: "her firm young breasts are all mixed up with the bowels of a dismembered policeman, and the embryo from her womb is splattered against the face of a dead bishop." This line did not make it into the film. Nor did Irene's declaration of conscience: "I'll tell you what you can do in these tragic circumstances. You can refuse to fight!" (Had *Idiot's Delight* been filmed as written, it would have answered Senator Nye's demand for films showing the "sons of mothers living legless, or lungless, or brainless, or sightless in hospitals," casualties of foreign wars.)

The film version of *Idiot's Delight* starred Clark Gable and Norma Shearer. Released in 1939, it was—despite the prissy expurgations—the last of a string of 1930s Hollywood movies embodying the Nye-ish belief that we'd been tricked into the First World War and we wouldn't get fooled again. When Clark Gable, playing the wisecracking American vet and two-bit impresario, sneers at the idea of "fight[ing] to make the world safe for democracy—again," he is rebuking Woodrow Wilson and his globalist heirs.

However, by the time the film *Idiot's Delight* was released, its author was blowing with the prevailing wind, recanting his antiwar convictions with alacrity, if not anguish. Sherwood's second Pulitzer Prize winner, *Abe Lincoln in Illinois* (1938; filmed in 1940), was based on Carl Sandburg's dubious biography and can be read as an allegory urging U.S. intervention in Europe. As pacifist sentiment became less fashionable, Sherwood went whole hog for war, writing the agitprop *There Shall Be No Night* (1940) and overseeing the propaganda machine in the Office of War Information.

Sherwood was one of the few talented American writers who had aligned himself with the New Deal; he even ghostwrote some of FDR's fireside chats. To his shame, Sherwood ghosted the president's infamous October 30, 1940, pledge to the "mothers and fathers" of America: "I have said this before, but I shall say it again and again and again: Your boys are not going to be sent into any foreign war."[13] Sherwood later confessed that he knew that this was a lie, but by that time the lofty old conceit about speaking Truth to Power (the writer's job, or so say hopeless idealists) had degenerated into speaking Falsehoods for Power.

Sherwood's apostasy was bitter. His script for William Wyler's overwhelming (and, at times, quite moving) homecoming epic, *The Best Years of Our Lives* (1946), contains a memorable scene in which Harold Russell, a non-actor portraying a vet who has lost both hands in the war, and Dana Andrews, a decorated hero now toiling as a soda jerk, get into a row with a nervous little man at a lunch counter who bears what cannot be a coincidental resemblance to Thomas E. Dewey.

"It's terrible when you see a guy like you who had to sacrifice himself—and for what?" the man at the counter says darkly, staring at Russell's prostheses.

"For what? I don't getcha, mister," replies Russell.

"We let ourselves get sold down the river. We were pushed into that war."

"Sure, by the Japs and the Nazis."

"No," gusts the man. "The Germans and the Japs had nothing against us. They just wanted to fight the limeys and the Reds, and they woulda whipped 'em too, if we didn't get deceived into it by a bunch of radicals in Washington."

Dana Andrews tells the loudmouth to beat it. The man, getting up to leave, grumbles, "And that's another thing. Every soda jerk in this country's got an idea he's somebody."

"Look mister," Russell demands. "Just what are you sellin'?"

"I'm not selling anything but plain old-fashioned Americanism," the man declares.

Russell snatches something from the man's lapel and it falls to the floor. They scuffle, and Andrews lands a roundhouse to the man's jaw, sending him sprawling. Russell retrieves the item from the floor. It is an American flag pin which Russell carefully sticks on his own lapel.

See how cleverly Sherwood has fixed the game. The Nye position—that Americans are dragged into foreign wars by external influences—is presented as reactionary poison peddled by impolite creeps who detest Roosevelt. Peace, it seems, is for right-wing cranks. The Nyes, populist Main Streeters, sneer at uppity soda jerks in Sherwood's world. "Americanism" is a hate crime, although the spunky crippled vet appropriates the flag lapel pin. Our hero was maimed by "those radicals in Washington," but he's still willing to fight on their behalf. Sherwood has come a long way from *Idiot's Delight*.

Frederic March had also traveled some distance. The actor, who won an Oscar for his performance in *The Best Years of Our Lives*, had starred in one of the grimmest Nye-era antiwar movies, 1933's *The Eagle and the Hawk*, in which he played a disillusioned flier who blows his brains out rather than drop bombs. A film with a similar theme, *Ace of Aces* (1933), directed by J. Walter Ruben from a story by John Monk Saunders, finds sculptor Richard Dix renouncing his humane ideals and pacifism to become a "self-glorifying cold-blooded butcher" in the skies of Europe—all because his fiancée called him "yellow." Dix learns his lesson—the Croix de Guerre and Legion of Honor are not worth even "one dead man"—but his muse has deserted him, and he is fated to live out a forlorn life without art.

Gary Cooper was even more versatile than March: an America First sympathizer,[14] Cooper won his first Academy Award for the 1941 film *Sergeant York* as the heroic Tennessee farmer who abhors fighting—"war's ag'in the Book"—but goes on to capture 132 of the Kaiser's men singlehandedly.

In later years the makers of these films were remarkably honest about their intentions. Jack Warner boasted of the tendentiousness of such Warner productions as *Espionage Agent* (1939), in which an American peace group is a Nazi front, and *Confessions of a Nazi Spy* (1939), which *The New Republic*'s Otis Ferguson denounced as "a hate-breeder" made for "playboy intellectuals . . . charging around proclaiming the duty to go into battle of somebody else."[15]

Director Irving Pichel's *The Man I Married* (1940) features Joan Bennett as the wife of a German-American who visits the fatherland on business and within a fortnight turns Nazi. Fortunately, Joan meets foreign correspondent Lloyd Nolan, who says knowingly, "The Nazis wanna include us out of the next war"—and so do Nazi sympathizers back home. Fritz Lang's

Man Hunt (1941), a favorite of mine, finds big-game hunter Walter Pidgeon being chased through the alleys of London by monocled Nazi George Sanders, who bellows, "Today Europe, tomorrow the world!"

The jewel of the Crown offensive, however, was Metro-Goldwyn-Mayer's *Mrs. Miniver,* based on Jan Struther's novel, which began shooting one month before Pearl Harbor. The masterly William Wyler directed; he later called the picture "perfect as propaganda." The English, we are told in the prologue, are a "happy, careless people," and every stock English character—the snobbish dowager, the g-dropping pubcrawler, the socially conscious Oxonian, the ditzy chambermaid—lives in the Minivers' cheerful village. Class differences melt in the crucible of war, and this cohesive community resists Nazi aggression with pluck and patriotism. England is represented by Greer Garson and the girl-next-door beauty Teresa Wright. (Miss Wright, minus the English accent, also played in *The Best Years of Our Lives.*)

Mrs. Miniver ends with the doughty villagers singing "Onward Christian Soldiers" in a ruined chapel. In a spicy irony, the stage version of *Idiot's Delight* ended with Irene and Harry humming the same hymn, to rather different effect.

Exposing the evils of Nazism (as Frank Borzage did in his fine movie *The Mortal Storm* [1940]; so, despite its cartoonish aspect, did *The Man I Married*) was not enough; nor was fitting Englishmen for haloes. American peace leaders—most of them old liberals opposed to war and regimentation—had to be recast as jackbooted heavies with suspicious five o'clock shadows. One of the most despicable such Hollywood efforts was the little-known Katharine Hepburn-Spencer Tracy film *Keeper of the Flame* (1942), scripted by wealthy Communist Donald Ogden Stewart from a novel by Ida A. R. Wylie, and directed by the talented "women's director," George Cukor.

The opening credits roll against louring clouds, as though we are piloting an airplane encountering frightful turbulence. As the story begins we see a car hurtling off a bridge in a rainstorm;

it strikes the ground and explodes into flames. A montage of newspaper headlines reveals that a national hero, Robert Forrest, has died. America mourns.

Forrest, as even the dullards in the audience must realize, is Charles Lindbergh. We hear testaments to his courage. He was a superman, worshiped by his countrymen; yet there was still a "simple, homely" Middle American quality about him. Spencer Tracy plays a noted war correspondent who wants to write the authorized biography of Forrest in order to stiffen the national backbone in these perilous times.

While studying "Forward America," Forrest's organization dedicated to "true Americanism," Tracy uncovers the startling truth: Robert Forrest was in fact a fascist traitor! It turns out that Mrs. Forrest, played by Katharine Hepburn, facilitated the killing of her own husband as an act of patriotism.

"Of course they didn't call it fascism," Hepburn sobs to Tracy. "They painted it red, white, and blue and called it Americanism." Hepburn is murdered at film's end by a crazed Forward America leader, but in death she is eulogized by a grateful nation for saving us from a cornfed Hitler.

Keeper of the Flame was a box-office disappointment. Director Cukor, a wholly apolitical man, called it "pure hokey-pokey."[16] Yet it remains a fascinating artifact. As a piece of celluloid slander *Keeper* is unmatched: it makes Orson Welles's *Citizen Kane* look like a tribute commissioned by William Randolph Hearst. (Hepburn later averred, lamely, that *Keeper of the Flame* had been based on Hearst, not Lindbergh.)

How could a major studio like MGM make a film crucifying the towering American hero of the age? The answer, of course, is that Lindbergh had just been reviled as "the Number One Nazi fellow traveler" by FDR's self-styled curmudgeon, secretary of the interior and head of the WPA, Harold Ickes. The hit, if not authorized at the top, was inspired by it. Lindbergh's father was a Minnesota congressman whose populist attacks on the merchants of death won him the sobriquet of the "Gopher

Bolshevik." Young Charles was his father's son, and his opinion, shared by so many in Middle America, was simply this: "What happens in Europe is of little importance compared with what happens in our own land. It is far more important to have farms without mortgages, workmen with their homes, and young people who can afford families, than it is for us to crusade abroad for freedoms that are tottering in our own country."[17]

This is hate and perfidy and treason?*

I know that I am stepping, none too daintily, among the land mines. I readily concede that anti-Semitism was a motive in later unjustified government investigations of Hollywood. For example, two of the martyred Hollywood Ten, Communist Party (USA) members Edward Dmytryk and Adrian Scott, were haled before the House Un-American Activities Committee (HUAC) largely because of their roles directing and producing *Crossfire* (1947), in which a psychopathic soldier (Robert Ryan) beats to death a Jewish man he has picked up in a bar.

Crossfire is a strange hybrid: a fast-paced film noir clogged with tedious moralizing by detective Robert Young. Nevertheless, making preachy films is not against the law, else Stanley Kramer and Richard Attenborough would be in the hoosegow, and besides, those Communists who on principle refused to betray their friends deserve a grudging respect. (Dmytryk did eventually squeal.) It should be noted, however, that the national security state of which the witch-hunting HUAC was a part was bequeathed us by the Roosevelt and Truman administrations. What comes around. . . .

Lest anyone think that the boys were heading back home once Hitler was vanquished, our celluloid heroes had news for them. Director Herbert J. Biberman's *The Master Race* (1944)

---

*The peace movement of the 1940s was slandered well into the next decade. In 1957's *A Face in the Crowd,* a collaboration of former Communists Budd Schulberg and Elia Kazan, cornpone TV personality Lonesome Rhodes—brilliantly played by Andy Griffith—meets his end when he tries to humanize Senator Fuller, a quasi-fascist known as the "last of the isolationists."

follows a Nazi colonel, Friederich Von Beck (played by George Coulouris), underground to a liberated Belgian village seemingly populated by beautiful models (anyway, they look much too fetching to have been just released from Nazi oppression). The colonel, posing as a crippled French soldier, tries to sow discord in order that Americans will cry "to bring their troops home."

This film is obscenely perverse: the Nazis come off as anti-imperialists supporting the supremely just idea of one Belgian mill owner that "the Germans are gone—and we don't want the Russians and Americans to take their place." Or as an American officer explains to a townsman who wonders why the "invalid" villagers aren't allowed to take care of themselves: "I don't think invalids should prescribe for themselves. That's why we have doctors."

After Coulouris is caught and shot by the American and Russian occupiers, the grizzled U.S. commander assures us, "Winning the war wasn't pretty. Maybe winning the peace won't be either." While he used to dream of just "going home," he now vows to stay in Europe and root out every last Nazi and malcontent. This is a bizarre speech for an American to make, but the presence of 250,000 U.S. troops on the European continent thirty and forty years later proved him nothing if not ahead of the curve.

Hollywood's evangels of interventionism discovered eventually that there were limits to the audience's credulity. One deserving flop was Darryl Zanuck's lavish *Wilson* (1944), a stiff and hilarious biopic intended to promote Zanuck's great enthusiasm, the United Nations. *Wilson* is hagiography gone haywire: Alexander Knox plays the great man as such a prig that even the most fanatical World Federalist must cheer as the pursed schoolmarmish president sees his League of Nations rejected by the benighted multitude. Thrown for a loss by *Wilson*'s disastrous showing at the box office—the people of Zanuck's hometown of Wahoo, Nebraska, site of the glitzy premiere, were so indifferent that the miffed film magnate vowed never to return—Zanuck shelved plans to film Wendell Willkie's internationalist *One World.*

Wilson bombed in 1944; so did Senator Nye, who lost his reelection bid. Nye went to his grave wearing the scarlet lettered cerements that shroud so many of our best dissidents. The gutsy radical who had crossed party lines to support the Red Harlem Congressman Vito Marcantonio, the consistent anti-imperialist who had denounced U.S. interventions in Nicaragua and the Philippines, the agrarian hell-raiser who called for a conscription of plutocratic wealth during wartime, was reviled as a sour right-winger. Nye's investigation was deemed a witch-hunt; nothing came of it but bad publicity.

The funny thing is, Nye had been right: Hollywood *was* run by European-born moguls; a disproportionate number of its directors *were* European immigrants; British actors *did* "swarm" all over the place; the monopolistic studios *did* have a powerful interest in keeping open their lucrative European markets; and American theaters *were* flooded with war propaganda. (One study done by College Men for Defense First of 553 defense-related newsreels in early 1941 found only seven that presented isolationist views.)

But his nativist zeal had led him astray. Robert Sherwood was a Yankee through and through, as were such sanguinary intellectual partisans as Archibald MacLeish and William Allen White. And the man in the White House was a patroon who made your average Plains isolationist look like a wetback.

The studio chiefs survived the republic, but only by a few years. The mini-empires they built are owned today by Japanese and Australians and the faceless conglomerates of the New World Order. Come the next war, a Nye for the 1990s won't know where to begin.

NOTES

1. Quoted in R. Baird Shuman, *Robert E. Sherwood* (Boston: Twayne, 1969), p. 70.

2. Erwin Leiser, *Nazi Cinema* (New York: Macmillan, 1979), p. 10.

3. Gerald Nye, "War Propaganda," *Vital Speeches,* September 15, 1941, p. 721.

4. Ibid., pp. 720–21.

5. Ibid., p. 721.

6. Quoted in Mark Lincoln Chadwin, *The Hawks of World War II* (Chapel Hill: University of North Carolina Press, 1968), p. 218.

7. Frederick Barkley, "Movies Feed Propaganda, Nye Charges at Inquiry," *New York Times,* September 10, 1941, p. 1.

8. Nye, "War Progaganda," p. 721.

9. *Congressional Record,* October 6, 1941, p. 7628.

10. Nye, "War Propaganda," p. 721.

11. Michael Korda, *Charmed Lives* (New York: Random House, 1979), pp. 154–55.

12. Frederick R. Barkley, "Flynn Says Films Bar Peace Side," *New York Times,* September 12, 1941, p. 24.

13. Quoted in Kenneth S. Davis, *FDR: Into the Storm 1937–1940* (New York: Random House, 1993), p. 621.

14. Letter to the author from Justus D. Doenecke, February 12, 1993.

15. Otis Ferguson, "They're Down! They're Up!" *The New Republic,* May 10, 1939, p. 20.

16. Patrick McGilligan, *George Cukor: A Double Life* (New York: St. Martin's Press, 1991), p. 169.

17. Quoted in *Profiles in Populism* (Greenwich, Conn.: Flag Press, 1982), p. 174.

Part Two

Let Us Now Praise Famous America Firsters

4

Alice of Malice:
The Other Side of Rooseveltism

"Irreverence is the champion of liberty and its only sure defense."
—Mark Twain, *Notes*

The true nature of the New Deal was revealed in one of those brilliant ironies that flash like lightning in a midnight storm.

It happened on September 13, 1933, the kickoff of a new secular holiday: NRA (National Recovery Administration) Day. An interminable parade up New York's Fifth Avenue celebrated the NRA, which was to set prices, fix wages, control production, and otherwise cartelize the economy. More than a quarter million happy serfs marched, many carrying the Blue Eagle, emblem of the NRA. Wolves whistled at the comely duo of Miss NRA and Miss Liberty, whose bathing suits encouraged monopolistic fantasies.

Yes, there was no doubt about it, the People were in charge now! The plutocrats were on the run; the common man, led by his paladin, Franklin D. Roosevelt, whose publicists merrily admitted him to be a "traitor to his class," was in the ascendant. The cortege filed past the reviewing stand. And looking down on the contented masses from high atop the platform of dignitaries stood the New York coordinator of the NRA, that notorious scourge of the money-changers, W. Averell Harriman.

The revolution was on.

No family did more to facilitate our passage from republic to empire than the Roosevelts, both the Hyde Park and Sagamore Hill branches. Our pious canting imperialism, the favoring of big over small business, the bloating of the executive branch, the centralization of power in Washington, permanent involvement in the affairs of Europe, conscription, confiscatory taxation—the cousins Roosevelt hammered gilt nails in our collective coffin.

Yet the Roosevelt coin has a reverse side, which we would do well to consider: it is patrician dissent, the self-assured radical criticism born of proprietary patriotism, and it has no more vivid incarnation than the Roosevelt stray who terrorized her kinfolk with frivolity and witty malice: Alice Roosevelt Longworth (1884–1980).

Theodore Roosevelt's daughter is today remembered, if at all, as a tart-tongued termagant tossing off bons mots boiled in acid. Her remark to an unattached woman at a dinner party—"If you haven't got anything good to say about anyone, come and sit by me"—was a nugget mined from the Philip Barry/ Noël Coward quarry; and, indeed, a thinly disguised Alice was the heroine of a crackling George S. Kaufman-Katharine Dayton play, *First Lady* (1935).

But there was much more to her than acerbic wit. Like all the best dissidents, Alice believed that this country belonged to her. As an old woman she said that she could still "hear my father and Cabot Lodge talking about Jefferson as if he were an obnoxious neighbor of theirs."[1] She was unimpressed by power, impervious to the discreet charms of the Potomacists. Alice had a blue bloodline, and she lacked, to put it kindly, the demotic touch; but her horror of internationalism drove her into the arms—literally, gossip had it, in a couple of cases—

of an Old Republic remnant that included such buckskin populists and reactionaries as Senators James Reed of Missouri, William E. Borah of Idaho, and Thomas P. Gore of Oklahoma.

There was little in her girlhood to indicate that Alice would be anything other than a luminous party flirt. "I can be President of the United States," her exasperated father told Owen Wister, "or I can attend to Alice. I can't do both." Alice was a pretty gamine of irrepressibly high spirits: she smoked, drank, danced, played the ponies, went to boxing matches, and honed her wit on the whetstone of mordancy. Popular songs celebrated her; fashion designers mass-marketed the Alice style.

As a teenager in the White House Alice was a legendary brat, an admitted "selfish and defiant" child, and something of a witch: on the last evening of her father's presidency she buried "a bad little idol" in the White House lawn to hex the stolid Ohio Tafts. (She later become young Robert's vociferous champion.)

She was funny, in the way that ostentatiously frank people are. Asked a few years after McKinley's assassination how she had felt when she learned that Leon Czolgosz and an incompetent Buffalo physician had effectively killed the president, admitting Theodore Roosevelt to the White House, Alice confessed to "utter rapture" and said she had danced "a little jig." She gaily admitted that if not for Czolgosz, "we would probably all have been back in our brownstone-front houses and I would have doubtless married for money and been divorced for good cause."[2]

As it was, she married the bald, boozing Congressman (later Speaker of the House) Nicholas Longworth of the dreaded city of "Cincin-nasty." Borah had once said, "I'd rather be right than president." Alice, adapting the remark to her husband, noted, "He'd rather be tight than president."[3]

Daughterly loyalties led Alice into her first, and most successful, political battle: defeat of U.S. entry into the League of Nations.

Part of it was personal: she still despised Woodrow Wilson

for his refusal to allow her father to raise a division of reconstituted Rough Riders at World War I's outset. "I never forgive the persons who injure those I love," she snarled.

But Alice was no longer the naughty hoyden boasting, "I care for nothing except to amuse myself in a charmingly expensive way." She was a budding nationalist, fearful, she said, that Woodrow Wilson wanted to submerge her father's country in a global world federation of which the dour Princeton moralist would be headmaster. The League, she argued, "would pledge us to active participation in the affairs of Europe—indeed, of the whole world—[and] would pledge us in advance regardless of our interests, to use our armed and economic forces when questions arose which were of no possible concern to us."[4]

"Alice in the anti-Wilson fight was a feline figure and one often ready with talons," recalled Jonathan Daniels, son of Wilson's Secretary of the Navy.[5] Her salon on Washington, D.C.'s, M Street became headquarters of the "irreconcilables": those senators unalterably opposed to joining the League, which Senator Borah called a "conspiracy to barter the independence of the American Republic."

This hardy band was tagged the Battalion of Death; Alice was dubbed "Colonel of Death." She and Ruth McCormick, wife of the senator, monitored the debate from the Senate gallery. (Ruth's father, Mark Hanna, might have saved us this trouble had he more forcefully pressed his doubts about empire on his Ohio client William McKinley in 1898.) Day in and day out Alice prowled the Senate, often conferring with Medill McCormick and her closest ally, Connecticut's rascally gentleman, Senator Frank Brandegee.

Closer, in a different way, was Borah, who is widely believed to have fathered Alice's only child. (Wags called her "Aurora Borah Alice.") The Lion of Idaho, the spearless leader, roared anathemas on the League and its internationalist sponsors. "Run up the American flag and let the traitors pull it down if they dare," he boomed, and Alice loved it. Alice herself employed less conventional methods. On the night of President Wilson's return from Paris, she stood outside the White House chanting the curse, "A murrain on him, a murrain on him." (This, truly, was American paganism's finest hour.)

She held no office and commanded no armies, but Alice—through lineage and personality—wielded power. Her incessant gossiping provided valuable intelligence. She learned who was leaning which way, and when suasion was necessary she stuck the needle as only she could. "Hello, Mr. Wobbly," Alice took to greeting Cabot Lodge, who she suspected—rightly—was not averse to compromise. ("You can't amend treason," said Borah of the proposed GOP treaty reservations, by which Lodge and other wavering Republicans sought to amend—and save—President Wilson's treaty and League.)

She told one and all that she was sure that "Fa-tha" would have opposed American membership in the League as a "complete surrender of our independence as a nation." (Or as Borah put it, "the League of Nations makes it necessary for America to give back to George V what it took away from George III.")

Alice probably misunderstood her father, thank God. "Megaphone of Mars," as novelist Henry B. Fuller mockingly described him, had been bully for war. In 1914, impatient for President Wilson to renounce neutrality, Roosevelt envisioned "a great world agreement among all the civilized military powers *to back righteousness by force*" (original italics).[6] This "World League for the Peace of Righteousness" was to adjudicate international disputes and, when necessary, bring "the collective armed power of civilization" to bear against recalcitrants. This global police force is the logical consequence of the collective security provision of Alice's hated Article X of the Covenant of the League of Nations, which provided for collective action to maintain peace (or enforce unjust League decrees). Alice's vehemence on the matter, while partly traceable to the enmity she bore Wilson, also shows the increasingly independent cast of her mind. The debutante who had gone gleefully "panting after my parent, longing to go into the First World War," was becoming a sharp critic of foreign entanglements. She would never become what her father most detested—a pacifist—but she did grow up to be one of those "little old ladies in tennis shoes" whose American soles ushered in the peace and comity that marked the 1920s and 1930s.

In the League fight we descry the contours of realignment, the scrapping of meaningless party distinctions and their replacement with . . . what? The provincial-cosmpolitan bipolarity is out, scuttled by the coupling of Idaho's Borah and soigné Alice. Centralist-decentralist is better, as are Little American-globalist and imperialist-republican. Whatever the taxonomy, and whether the treaty marked a sellout of our independence, as Alice asserted, or if, as La Follette charged, it was "a treaty of financial imperialists, of exploiters, of bankers, of all monopolists, who sought through mandates to sanctify and make permanent a redistribution of the spoils of the world and to cement forever the stranglehold of the power of gold on the defenseless peoples of the earth,"[7] natural allies did battle under the Americanist banner.

The victorious patriots gathered at the Longworths' residence on November 19, 1919, to celebrate the Senate defeat of the Versailles Treaty over a midnight dinner of scrambled eggs. The whole gang was there: atrabilious Missouri Senator Reed, the brilliant Jeffersonian toper; Oklahoma populist Senator Gore and his wife; the McCormicks; the Hardings; Senator and Mrs. Frelinghysen; Borah (without his wife); and aristocratic Senators Lodge, Brandegee, and Wadsworth, among others. "Mrs. Harding cooked the eggs," Alice archly recalled in her 1933 autobiography, *Crowded Hours,* a listless effort which Maxwell Perkins cajoled her to write.

The lion lay down with the Longworth; the sons of the wild jackass (i.e., the Western Populists of the 1910s and 1920s) drank cocktails with the daughters of Pilgrims. The League issue was of such magnitude that the detritus of past quarrels over domestic issues was swept aside.

In 1920, Alice supported an unprepossessing family friend, General Leonard Wood, for the Republican presidential nomination, although she was also fond of her father's Bull Moose running mate, California Senator Hiram Johnson, whose campaign theme was his "100 percent Americanism." He did not mean by this a petty xenophobia or insistence upon loyalty oaths that no real patriot would ever dream of signing; rather, Johnson upheld fidelity to one's little corner of the world.

Johnson's platform was normalcy itself. "It is time for an American policy," he declared in 1919. "Bring home American soldiers. Rescue our own democracy. Restore its free expression. Get American business into its normal channels. Let American life, social and economic, be American again."* Although he polled the most primary votes, Johnson's bid fell short, as did Wood's. Alice withheld the endorsement of the Sagamore Hill Roosevelts until eventual Republican nominee Warren G. Harding, whom she liked as a poker pal but dismissed as a lightweight, promised a hard-line anti-League stance.

Alice roared through the 1920s carrying a flask of bootleg bourbon and a copy of the Constitution in her capacious purse. Borah sounded, at times, like her father, as he denounced "this weakening, simpering, sentimental internationalism which would destroy national character and undermine nationalism," and insisted upon the cultivation of "an American mind, an American purpose and American ideals."[8] This was Rooseveltian phraseology in service of an anti-Rooseveltian program.

"I am a Republican with a Progressive tradition-inclination," Alice said in 1932. She deplored "lavish federal spending and drastic federal control of business and agriculture" and, most of all, any diminution of American sovereignty. Her progressivism was the forgotten kind, that of Amos R. E. Pinchot and *The*

---

*The tragedy of twentieth-century American politics is that the faithless took over, and men like Hiram Johnson were cast out into a wilderness in which they died, graves unmarked, and from which their heirs have yet to return.

Nation's William Hard and the New Jersey dynamo George Record. It stood for parsimonious expenditure; for "equal rights for all, special privileges for none"; for the destruction of monopoly by democratically controlled local governments; and for the Founders' coiled rattlesnake foreign policy of armed neutrality. That this progressive tradition was completely at odds with her father's never seemed to cross Alice's mind. (Others understood. The Republican party of North Dakota, deep-dyed in agrarian antimonopolist radicalism, tried, but failed, to start an "Alice for Veep" boomlet in 1932.)

And then along came her father's fifth cousin, "Feather Duster" Roosevelt, whom Alice had long ago dismissed as "the kind of boy whom you invited to the dance but not the dinner."[9] Alice had been Eleanor's maid of honor and it was she who introduced Franklin to the elongated cigarette holder, but she could not abide their reign. Alice sighed, "When I think of Franklin and Eleanor in the White House, I could grind my teeth to powder and blow them out my nose."[10]

The new president, she complained, was "ninety percent mush and ten percent Eleanor."[11] He was hobbling our hale republic. "My poor cousin, he suffered from polio so he was put in a brace; and now he wants to put the entire U.S. into a brace, as if it were a crippled country—that is all the New Deal is about, you know," Alice said, typically impolitic.[12] Her animus, however, didn't keep her from abetting Franklin's affair with Lucy Mercer Rutherford; after all, she later explained, he "deserved a good time. He was married to Eleanor."

Alice undertook a syndicated column that was every bit as insipid as Eleanor's "My Day." She meant to write corrosively funny attacks on the New Deal but, as with *Crowded Hours,* her lively wit sputtered and died somewhere in transit between mind and paper. Besides, Alice's country had become "all body and no soul," and she despaired of the mostly fourth-rate men who stood quakingly in opposition.

She reserved her most withering scorn for the Republican

panjandrums who made the party so ineffectual during the critical middle decades of the century. Thomas E. Dewey, of course, was the "bridegroom on a wedding cake"; John Bricker was "just an honest Harding"; and Wendell Willkie "sprang from the grass roots of a thousand country clubs." Alice did approve of Calvin Coolidge, but he was dead.

Alice also admired Senator Robert A. Taft, even if she conceded that he suffered from "an abundance of lack and shortage of luster." With Taft, at least, we could "return to the ways of our old self-reliance," she told readers of *The Saturday Evening Post* in May 1940. Yes, he was phlegmatic, but "Miss Columbia has had a long and giddy spell being the girl friend of the whirling dervish. It's time she stopped revolving, chose another partner." (Alice's paean to Taft is sprinkled with other metaphors of physical activity, an obvious taunt to the wheelchair-bound president. Alice did have a mean streak.)

She lobbied energetically against the Supreme Court-packing scheme that backfired on FDR in 1937, and the friendships she forged in that fight with independent liberals like Senator and Mrs. Burton K. Wheeler flowered over the next quadrennium, as old republicans of both the Left and Right merged to halt the drift toward war.

The friends Alice acquired in this phase of her life perplex those chroniclers who regard her as a bipartisan bon vivant. Borah was strange enough, but another rumored swain, United Mine Workers President John L. Lewis, boggles the mind. About the Iowa-born Congress of Industrial Organizations (CIO) leader she quipped, "He loved making trouble, and I loved watching him make it. It was natural that we should get together."[13]

Lewis also loathed Franklin, but there was more to it than beefy petulance. He was anti-imperialist to the bone. Lewis understood that working men pay war's wages in blood; he was a patriot who believed FDR was a "would-be dictator" under whose misrule "the United States first becomes a militaristic nation, and second, becomes an imperialistic nation."[14] Lewis called them the way he saw them for the rest of his tumultuous life; even in the Cold War's most frigid phase, he denounced the transfer of wealth from American taxpayers to European governments.

Alice bolstered her men in their anti-FDR efforts; the fortifying effect of her slashing Old Right wit is impossible to calculate. She never brought Lewis over to Robert Taft—like Hiram Johnson, he was for Wheeler in 1940—but her charm and magnetism helped to unite the antiwar movement.

Once more her salon, now in a four-story sandstone just off DuPont Circle, was a hospice for Americanists who, like Alice, wanted to "keep out this time." Alice was on the national America First Committee and she was a constant presence at America First rallies, sitting on stage beneath a broad-brimmed hat. She was a director of the potent Washington, D.C., chapter of America First; her manner gave the dowdy committee a welcome dash of flair.

Apologists—the kind who believe "America First" is a code name for Nazi, and scramble to explain away their beloved Mrs. Longworth's fervent isolationism—point to her retrospective crack, "Family feeling enters into it; anything to annoy Franklin." But this was a calculated exculpation of what had come to be defined as a sin, for Alice, like most self-consciously outrageous persons, had a keen sense of boundaries. She knew better, once the myths had hardened, than to advertise her objections to the holiest enterprise ever undertaken by man.

Family feeling did enter it into it, of course: Alice regarded herself as keeper of her father's flame, though it's hard to imagine "Rough Rider" Teddy wanting to sit out the European War of 1939. Richard Nixon noted of Alice, "As a devoted admirer of her father, she was first, last, and always a nationalist. Her father, of course, was America's first truly internationalist President."[15] (From her ebullient father Alice did inherit a passion for learning and life. One can easily imagine Teddy spending a magnificent evening with Edwin Hubble on Mount Wilson at the eyepiece of the 100-inch reflector, as Alice did.)

Once war came, America was not to be first again. "Well, Franklin asked for it. Now he's got it," Alice remarked at lunch on December 7, 1941.

After the war Alice continued to dabble in Americanist activities (she helped organize a "United States Day" in 1954 to counter United Nations Day), but mostly she reveled in her role as what she termed "a rather loathsome combination of Marie Dressler and Phyllis Diller."

Alice grew older and more cantankerous and, ultimately, harmless. John F. Kennedy called her "the best company in town." She voted Democrat for the first time in 1964 because she thought Goldwater humorless. She enjoyed the student rebellion because it gave her old nemeses in the Democratic Establishment fits. According to her relatively unsympathetic biographer Carol Felsenthal, Alice as dotard extinguished her father's flame. When a reporter asked in 1977 about the Panama Canal Treaty, she replied, "I don't care what they do with the canal. Who cares? It's there and I don't give a damn. Nothing could bore me more."[16]

Near the end of her life Alice recalled, "We were against the League because we hated Wilson. . . . All that nonsense about my killing the League with a bunch of diehard cronies is ridiculous."[17] The earlier self she reimagined belonged in the George S. Kaufman play; it was motivated by spite and jealousy and the desperate need to be an intrigant in the court. This did no justice to the hellcat princess who had thrown herself into valiant battles against "the internationalism that we felt menaced our very existence as an independent nation."

Alice Roosevelt Longworth did not lead a blameless life. She was, it seems, a horrible mother, by turns domineering and neglectful, and her shy daughter, Paulina, committed suicide at age thirty-one, although not before the girl found the bridge between Left and Right by being active in both Twenties for Taft and the anarchist Catholic Worker movement. In this sense, at least, Paulina was very much the daughter of the Republican dame who had loved John L. Lewis.

However imperfect, Alice had a soul. She laughed, and made others laugh. She brightened the corner where she was, and the light she generated was, as Anne Morrow Lindbergh might say, American . . . American . . . American.

She concluded in *Crowded Hours,* "Anyway, the show is there for us, and we might as well get what entertainment we may out of it." That is how one lives to be ninety-six years of age, sunnily dispensing wicked apothegms as the empire slides into night.

NOTES

1. Quoted in Michael Teague, *Mrs. L.* (Garden City, N.Y.: Doubleday, 1981), p. 52.

2. Ibid., p. 159.

3. Quoted in Carol Felsenthal, *Alice Roosevelt Longworth* (New York: Putnam's, 1988), p. 162.

4. Alice Roosevelt Longworth, *Crowded Hours* (New York: Scribner's, 1933), p. 276.

5. Jonathan Daniels, *The Time between the Wars* (Garden City, N.Y.: Doubleday, 1966), p. 38.

6. Quoted in Harold Howland, *Theodore Roosevelt and His Times* (New Haven: Yale University Press, 1921), pp. 257–58.

7. Quoted in David Green, *The Language of Politics in America* (Ithaca: Cornell University Press, 1987), p. 94.

8. Quoted in LeRoy Ashby, *The Spearless Leader* (Urbana: University of Illinois Press, 1972), p. 98.

9. Quoted in Howard Teichman, *Alice: The Life and Times of Alice Roosevelt Longworth* (Englewood Cliffs, N.J.: Prentice-Hall, 1979), p. 50.

10. Ibid., p. 163.

11. Ibid., p. 156.

12. Quoted in Felsenthal, *Alice Roosevelt Longworth,* p. 171.

13. Teichman, *Alice: The Life and Times of Alice Roosevelt Longworth,* p. 192.

14. Quoted in Melvin Dubofsky, "John L. Lewis and American Isolationism," in *Three Faces of Midwestern Isolationism* (Iowa City: Center for the Study of the Recent History of the United States, 1981), p. 28.

15. Felsenthal, *Alice Roosevelt Longworth,* p. 197.

16. Ibid., p. 264.

17. Teague, *Mrs. L.,* p. 167.

5

Sinclair Lewis: It's a Grand Republic

"To its fugitive children, Grand Republic will forgive almost anything, if they will but come back home."
—Sinclair Lewis, *Cass Timberlane* (1945)

Late in life, Sinclair Lewis of Sauk Centre, Minnesota, figured something out: he would soon be forgotten. In a mock self-obituary, Lewis foresaw that he would leave "no literary descendants. . . . Whether this is a basic criticism of [Lewis's] pretensions to power and originality, or whether, like another contemporary, Miss Willa Cather, he was an inevitably lone and insulated figure, we have not as yet the perspective to see."[1]

Half a century later, we have the proper perspective but Lewis, the first American to win the Nobel Prize for literature, has vanished. He is heirless and unread; Mark Schorer, his principal biographer, allowed that Lewis "was one of the worst writers in modern American literature," and a truculent acne-ridden boozer to boot.[2]

What's more, Lewis was a garrulous drunk, an inattentive father, and possibly a bad husband. (In Lewis's defense, his first wife, Grace Hegger, was "a poisonous woman" who "converted herself into a fake English duchess," as H. L. Mencken wrote in his abortive professional autobiography. His second wife, the newspaper oracle Dorothy Thompson—"the Talking Woman," Lewis called her—was no saintly helpmeet either. Alice Roosevelt Longworth called Thompson "the only woman in history who has had her menopause in public and made it pay."[3])

But Sinclair Lewis did write several excellent novels about people from the places he knew best: the one-horse towns and bustling small cities of Minnesota. He trained his mordant wit upon them because he loved them—because to Sinclair Lewis, Zenith and Gopher Prairie and Grand Republic were the only places in the world that really mattered. In his declining years he lamented,

> My father has never forgiven me for *Main Street*. . . . He can't comprehend the book, much less grasp that it's the greatest tribute I knew how to pay him. . . . *Main Street* condemned me in his eyes as a traitor to my heritage—whereas the truth is, I shall never shed the little, indelible "Sauk-centricities" that enabled me to write it.[4]

Deliciously, appositely, Sauk Centre is the keeper of the Sinclair Lewis flame. The novelist's boyhood home is a museum; the high school football team is called the Main Streeters. Some find this ironic but I think it's perfect, for Sinclair Lewis was a hayseed of the sort found in every crossroads burg: the debunker, the scoffer, the town atheist whose deepest secret (which his neighbors know, which is why they tolerate, even cherish him) is that he loves his village with almost embarrassing ardor.

Harry Sinclair Lewis was born in 1885, the son of a country doctor. He had the gift of seeing himself as both of and apart from his surroundings. "While I was a mediocre sportsman in Boytown, I was neither a cripple nor a Sensitive Soul,"[5] Lewis recalled with an odd pride that any small-town lad can understand. His memories of childhood were invariably happy, much to the puzzlement of a clerisy that consistently misread his books. A middle-aged Lewis told the Sauk Centre high school yearbook in 1931: "I could have been born and reared in no place in the world where I would have had more friendliness. . . . It was a good time, a good place and a good preparation for life."[6]

Young Lewis enjoyed reading H. G. Wells and Thomas Hardy, but his imagination was fired by Hamlin Garland's stories of hardscrabble Dakota farms and families. "If I ever succeed in expressing anything of Minnesota and its neighbors, you will be largely responsible," he wrote to Garland in 1915, "for it was in your books that the real romance of that land was first revealed to me."

It takes a keen eye and sympathetic heart to find romance on Garland's plains; I suspect that Lewis was inspirited most by Garland's 1894 manifesto *Crumbling Idols,* a full-throated war cry for an American literature of place. "Be true to yourself, true to your locality, and true to your time," Garland exhorted, and for all his biliousness and vagaries and venom, Sinclair Lewis kept that faith.

He was proudly, defiantly Midwestern. As a green newsman in 1908, Lewis prophesied in the Waterloo, Iowa, *Daily Courier*: "The artist capable of the really vital and American play is far more likely to hail from the fresh brightness and unscoured genuineness of the Corn Belt than he is from the New York millions."

Lewis's first vital and American novel was his fifth, *Main Street* (1920). When he placed the vivacious newlywed Carol Kennicott in Gopher Prairie with her stolid husband, Will, a country doctor, the Minnesotan Lewis was working within a regional realist field plowed years before by Garland, Joseph Kirkland, Mary Wilkins Freeman, Edgar W. Howe, Harold Frederic, and others. What set *Main Street* apart from its predecessors was its astringent humor; earlier novels had measured the spiritual poverty of frontier villages, but never with Lewis's tartness. (Hamlin Garland hated the book for "belittling . . . the descendants of the old frontier.")

There are passages of pure vitriol in *Main Street,* although the bitterest observations are usually attributed to the foolish Carol. She sees in Gopher Prairie

> an unimaginatively standardized background, a sluggishness of speech and manners, a rigid ruling of the spirit by the desire to appear respectable. It is contentment. . . . the contentment of the quiet dead, who are scornful of the living for their restless walking. It is negation canonized as the one positive virtue. It is the prohibition of happiness. It is slavery self-sought and self-defended. It is dullness made God.[7]

Harsh, yes, but even the rankest Valley of Democracy sentimentalist must recognize its ring of truth. If one really *belongs* to a village, is a part of that corporate whole, then all sorts of crotchets and queer behavior are permitted. But if, like Carol, one is from outside—and if the outsider is headstrong and outspoken—then life can be miserable, and her straining will cause the witches of every American Gopher Prairie to sneer: "Who does she think *she* is?"

Lewis claimed that his novel was an act of fealty; he wrote it, he said, from "a love of Main Street, from a belief in Main Street's inherent power." Lewis's next novel, *Babbitt* (1922), his grandest achievement, validated this claim.

Our guide through the city of Zenith is George Babbitt, real-estate booster and incorrigible joiner, and the greatest character Lewis ever created. Babbitt is the apostle and the apotheosis of the Standardized American Citizen. He is bully for progress: Zenith has "the finest school-ventilating system in the country," he brags; its oustanding flaw is its slowness in "extending the paving of motor boulevards." Babbitt extols the new, the big, the efficient; yet in his heart of hearts he is loyal to the smallest and homeliest piece of his world: his family and friends.

With *Babbitt,* a critical refrain developed: all of Lewis's Midwestern characters talk alike. That's the highbrow line, and say, maybe fer once them Greenwich Village birds are posolutely, absotively right. Darned if a reg'lar captain of industry like Sam Dodsworth don't talk an awful lot like that dub Lowell Schmaltz and that four-flusher Elmer Gantry and even a real he-American like George Babbitt, yessirree!

Was Lewis lazy, or was there a method to this sameness? In his unpublished introduction to *Babbitt,* Lewis noted, "Differences [between cities] have for a long time now tended to decrease, so powerful is our faith in standardization. . . . Hartford and Milwaukee—the citizens of those two distant cities go to the same offices, speak the same patois on the same telephones, go to the same lunch and the same athletic clubs, etc."[8]

Zenith had joined the mad scramble to imitate the big cities; it was losing its provincialism—and Lewis, contrary to myth, was a provincial of the first water. The disease of universal culture was spreading even to the Gopher Prairies. Small towns "all want to be just like Zenith," Vergil Gunch crowed to George Babbitt over a poker pot. Zenith, in turn, wanted to be just like Chicago, which wanted to be just like New York. (*Babbitt's* original title was *Population 300,000*; Lewis hoped to inspire rude young bards in places like Omaha, Rochester, Cincinnati, and Louisville.)

Babbitt is a kind of regionalist dystopia. The sons of the pioneers had traded in their buckskins for the the drab dress grays of conformity. George Babbitt is a fool not because he is provincial but because he has bought into the lie of mass culture.

Lewis walked it like he talked it: he used his fame to promote fellow novelists of place. Besides Willa Cather, he championed Booth Tarkington, the gentleman from Indiana; Ruth Suckow, with her German Iowa farmers; and Wisconsin's indefatigable August Derleth. In an illuminating and shamefully neglected memoir, *Three Literary Men* (1963), Derleth describes how Lewis beat the bushes in the upper Midwest in support of unknown regional novelists. "The general lack of recognition given authors by their home states" bothered Lewis, Derleth recalled, and "he was doing all in his power to encourage and stimulate the young writers" of his region. One of the many shortcomings of Schorer's biography is to neglect Lewis's avuncular solicitude for his nieces and nephews in Green Bay, Sioux City, and all the little prairie towns with Indian names and restive children.

Lewis urged young writers to stay put and to avoid New York City at all costs. He remarked:

> America—the literary map of it, apparently, shows three cities, New York, Chicago and New Orleans; then a stretch inhabited by industrious Swedes who invariably (after an edifying struggle) become college professors or rich farmers; then a noble waste still populated by cowpunchers speaking the purest 1870; finally, a vast domain called Hollywood. But actually there are portions of the United States not included in this favorite chart.[9]

America deserved a "literature worthy of her vastness," Lewis declared in his 1930 Nobel acceptance speech. (This fine address was marred by an unfair swipe at William Dean Howells for having "the code of a pious old maid whose greatest delight was to have tea at the vicarage." Funny, but unfair. Howells was not only Hamlin Garland's mentor but also an enthusiast for the Midwestern realists so admired by Lewis.)

Lewis's vagabondage carried him across the vast American continent many times. Although his happiest adult years were spent on his Vermont farm, Lewis tried to come home to Minnesota in the 1940s. He spoke to numerous civic groups: "Stay West, Young Woman," he urged the University of Minnesota's coeds, and he earnestly promised the citizens of Duluth his "help in setting up a few stones in what may be a new Athens."[10]

Lewis became—no, he always was—a booster par excellence. He memorized Minnesota's eighty-seven counties and county seats, alphabetically, just like the eponymous hero of *Cass Timberlane*. Lewis's friend, the artist Adolph Dehn, recalled, "He looked at all my Minnesota scenes but wasn't interested in land-scapes outside the state, or pictures of anything non-Minnesota." As one appalled Duluth matron exclaimed, "The man who wrote *Babbitt* actually loved Babbitts."[11]

Like other independent American writers (Jack Kerouac the Catholic Taft Republican, Garland the Jefferson-Jackson pop-ulist, and Gore Vidal the patrician republican), Lewis befuddled the literary mafia with his politics. Dorothy Thompson called him "an old-fashioned populist American radical" with "a deep feeling for tradition." Lewis was a cultural and political America Firster: part upper Midwest maverick, part George Babbitt Rotary Republican. "Intellectually, I know America is no better than any other country," Lewis wrote in 1930. "Emotionally, I know she is better than every other country."[12]*

He was a welter of contradictions, a caustic sentimentalist. "He mocked the cruder manifestations of Yankee imperialism because he was, at heart, a fanatic American," the novelist wrote of himself in his 1941 essay "The Death of Arrowsmith." Lewis kidded George Babbitt for his indifference to Europe but then turned around and joined the America First Committee. When *The Nation* asked Lewis, a La Follette man, to return to Gopher Prairie and cover the 1924 election, he submitted a piece titled "Main Street's Been Paved" (*The Nation,* September 10, 1924), in which the Coolidge supporter Doc Kennicott gets off all the best lines.

Lewis was a devotee of Henry David Thoreau, although his Walden included a mansion and servants. His most poignant characters, whether Sam Dodsworth or George Babbitt or Fred Cornplow of *The Prodigal Parents* (1938), long to ignore the crowd and follow the inner light. "Why is it that nobody ever

---

*Lewis's Americanism flared when he was attending a magic show in England in 1921. When the magician made a snide crack about America, Lewis stood up and shouted, "Take that back! Take that back!" The flustered thaumaturge apologized and left the stage.

does do any of the things that he's free to do?" is the Thoreauvian question haunting almost every Lewis novel. Babbitt would flower if he just had the confidence to be his hick self.

Much as his friend H. L. Mencken committed public suicide with his anti-New Deal polemics, so did Sinclair Lewis slit his throat with the publication of *The Prodigal Parents*.

This unjustly obscure novel—in some ways a rewrite of *Babbitt*—features a wholly sympathetic upstate New York auto dealer named Fred Cornplow, self-declared president of the "Mind Your Own Business Association." Fred's children are spoiled lotus-eating Reds: when not cadging money from Pop, Fred's son drones at the dinner table: "Dad, did you realize that in the past year . . . the growth in production in heavy industry in the Ural section of Russia has been two hundred and seventeen percent?"13

Slowly it dawns on Fred that his family is not atypical: America is being remade, and the Cornplows—the small independent businessmen, backbones of the fading republic—are an endangered species. The Communists will bury him, the brain trusters jeer at him, a New York City psychiatrist wants to put him away (only a crazy man, the shrink reasons, could enjoy a middle-class life in dowdy Sachem Falls, New York). The country has passed to the likes of Fred's son, who dad thinks would "make a first-rate coat holder for some posthole digger on a WPA project that ain't started yet."14

The Prodigal Parents contains more laughs per page than any of Lewis's post-*Babbitt* novels, but the author was roasted for its homely slant. Lewis had tipped his hand; the heretic had been a Main Streeter all along. He infuriated reviewers with passages such as this:

From Fred Cornplow's family, between B.C. 1937 and A.D. 1937, there came, despite an occasional aristocratic Byron or an infrequent proletarian John Bunyan, nearly all the medical researchers, the discoverers of better varieties of wheat, the poets, the builders, the singers, the captains of great ships. Sometimes his name has been pronounced Babbitt; sometimes it has been called Ben Franklin. . . . He is the eternal bourgeois, the bour-joyce, the burgher, the Middle Class, whom the Bolsheviks hate and imitate, whom the English love and deprecate, and who is most of the population worth considering in France and Germany and these United States.[15]

(These same independent freeholders—farmers, shopkeepers, printers—are the bulwark of Vermont's resistance to a fascist takeover in Lewis's crude cautionary novel, *It Can't Happen Here* [1935].)

After *The Prodigal Parents,* it was open season on Sinclair Lewis. His last novels, with the exception of *Cass Timberlane,* were anemic. Like Mencken, he was dismissed as a young radical grown crusty and conservative. *Main Street* and *Babbitt,* once wrongly praised as exposés of the barrenness of Mid-America, were now condemned (by Mark Schorer) for "sugar-coating [the] loneliness, monotony, and boorishness" of small towns. The village atheist was discovered kneeling in the church, and for this sin of Main Street devotion he has never been forgiven.

To the end, Lewis stayed true to his time and his locality. He insisted, despite the naysaying of the folks who run things in this country, on the romance of the "Average Citizens of the United States." His crime, it seems, was that he *liked* them. He thought them funny and tragic and worthy of a lifetime's work.

In a preface to his ludicrous race novel, *Kingsblood Royal* (1947), Lewis wrote:

The Knights of the Crusade no more sang poetry about themselves than does my hero, the young banker of Grand Republic, Minnesota. It is only centuries later that the epic poet comes along and finds them elevated and given to speaking in blank verse. . . . Some future Mr. Homer or Milton (born in North Dakota) . . . will make ringing heroic couplets out of him. The ring and the heroism are there all right, and I hope they are implicit in my own sardonic cataloguing.[16]

Lewis was not the sophisticate mocking the bumpkins. (Compare his affectionate treatment of his fire-and-brimstone scoundrel, Elmer Gantry, with Mencken's vicious requiem for William Jennings Bryan.) Lewis loved the Bryans and the Babbitts, the Gantrys and the Kennicotts. He died alone in Italy in 1951, but the long arm of the small town reached out and brought him back to Sauk Centre, where he belonged. The funeral took place on a blustery day, and Sinclair Lewis's ashes were accidentally scattered all over his native ground. The prodigal son, home at last.

NOTES

1. "The Death of Arrowsmith," in *The Man from Main Street,* edited by Melville H. Cane and Harry Maule (New York: Random House, 1953), p. 105.
2. Mark Schorer, *Sinclair Lewis: An American Life* (New York: McGraw-Hill, 1961), p. 813.
3. Quoted in James Brough, *Princess Alice* (Boston: Little, Brown, 1975), p. 297.
4. Schorer, *Sinclair Lewis: An American Life,* pp, 461–62.
5. Ibid., p. 19.
6. Ibid., p. 7.
7. Sinclair Lewis, *Main Street* (New York: Harcourt Brace Jovanovich, 1920), p. 265.
8. "Unpublished Introduction to *Babbitt,*" in *The Man from Main Street.*
9. Cane and Maule, *The Man from Main Street,* p. 144.
10. Schorer, *Sinclair Lewis: An American Life,* p. 732.
11. John J. Koblas, *Sinclair Lewis, Home at Last* (Bloomington, Minn.: Voyageur Press, 1981), p. 138.
12. Quoted in D. J. Dooley, *The Art of Sinclair Lewis* (Lincoln: University of Nebraska Press, 1967), p. 177.

13. Sinclair Lewis, *The Prodigal Parents* (Garden City, N.Y.: Doubleday, Doran, 1938), p. 12.

14. Ibid., p. 31.

15. Ibid., p. 100.

16. Sinclair Lewis, preface to *Kingsblood Royal* (New York: Random House, 1947).

6

Patriotic Gore Vidal

"Whoso would be a man must be a nonconformist."
—Ralph Waldo Emerson, "Self-Reliance"

We do not live in a golden age for homegrown and cornfed radical critics. Legal restrictions on political speech remain few, but informal strictures and the passage of time have muted those who remember—and like—the free, landed republic that this country used to be, before World War II and the monolithic Cold War state. We are an empire today, the antipode of the virtuous agrarian society that our forefathers envisaged.

Woe betide the independent man, unbeholden to university or think tank, who speaks these truths. Whether left or right, blueblood or fieldhand, dullard or high wit, the foe of empire invites the pillory.

Enter Gore Vidal.

No public figure in present-day America takes a more brutal thrashing from the arbiters of acceptable opinion than Gore Vidal: novelist, essayist, acidulous celebrity. Although his work, particularly his remarkable chronicle of American history (*Burr; Lincoln; 1876; Empire; Hollywood; Washington, D.C.*), is wildly popular with the Middle American reading public, Vidal is vilified by the "vital center," that loud and puissant band of Cold War liberals and power-worshiping conservatives.

These attacks have all the subtlety of a commode flushing. For instance:

• *The New Republic* branded a Vidal essay on Israel's U.S. supporters, notably the polemicist Norman Podhoretz, as "brazen racist hate" and pronounced the essayist "ready for the funny farm."

• *National Review* labeled that same essay "anti-Semitic screaming" by an author who "enjoys a special immunity as an avowed homosexual."

• Irving Howe of the socialist journal *Dissent* found the disputed essay "a racist diatribe."

There is more, in the same vein, but you get the gist. Vidal has offended all three pointy-heads of the regnant American political triangle: the Manhattan-Washington-based neoconservatives, the Manhattan-Washington-based corporate-state socialists, and the Manhattan-Washington-based New Class conservatives—in short, the power elite.

Why the Vidal-hatred?

Let us first dispose of the obvious, and wholly unsatisfactory, explanation: his open homosexuality. Vidal has never concealed what he calls his "same-sex" preference; indeed, he published *The City and the Pillar* in 1948, at no small risk to his career. Too, he has baited William F. Buckley, Jr., on this subject, so deftly that the normally imperturbable Buckley threatened him on national television in 1968: "You queer . . . I'll sock you in the goddam face."[1]

But Vidal is a citizen of America, not Queer Nation. He scoffed at the idea of a "gay political identity" in his quixotic 1982 California campaign for the Senate; apart from endorsing the repeal of sodomy laws on libertarian grounds, Vidal has ignored the gay rights agenda. Moreover—and anyone who has spent any amount of time in Washington, D.C., can attest to this—the grant-grazing conservative herd is rife with closeted gay men who sing the praises of Republican "family values" by day and cruise for boy prostitutes by night.

So the Vidal-loathing has much deeper roots than the Beltway Right's purported aversion to homosexuality. The real source of the rancor is the American past, an epoch that Gore Vidal has spent the last two decades excavating and explicating in his self-described role as "current biographer" of the United States.*

Identifying the inspiration for his historical novels, Vidal told a young interviewer in *The Progressive* in 1986: "It's thirty-five years we've been a garrison state. Somebody your age doesn't even remember what the country was like before. I do, and the country was a very good one. It had its problems, but the place worked. For one thing, we believed in the country more. Now nobody understands it. It isn't taught."[2]

We have forgotten our past. In Vidal's words, "We have no public memory of anything that happened before last Tuesday." Pre-Depression America has been surgically excised from the national memory, save its quainter aspects. We are not supposed to know that alternatives once existed—indeed, still exist—to industrial capitalism, the permanent war economy, and rootless man. Gore Vidal, bless his contumacious heart, has not forgotten, and his work is monument to that past, witness to the climacteric events that marked the way from republic to empire . . . and, maybe someday, back again.

Just as the key to understanding Charles Lindbergh is the aviator's father, the "Gopher Bolshevik" Congressman from Minnesota, so was Gore Vidal molded in the person of an ancestral

---

*Unlike his critics, who are generally contemptuous of all American literature outside the corpus of Saul Bellow, Vidal has written dozens of appreciative essays about American writers he admires, from Henry James to L. Frank Baum of the Oz books, and from William Dean Howells to Dawn Powell, the satirist whose rediscovery is traceable to Vidal.

politician: his grandfather, the blind populist Roosevelt-hating Oklahoma Senator Thomas P. Gore. Young Vidal read to his grandfather, escorted him around the Senate, and drank up the wisdom of a man who was at once socialistic (like many populists, he was avid for the nationalization of certain industries, especially in the teens) and an old-fashioned American independent (he ranked with petrified Virginian Carter Glass as the most consistent Democratic New Deal foe in the Senate).

Grandfather Gore was, at once, a warm defender of the people and a witty misanthrope who used to say, "If there was any race other than the human race, I'd go join it." He was defeated for reelection in 1936, and shortly thereafter he passed the populist baton to his grandson Eugene, who later took the old man's surname as his first name in patronymic homage. Young Vidal's first battle in the political wars came at Exeter, where he was active in the America First chapter. In a long, strange, and wonderful journey he has always kept to that path.

"The historic novel," Henry James wrote Maine novelist Sarah Orne Jewett in 1901, "is condemned . . . to a fatal *cheapness*. . . . You may multiply the little facts that can be got from pictures and documents, relics and prints as much as you like— the *real* thing is almost impossible to do."[3]

The audacious Gore Vidal has done it. Grandson of Thomas P. Gore, friend of Eleanor Roosevelt, slashing wit of the Kennedy demimonde, Vidal has ever regarded politics at close range. He perfectly comprehends the constitution of the statesman: he is a lucent and experienced anatomist of power. An anatomist, moreover, who appreciates Henry Adams's twin dicta: "Power is poison," and politics is "the systematic organization of hatreds."

With brio, intelligence, and mordacious humor, Vidal has vivified American history and its great actors. He relumes even the dimmest politicians by peopling his chronicle with men of letters—radical libertarian journalist William Leggett, poet William Cullen Bryant, John Hay, Henry Adams—who are quick with the epigram, the gnome, the illuminating quip.

Beyond his flair for reanimating dead statesmen, Vidal succeeds because he has found a grand unifying theme: the growth of the American empire. He has descried, as have few others, the irreconcilable conflicts that delivered us unto that empire: the early tension between republican ideals and the lure of the western lands; Lincoln's cataclysmic destruction of the loose confederation of states and annealment of a brand-new centralized and unitary state; the withering of republican virtue in the flames of the Great Barbecue; Teddy Roosevelt's vanquishment of the principles of 1776; the assumption of dictatorial powers by Woodrow Wilson and his Hollywood handmaidens (i.e., the Hun-hating movie producers); and the exponential growth of government in the wake of the Second World War.

Vidal has plaintively summarized his politics as such: "I hate the American Empire, and I love the old republic."[4] He is emphatic, sometimes didactic, on this point. In *Washington, D.C.* (which is, with the possible exception of *Two Sisters,* his only semi-autobiographical novel), Vidal deplores how Franklin Roosevelt "had managed by force of arms and sly maneuvering to transform an isolationist republic into what no doubt would be the last empire on earth."[5] Or witness this exchange, from the turn-of-the-century novel *Empire,* between Secretary of State John Hay and Henry Adams, who in so many ways is Vidal's kindred in spirit.

> "John, it is empire you all want, and it is empire that you have got, and at such a small price, when you come to think of it."
>   "What price is that?" Hay could tell from the glitter in Adams's eye that the answer would be highly unpleasant.

---

*I do not invent my literary ancestors. If anything, they invented me," wrote Vidal in his appreciation of William Dean Howells. Although not related, Vidal and John Jay Chapman, the tartly independent essayist whom Vidal regards as his era's best critic, lived in the same home: Edgewater, on the Hudson at Barrytown. Chapman spent the 1920s warding off charges that he was a nativist—an indictment later visited upon Vidal.

"The American republic. You've finally got rid of it. For good."[6]

The parallels between Vidal and Henry Adams are many and significant: aristocratic families, lengthy European residences, arraignments on charges of anti-Semitism, and hostility to formal education. To emphasize the affinity, Vidal has made Adams the grey eminence of the middle chronicles, offering droll—and very Vidalian—commentaries.

The most pertinent kinship between the two is ideological. Vidal and Adams are conservatives in a singularly American vein. They are exponents of Ben Franklin's notion of republican virtue: disparage "the love of power and the love of money," as the bon vivant told the Constitutional Convention, and elect to office "a sufficient number of wise and good men."[7]

Underneath Gore Vidal's cynical skin beats the heart of a good-government Mugwump, surrounded by fetid grafters and power-seekers, forlornly seeking those fabled few good men. The Mugwump need not be as ineffectually idealistic as the reformers of the 1880s; he may be harsh and caustic, as in Adams's novel of the Gilded Age, *Democracy* (1880), but the flame of idealism is never quite extinguished.

Thus Adams, the self-proclaimed "conservative Christian anarchist," and Vidal, whom we might tag a "patrician atheistic republican," share an ardent and anachronistic passion for the old republic. They are not naifs or goo-goos, blind to the evil that men do; indeed, for sworn enemies of power, both spent an inordinate amount of time within power's ambit. But they evince a familial concern for their country. They bleed richly for it, and when they see its government acting the bully or the slattern they inveigh and protest in plaintive voices, with the outrage of one who witnesses the desecration of an ancestral tombstone.

"Today's man knew no motive but interest, acknowledged no criterion but success, worshipped no god but ambition," Vidal lamented in *Washington, D.C.* (1967), the first written (but chronologically last) novel of the series, and in the quarter-century since he has traveled back to more congenial times.

In *Empire* (1987), an extended wake for the old republic, Vidal finally finds his milieu in the dimming twilight of the native aristocracy. Sitting in a parlor with the Henrys, Adams, and James, and John Hay, the salon lighted by lambent banter, belittling the Blaines and Roosevelts, the corrupt and imbecilic, the parvenu enemies of the republic—this is Gore Vidal's home.

Gore Vidal's historical novels are object lessons in the uses of political power. His Abraham Lincoln has all the depth and appeal of the mythic character found in history books, but the novelist's Father Abraham differs sharply from the hagiography read by American students. Vidal's Lincoln is a *politician*: a skillful manipulator of men, to be sure, but even more he is the grand reconstructor of our polity. He effaces the bequest of the Founders and substitutes, in the bloody birthpang of war, a national government muscular and triumphant, bound for glory and conquest.

Vidal conveys the grandeur of the Railsplitter's achievement through the eyes of Lincoln's secretary of state: "For the first time, Seward understood the nature of Lincoln's political genius. He had been able to make himself absolute dictator without ever letting anyone suspect that he was anything more than a joking, timid backwoods lawyer."[8]

His Lincoln is a tyrant, preternaturally shrewd and personally engaging, but a tyrant nevertheless. Vidal's obvious affection for the protean and undeniably great Lincoln perhaps accounts for the book's reverent tone; the author's awe, however, does not cloud his lyncean and quite unfashionable understanding of the centrality of the Civil War to what the textbooks call the American Experience.

Vidal captures the overriding political significance of the war in this brief exchange in *Empire* between diplomats John

Hay and Elihu Root, archaic exemplars of fast-fading republican virtue.

> "Poor Jefferson thought that he had won, and now we are all Hamiltonians."
> "Thanks to the Civil War."[9]

The incident that roused Vidal to his attack on Norman Podhoretz was the *Commentary* editor's boast that "to me, the Civil War is as remote and irrelevant as the War [sic] of the Roses."[10] The Civil War! *The* watershed event in our history, the fork in the American road at which union and decentralism, liberty and equality, capitalism and agrarianism, forever parted company.

To write lively history, one must prefer the past to the present, an inexpiable sin in an era in which America sits astride the world. Podhoretz's disdain of American history galls Vidal, who is guilty of uttering the one unforgiveable phrase in the public lexicon: "I remember." (In interviews, Vidal upholds the Confederacy's right to secede—thus joining the distinguished band of literary Copperheads including Edmund Wilson, Harold Frederic, and John Updike.)

The compromised but noble republican character James Burden Day, vanquished by a shallow Kennedyesque comer in *Washington, D.C.,* "noticed that since the war interest in the American past had waned. . . . For the majority, history began with the New Deal, and any contemplation of the old Republic was downright antipathetic to those who wanted reform in the present and perfection in the future."[11] Today, of course, even the New Deal is antediluvian. Our history now is considered to have begun at daybreak, December 7, 1941, and to cite persons or events prior to that sublime moment is an act of appalling tactlessness, if not blasphemy.

*   *   *

The most disabling smear against Vidal is that he is anti-Semitic. The evidence, as it were, consists of a hilarious 1986 essay in *The Nation,* titled "The Empire Lovers Strike Back," excoriating Israel and her American supporters and demanding, in best Mugwump isolationist fashion, that we adopt a foreign policy of America First.

Responding to this causerie, critics attacked Vidal for his "tone" rather than his policy prescriptions, always a neat way of stifling the heretic. The sentence that drew the most flak— and that serves as a fair summary of the rest of the piece— was Vidal's charge that "Like most of our Israeli fifth columnists, Midge [Decter, Norman Podhoretz's wife] isn't much interested in what the *Goyim* were up to before Ellis Island."[12]

In my opinion, the anti-Semite charge is merely a convenient rope with which to hang the renegade. Anti-Semitism simply cannot be inferred from Vidal's writings on Israel—unless one equates a dislike of Norman Podhoretz and the Israeli state with a dislike of Jews qua Jews.

Certainly Vidal is "insensitive," to borrow the limp adjective used by the clucking hens of the media to destroy any hearty soul who uses blunt language or cracks off-color jokes. Public figures in America are forbidden to have authentic (by definition, coarse) senses of humor, and if a joke offends even one tender ear the joker must lie prostrate and penitent while editorialists read him the quiet act.

But the overlooked substance of Vidal's essay resounded with the good sense of Americanists of another age. "The time has come," he ended his *Nation* essay, "for the United States to stop all aid not only to Israel but to Jordan, Egypt, and the rest of the Arab world. The Middle Easterners would then be obliged to make peace, or blow one another up, or whatever. In any case, we would be well out of it."[13]

Is it any wonder that Vidal is the most popular "serious" novelist in America? His sentiments perfectly echo those of the silent American majority. Call it isolationist, nativist, whatever, but our humble countrymen simply do not want the United States entangled in the affairs of far-off countries, whether Israel, Angola, or Vietnam. On this issue, Vidal speaks with the *vox populi.*

In *Empire* he has his antecedent Henry Adams saying: "I want us to build a sort of Great Wall of China, and hide behind it as long as possible." So, too, did—and do—the people of these United States. (Interestingly, Adamsian isolation was the original justification for the Strategic Defense Initiative, before it degenerated into just another defense boondoggle.)

Gore Vidal is a tempting target for slander because his fellow intellectuals in this century of slaughter, without much difficulty, have been silenced. Most were bought off with grants or tenure or paychecks signed by the federal government. From Mencken on, independent critics of foreign entanglements have been thrashed by the elite press.

"I don't give a God damn what other countries do," the novelist told *The Spectator* of London in 1986,[14] and that frank declaration of indifference blends very nicely into the American grain.

Vidal's knotty political iconoclasm has long perplexed liberal observers. (Indeed, Vidal has called himself a conservative cross that his liberal friends have to bear.) He was one of the precious few with the courage to praise Edmund Wilson's anguished *The Cold War and the Income Tax* (1964). Wilson's lament for his beloved country was met with averted eyes and whispers of senility when it appeared, at Camelot's zenith: fancy an educated man complaining that the national government was accumulating too much power!

Vidal seconded Wilson's testament, warning that Washington's postwar power-grab was creating "a rigid Byzantine society where the individual is the state's creature, his life the property of a permanent self-perpetuating bureaucracy."[15]

Vidal's sympathy for rebels and nonconformists extends to

those on the right, from tax protesters to populist tribune George Wallace. He was long ago sharp enough to detect sweet indigenous radicalism in the Wallace campaigns, prefiguring revisionist assessments of this bantam populist's message by social critic Christopher Lasch and others.

Vidal endorses Wallace's sage adage that "there ain't a dime's worth of difference between the Republicans and Democrats." "There is only one political party in the United States," insists Vidal, "and it is the Property party," controlled by a vital center directorate of plutocrats, bureaucrats, generals, and various well-off evil doers. A central function of the Property party is the stigmatization of *real* dissent—exemplified by maligning Wallace as a malevolent racist, or Barry Goldwater as a bloodthirsty nuke-crazed monster (when it was a liberal Democrat who dropped the Bomb), or Gore Vidal as a raving anti-Semite.

Vidal elucidates his conspiratorial view in the 1972 essay "Homage to Daniel Shays," included in the collection of the same name. If the aroma of crankiness sometimes intrudes, we must remember Delmore Schwartz's truism that "paranoids have real enemies, too." Besides, the Property party can do that to a man: Henry Adams tells us that he "had become little better than a crank" after inhaling the rank smoke of the bankers and politicians in the 1870s' brave new world that Abraham Lincoln had wrought.

The shameful abandonment of early American political values— liberty, decentralism, self-rule—explains, I submit, the strident hostility to Gore Vidal. For Vidal is an authentic champion of a peculiarly American patriotism, vastly nobler than that of the typewriter hawks and blow-dried Republicans of Washington, D.C.

With the countenance of an antebellum aristocrat and a flair for the eloquent savagery once so common in American political writing, Gore Vidal is the avenging wraith of Henry Adams made flesh, merciless in dissecting the empire-lovers and power-lusting intellectuals. He is the finest writer of our age, and the "Paleolithic conservatives" with whom he claims kinship in his brilliant meditation on life and war and movies, *Screening History* (1992), have in him a polemicist at least the equal—probably the superior—of Mencken and Paine.

So let the heathen rage. Vidal's historical novels and fulgurant essays will outlast his carping contemporaries. *Burr, Lincoln, Empire,* and even "The Empire Lovers Strike Back" will be read long after back issues of *The New Republic* molder unread between unopened covers. But it remains for conservatives and radicals of future generations to read Gore Vidal as a discerning critic of the empire that Abraham Lincoln, by crushing the localist Confederate rebellion, sired so many years ago. May the blind give birth to the sighted!

Someday the American Empire, like all empires, will collapse. The republic will probably be buried under the debris. And in the ruins of what once constituted humankind's finest political achievement, archaeologists will discover in the witty dissections of Gore Vidal a prolonged and heartfelt jeremiad. The pity, you will understand, is that he was not heeded.

NOTES

1. Quoted in Jere Real, "Gore Vidal, Roman Senator," *Inquiry,* May 17, 1982, p. 9.
2. "Gore Vidal: The *Progressive* Interview," *The Progressive,* September 1986, p. 39.
3. Quoted in John Updike, *Buchanan Dying* (New York: Knopf, 1974), p. 257.
4. Quoted in Charles Glass, "Gore, Poddy, and Midge," *The Spectator,* September 20, 1986, p. 13.
5. Gore Vidal, *Washington, D.C.* (Boston: Little, Brown, 1967), p. 243.
6. Gore Vidal, *Empire* (New York: Ballantine, 1987), p. 387.
7. *Notes of Debates in the Federal Convention of 1787, Reported by*

James Madison, edited by Adrienne Koch (Athens, Ohio: Ohio University Press, 1984), pp. 52–55.

8. Gore Vidal, *Lincoln* (New York: Ballantine, 1984), p. 460.

9. Vidal, *Empire,* p. 166.

10. "The Empire Lovers Strike Back," *The Nation,* March 22, 1986, p. 350.

11. Vidal, *Washington, D.C.,* p. 336.

12. "The Empire Lovers Strike Back," p. 350.

13. Ibid., p. 353.

14. Glass, "Gore, Poddy, and Midge," p. 13.

15. Gore Vidal, "Edmund Wilson, Tax Dodger," in *Homage to Daniel Shays* (New York: Vintage, 1973), p. 155.

7

Fulbright: The First Arkansas Bill

"The price of empire is America's soul and that price is too high."

—Senator J. William Fulbright, August 8, 1967

A rich boy from a poor state, a bookish football hero, an Ozark Anglophile, Senator William Fulbright (1905–1995) operated outside the dismal confines of Left and Right. He was a Confederate anti-imperialist. A well-bred foreign-policy realist of the George Kennan kidney. The Prince of Fayetteville. A Southern Whig. And the most trenchant senatorial critic of empire since Robert A. Taft departed this vale of tears.

I. F. Stone conferred upon Fulbright in 1966 the dubious title of "the most civilized and urbane man in the U.S. Senate." Fulbright was tough to peg, Stone wrote, "because he does not fit the easy stereotypes of American politics. He is not a rebel, a dissenter, a crusader, or a fighting liberal. He is not a liberal at all."[1] In Britain this "well-educated young country squire of minor but inherited and ample wealth" would have been a respectable if maverick Tory.

Well, perhaps. The issue of another of Arkansas's great families, the agrarian aristocrat John Gould Fletcher, commended

143

Fulbright for his "enlightened conservatism," which, when the light slants just right, blends into the poet's own "rebellious Americanism, my individualistic anarchism." Sweet dreams—and pariahs—are made of these.

J. William Fulbright was the golden boy of Fayetteville, Arkansas. Moody scion of the wealthiest family in town, he starred as halfback on the University of Arkansas football team, won a Rhodes scholarship, married a girl from Philadelphia's tony Main Line, earned a law degree at George Washington, and worked in a minor way for the New Deal-era Department of Justice before moving back to Arkansas to teach law and practice gentleman farming. Quite unexpectedly—and with his mother running interference—Fulbright acceded to the University's presidency in 1939 at the tender age of thirty-four.

The green president jumped into extracurricular frays. An ardent warhawk, he denounced "the weasling, timid, and fearful policy of the isolationist senators." Fired the next year at the behest of a new governor, Fulbright ran for Congress in 1942 on the family money. Although he had never set foot in six of his Ozark district's ten counties, he won, and began a thirty-year career representing a constituency he viewed as "self-reliant, industrious farmers and small businessmen."

Fulbright was an internationalist. He joined the Foreign Affairs Committee and gained early note as sponsor of a 1943 House resolution favoring U.S. participation in whatever worldwide organization might emerge from what he queerly termed a "creative war." (This fabled Fulbright Resolution was so vague that even isolationist tackle Hamilton Fish, another football hero-turned-congressman [from New York's Hudson Valley], voted for it.)

Fulbright rapidly became the pet Southerner of Eastern liberals. "This man is destined for greatness," journalist Dorothy Thompson raved. Fulbright's high-minded internationalism provoked Colonel McCormick's *Chicago Tribune* to castigate him as the "first-termer from Arkansas, who in his formative years was sent as a Rhodes scholar to Oxford to learn to betray his country and deprive it of its independence. In this instance, as no doubt in many others, Mr. Rhodes appears to have got his money's worth."[2]

It was a good decade for Anglophiles. In 1944, when Fulbright took the Senate seat away from Huey Long protegée Hattie Carraway, so passionate was his Atlanticism that populist foes derided him as "British Billy" and "Lord Flushbottom."

Young Fulbright was no heretic, although as a young senator he caught hell from Harry Truman when he mused aloud that because the GOP had captured both houses of Congress in the 1946 election, the president might want to appoint a distinguished Republican as secretary of state and then resign. (There was no vice president at the time.) Truman was not amused by British Billy's parliamentary daydreams. He called the freshman senator "an overeducated Oxford S.O.B." who'd have been better off going to a good land-grant college (which the University of Arkansas was).[3]

Fulbright trod an unusual path, compiling a standard Southern Democrat voting record while making a reputation with his highfalutin' speeches. (This is not to give Fulbright— or any contemporary politician—credit for the style of his "writings," which are usually done by a factotum.) Like the Beats, he lamented the subtle strictures that were squeezing out free speech. In January 1955 Fulbright decried

> the narrowing effect inherent in the concentration of managerial control of the press, the radio, the movies—and, in the foreseeable future, television. . . . People hear, see, watch, read, and listen to only one side of public questions. . . . The public man . . . may know the truth and want to speak it. Yet he doubts whether his views, as transmitted to his constituents by those who control communications channels, will be fairly presented, or presented at all.[4]

This hymnodist of dissent had as yet done little of it himself. In foreign and defense matters Fulbright clove to the Cold War consensus, even urging the more sensible President Eisenhower to send ground troops to Indochina in 1954. Like other mid-century enthusiasts for a muscular presidency he called for "a more assertive exercise of executive power" in international affairs. "The consequences of our global interventionism were not a major concern for me in the 1950s," he later admitted.[5] Then in 1959 Fulbright assumed chairmanship of the Senate Foreign Relations Committee, and the world turned.

To his great and everlasting credit, Fulbright recoiled from the adventurism of Democratic presidents Kennedy and Johnson. Disturbed by the Bay of Pigs, distressed by the invasion of the Dominican Republic, the chairman at first played the good soldier with respect to Vietnam; in 1964 he shepherded through the fraudulent Gulf of Tonkin resolution.* But two years later, Fulbright had become the chief "nervous nellie" in Johnsonian demonology; meanwhile, Warren Hinckle in the New Left journal *Ramparts* was hailing him for sailing "in the mainstream of native American radicalism." He had broken, finally and fully, with the Democrats' Vietnam War, and the series of hearings on U.S. foreign policy which Fulbright chaired over the next lustrum legitimized the dissent whose praises he had sung so hollowly a decade before.

Fulbright was the first Foreign Relations chairman to defy a president of his own party since the great spearless leader of the Western progressives, Idaho's William E. Borah, took on Calvin Coolidge over his gunboat diplomacy in Nicaragua in the 1920s. Borah and Fulbright both emphasized the paramountcy of domestic affairs. Empire, the Arkansan complained, has forced us to "reverse the traditional order of our national priorities,

---

*The Tonkin resolution—based on a reported North Vietnamese attack on U.S. destroyers—gave President Johnson a virtual license to escalate the war. The "attack" was later revealed to be a fiction. "I have had little confidence in what the government says since then," Fulbright wrote in *The Price of Empire.*

relegating individual and community life to places on the scale below the enormously expensive military and space activities that constitute our program of national security."

Borah was a congenital dissident, a leader of the GOP's trans-Mississippi populist faction. His defiance, while noble, was unsurprising. A better analogue to the Bourbon Fulbright was Massachusetts Senator George Hoar (1826–1904), a gentleman Republican who with bitter eloquence had split with his friend William McKinley over the president's decision to suppress the Filipino independence movement.

At least George Hoar had company; the Anti-Imperialist League was chock-full of Mugwump Republicans. Fulbright's lonely apostasy came at a time when the sane mind-our-own-business voices of Main Street had been silenced. Our two-for-the-price-of-one political parties were united in their support of American Empire: the Western isolationists were all superannuated or dead, the Midwestern Republicans (with the shining exception of Iowa's irascible reactionary H. R. Gross) had stolen the 1948 Democratic party foreign policy platform, and the shrunken Henry Wallace* peace wing of the Democracy was sponsoring Ban the Bomb rallies at which doe-eyed liberals held hands and sang Negro spirituals.

Enter J. William Fulbright, erstwhile booster of "creative wars," now a Southern constitutionalist dove.

The breed is rare, though the pedigree is honorable. The great Southern populists stood foursquare against war: Georgia's congressman Tom Watson (1856–1922) was a ferocious foe of the Spanish-American and First World wars, and Louisiana's Huey Long (1893–1935) promised to make the legendary Marine Corps Major General Smedley "War is a Racket" Butler his secretary of (anti)war.† Yet with few exceptions the states' rights Democrats of the South—whose belief in limited constitutional

---

*Henry Agard Wallace (1888–1965). U.S. vice president, 1941–1945.

†Long planned to challenge FDR for the presidency in 1936.

government ought to have engendered a skepticism of empire—
whooped it up for our frequent overseas interventions.

"No other section of the nation gave President Franklin
D. Roosevelt such unified support in his efforts" to involve these
United States in the Second World War, historian Wayne S.
Cole writes of the South.[6] The overwhelming support of Southern
members of Congress saved such critical 1941 measures as the
draft extension and the revision of the Neutrality Act. Only at
the region's periphery—beyond Arkansas—did antiwar groups
such as the America First Committee enjoy even meager support.

Something—Democratic party loyalty, an ingrained respect
for things military, the need to preserve foreign markets—kept
even the wisest of Southern conservatives quiet. For example,
Georgia Senator Richard Russell, chairman of the Armed Services
Committee, was a thoughtful states' rights advocate who drily
observed that "if it is easy for us to go anywhere and do anything,
we will always be going someplace and doing something."[7]

Alas, like the Fulbright of 1955, Senator Russell never
translated this wise maxim into practical action. Harshly critical
in private of our Vietnam conflict, he played the dutiful hawk
in public, caught up in the idiotic delusion that politics stops
at the water's edge.

Fulbright was a friend and admirer of Russell, and though
the Georgian was regarded as the apotheosis of the courtly
Southern senator, Fulbright, in his own way, was an even truer
son of the Old South. What liberals viewed as the wart on the
great man's profile was in fact the source of his greatness.

Let's step back for a moment. Even at his career's apex,
J. William Fulbright made a lousy saint. He took a states' rights
position on integration and stuck to it, much to the discomfort
of otherwise worshipful Northerners. Relations between blacks
and whites in Arkansas were the business of Arkansans, Fulbright
said, and none of the federal government's business. He signed
the March 12, 1956, Southern Manifesto in which members of
Congress attacked the Supreme Court's *Brown* v. *Board of*

Education decision for its exercise of "naked judicial power"; unlike nimble opportunistic old segregationists like Strom Thurmond, Fulbright never recanted.

His obduracy consisted of equal parts expedience and principle. There was an element of cowardice in Fulbright's position; to have come out for the various civil rights measures would have been "political suicide," he said. And "I did not feel like giving up my career in politics because of it."[8] This is a frank admission—of gutlessness.

On the other hand, one finds in the Fulbright record residual Confederate resentment of Yankee meddlers. Looking back, he says of the Manifesto signatories, "There was a sense that we were the poor part of the country, that we had historic reasons to band together against northerners who were imposing on us."

For all his aristocratic suavity, Senator Fulbright was capable of regional defenses that have the populist flavor of South Carolina's legendary Pitchfork Ben Tillman. "The people of the North are extremely solicitous of our welfare and progress," he said in 1948.

> They assure us that if we will furnish better schools and abolish poll taxes and segregation that strife will cease and happiness reign. They are critical of our relative poverty, our industrial and social backwardness, and they are generous in their advice about our conduct. Their condescension in these matters is not appreciated . . . because these people . . . have for more than half a century done everything they could to retard the economic development of the South. It is no secret that the South was considered like a conquered territory after 1865. Since that time, the tariff policy and the freight rate structure were designed by the North to . . . keep [the South] in the status of a raw material-producing colony. Above and beyond these direct restrictions, the most insidious of all, the most difficult to put your finger on, is the all-pervading influence of the great financial institutions and industrial monopolies.[9]

This self-aware Southernness (which, despite James Carville's cosmetic magic, one *never* descries in Bill Clinton) was Fulbright's saving grace. His Northern friends thought it to be his handicap; indeed, his anti-imperialism received its stimulus from the South. "Small countries wish to find their own way, make their own mistakes," Fulbright said by way of explaining why our presence in Vietnam was unwise. So, too, for the South, whose autonomy and independence—even in the years 1861–1865—he always defended.

Revolted by the swollen, belligerent leviathan that was crushing the states' rights democracy in which he believed, Fulbright emerged as a full-fledged Confederate anti-imperialist by 1966. He was never labeled as such, of course—it would have raised too many unsettling questions—but in his unread valedictory, 1989's *The Price of Empire,* the senator explained himself:

> Maybe I am the heir of the South with regard to the Civil War period. I may have absorbed an attitude towards big powers and big countries that has its roots in my Arkansas cultural background. You were not inclined, if you came from Arkansas in the years when I was growing up there, to be very arrogant. We were poorer than almost anyone else and there was a tendency to look down on Arkansas as backward and uneducated. It seems logical to me that this should have had an effect on my attitudes when I considered relationships between the United States and smaller, underdeveloped countries.[10]

Given the cosmopolitan surroundings Fulbright chose from early adulthood—Oxford, Georgetown parties, and all that rot—*only* his Arkansas roots immunized him against the disastrous "pay any price, bear any burden" globalist virus that was going around in enlightened Democratic circles.*

---

*The scariest thing I find about Bill Clinton is that despite the "Man from Hope" campaign theme, his veins were long ago drained of Arkansas blood. He has nothing left of the Confederate or rebel. When, in the 1992 campaign, the *Wall Street Journal* asked him, "What event before 1900 shaped your vision of American society? Your

Fulbright's Confederate anti-imperialism was fortified by the surety that comes from being the fair-haired son of the biggest family in a small city. One pictures young Bill as the Georgie Amberson Minafer—the most magnificent Amberson—of Fayetteville. "You'll never understand Bill until you realize what a secure basis he had," a friend told biographer Tristam Coffin. "The most important family in town. Never had to worry about money. Tremendous support from the family."[11]

Fulbright fits into Kenneth Rexroth's pattern of patrician American dissent: "Most American families that go back to the early nineteenth century . . . have a sense of social and cultural rather than nationalist responsibility. The sense that the country is really theirs, really belongs to them, produces radical critics, rebels, reformers, eccentrics."

Looked at this way, Fulbright's behavior is seen to be of a piece: his sense of cultural responsibility was ultimately so strong that he broke loose from the shackling postwar conventions and drifted back to the glorious tradition of localist Southern dissent. If Fulbright never quite got around to prescribing "a wise and masterly inactivity" for Washington, as did Virginia's John Randolph, he did offer what he termed a conservative "defense of traditional values and protest against the radical departure from those values embodied in the idea of an imperial destiny for America."[12] That Fulbright's fellow conservatives vilified him for this only goes to show that Empire blinds as well as bankrupts.

Fulbright's transformation ran counterclockwise. He was no Arthur Vandenberg, helping President Truman "scare hell out of the American people" and pasting laudatory press clippings

---

view of America's place in the world?" Clinton, blithely ignoring history, answered, "None, because most of the things the U.S. did before 1900 were totally inconsistent with the global role I'd like us to play, or were narrow disputes over territory."

Why Clinton—whose trajectory from Hot Springs through Georgetown and Oxford and Yale to Washington is a lot like Fulbright's—seems bereft of even vestigial sympathy for smallness remains an interesting question, one perhaps answered by the glimmer from Virginia Kelley's zircon-studded fist.

in his scrapbook. (As Vandenberg learned, the wages of conformity are great indeed.)

By the late 1960s, court journalists such as William S. White had caught on that "what the Fulbright people really represent is a new and embittered crypto pacifism-isolationism."[13] While this is a bit much, Fulbright did come tantalizingly close to advocating something like the paleo-isolationism he had fought two decades earlier. He was now saying that becoming a "global interventionist power" after the Second World War was "a mistaken ideal."[14] Weary of America's pious interventionism, Fulbright remarked: "I think the world has endured about all it can of the crusades of high-minded men bent on the regeneration of the human race."

The whole Vietnam episode seemed to him a burlesque of misguided liberalism:

> Lyndon Johnson, Hubert Humphrey, and others used to say that I was a racist, and that was why I didn't like the war in Vietnam. I didn't think "the little brown people" were entitled to democracy. "We want to bring them the Great Society," Hubert would say. "We're not racists. We have a great interest in those brown people." And all the time bombing them from five miles up.[15]

Fulbright, like most men who taste power, hung around its corridors too long. His reputation for aloofness grew—"no man, however strong, can serve ten years as schoolmaster, priest, or senator, and remain fit for anything else," said Henry Adams, who should know—and toothless populist Dale Bumpers routed Fulbright in the 1974 Democratic primary.

Although it cannot have been the critical factor, given the margin of defeat, outside money helped do in the senator. Fulbright committed the capital crime of candor in 1973 when he said on "Face the Nation" that when it comes to Middle East policy, "Israel controls the Senate" and "we should be more concerned about the United States' interests." The pro-Israel lobby thereupon directed its considerable energy toward teaching Fulbright the high price of dissent.

The experience made Fulbright, in retirement, a sharp critic of "the subservience of our foreign policy to domestic lobbies." Liberated by age and irrelevance, and insisting that he was "pro-American" and not "anti-Israel," Fulbright declared, "We have lost our freedom of action in the Middle East and are committed to policies that promote neither our own national interest nor the cause of peace. AIPAC [The American Israel Public Affairs Committee] and its allied organizations have effective working control of Congress. They can elect or defeat nearly any congressman or senator that they wish."[16]

This may be overstatement, but President Clinton has not provided us with a test case. He pledged to Prime Minister Yitzhak Rabin in March 1993 that our five-billion-dollar annual subsidy of Israel and Egypt would remain inviolate. Clinton's timorous budget cutters will swipe food from the mouths of destitute children before they'll slice a sacred piece of the foreign aid pie.

Fulbright's row with the Israel lobby probably explains why Bill Clinton never really honored Arkansas's towering statesman until he was safely dead. If Fulbright was half the man I think he was, he didn't care. At a Clinton inauguration party, he told a *New York Times* reporter that the recent Arkansas governor who'd really impressed him was . . . the infamous 1950s left-wing segregationist Orval Faubus.

Wendell Berry counsels:

> As soon as the generals and the politicos
> can predict the motions of your mind,
> lose it.[17]

Senator Fulbright did. His detractors said so for years. His admirers cherished him for the wisdom gained in loss.

NOTES

1. I. F. Stone, "Fulbright of Arkansas," *The New York Review of Books*, December 29, 1966, p. 5.

2. Quoted in Haynes Johnson and Bernard M. Gwertzman, *Fulbright the Dissenter* (Garden City, N.Y.: Doubleday, 1968), p. 73.

3. J. William Fulbright and Seth P. Tillman, *The Price of Empire* (New York: Pantheon, 1989), p. 49.

4. Quoted in Johnson and Gwertzman, *Fulbright the Dissenter*, p. 281.

5. Fulbright and Tillman, *The Price of Empire*, p. 160.

6. Wayne S. Cole, "America First and the South," *Journal of Southern History* (February 1956): 36.

7. Quoted in Noam Chomsky, *Towards a New Cold War* (New York: Pantheon, 1982), p. 191.

8. Fulbright and Tillman, *The Price of Empire*, p. 93.

9. Johnson and Gwertzman, *Fulbright the Dissenter*, p. 149.

10. Fulbright and Tillman, *The Price of Empire*, p. 154.

11. Tristam Coffin, *Senator Fulbright: Portrait of a Public Philosopher* (New York: Dutton, 1966), p. 41.

12. J. William Fulbright, "The Price of Empire" (speech), in Johnson and Gwertzman, *Fulbright the Dissenter*, p. 310.

13. Coffin, *Senator Fulbright: Portrait of a Public Philosopher*, p. 14.

14. Fulbright and Tillman, *The Price of Empire*, p. 153.

15. Ibid., p. 169.

16. Ibid., p. 183.

17. Wendell Berry, "Manifesto: The Mad Farmer Liberation Front," in *Collected Poems: 1957–1982* (San Francisco: North Point, 1985), p. 152.

8

Edward Abbey:
Parched in the American Desert

> "Up with Spring
> Down with Empire"
> —Edward Abbey, *Hayduke Lives!* (1990)

"Resist much, obey little," Walt Whitman entreated, and if some Americans listened, most did not. Certainly our writers have learned that obedience pays, as they fill out grant forms in triplicate and curry favor with the political wives who seemingly run all fifty state arts agencies.

Yes, there are resisters—from Ray Bradbury to Cormac McCarthy and the lone eagles of the great gray vastitude between—and while they have avoided the reeducation camps they are solitary and unaffiliated. Rebel Americans do not believe that there is strength in numbers.

Edward Abbey, a true son of Whitman, was such an American: a hillbilly intellectual, an adopted son of Arizona, a craggy-faced old man with a great bushy beard who wrote passionate comic novels—didacticism was never so much fun—and irreverent lovesongs to the desert.

Ed Abbey was a *man,* a free-swinging iconoclast, disrespectful of idols, who combined a commitment to the writers' craft with a homespun anarchism that still inspires young rebels to feats of sabotage and courage in the American West—an American West belonging not to Ananconda Copper or backpacker Bruce Babbitt but to the sons of American explorers Lewis and Clark and John Wesley Powell.

Edward Abbey was born in 1927, on hardscrabble acres in Appalachian Pennsylvania. His father, Paul Revere Abbey, who survived his son, was a Wobbly and a farmer. His mother, Mildred, was a partisan of the Woman's Christian Temperance Union. What she thought of her son's archetypal hero—a booze-guzzling anarchist outlaw tossing beer cans out of car windows—Lord only knows.

Young Ed left the farm for college, that great quasher of man's spirit. He studied philosophy in New Mexico, where he fell in love both with many women and with the untamed Southwest. He worked at a series of jobs, including park ranger and fire lookout, but his true vocation was writing: in his lifetime Abbey produced nine novels, seven essay collections, and five oversized coffee-table books.

His greatest achievement was the angry National Park Service memoir, *Desert Solitaire,* large portions of which were written in a Death Valley cathouse. The book was acclaimed as a Thoreauvian masterpiece of naturalism and reflection upon its publication in 1968; but the critics never quite knew what to make of Mr. Abbey, and over time his ornery wit and scorn for liberal pieties alienated practically everyone. The *New York Times* called him a "smirking pessimist"; *The Nation* averred that he was "puerile, arrogant, xenophobic, and dopey." To which Edward Abbey laughed, and replied, in his grand, self-mythicizing, Whitmanesque way, "Death before dishonor. Live free or die."

Abbey peppered *Desert Solitaire* with ill-tempered political opinions, adumbrating the themes that were to dominate his

work. An American dictator, he wrote, should take the following steps:

1. Concentrate the populace in megapolitan masses so that they
can be kept under close surveillance and where, in case of trouble,
they can be bombed, burned, gassed, or machine-gunned with
a minimum of expense and waste.

2. Mechanize agriculture to the highest degree of refinement,
thus forcing most of the scattered farm and ranching population
into the cities. Such a policy is desirable because farmers, woods-
men, cowboys, Indians, fishermen, and other relatively self-
sufficient types are difficult to manage unless displaced from their
natural environment.

3. Restrict the possession of firearms to the police and the regular
military organizations.

4. Encourage or at least fail to discourage population growth.
Large masses of people are more easily manipulated and dominated than scattered individuals.

5. Continue military conscription. Nothing excels military training for creating in young men an attitude of prompt, cheerful
obedience to officially constituted authority.

6. Divert attention from deep conflicts within the society by
engaging in foreign wars; make support of these wars a test
of loyalty, thereby exposing and isolating potential opposition
to the new order.

7. Overlay the nation with a finely reticulated network of communications, airlines and interstate autobahns.

8. *Raze the wilderness.* Dam the rivers, flood the canyons, drain
the swamps, log the forests, strip mine the hills, bulldoze the
mountains, irrigate the deserts, and improve the national parks
into national parking lots.[1]

Edward Abbey was a self-described agrarian anarchist who loved his country and hated its government. He deplored mass migration—*from any source*—into the frontier Southwest, and in one notorious essay he urged the U.S. Border Patrol to "stop every campesino at our southern border, give him a handgun, a good rifle, and a case of ammunition, and send him home. He will know what to do with our gifts and good wishes. The people know who their enemies are."[2]

Abbey deplored the Mexicanization of Southwestern culture: he once said that our neighbors to the south had contributed little to our estate beyond dashboard Jesuses and burritos.

Such frank sentiments made Abbey a pariah. His travel pieces regularly appeared in the glossy magazines of prestige, but—like Gore Vidal; Murray Rothbard; Noam Chomsky; Thomas Fleming; Christopher Lasch; Abbey's archenemy, the bookish anarcho-socialist Murray Bookchin; and, come to think of it, nearly every independent thinker in the land of the free— his political musings were rarely found on the pages of our listless and servile press.

The novel that first catapulted—well, nudged—Abbey to fame in 1956 was *The Brave Cowboy,* a threnody for man in the age of mechanized totalitarianism. The hero is Jack Burns, an itinerant and prickly loner. Jack is a cowboy anachronism wandering through the 1950s, a man stubbornly apart, as this exchange with a police officer shows:

"No driver's license, no social security card, no discharge card, no registration card, no insurance card, no identification at all? . . . My god, he must have *something* on him! A man can't walk around without any I.D. at all? . . . Where're your papers?" he said.

"My what?"

"Your I.D.—draft card, social security, driver's license."

"Don't have none. Don't need none. I already know who I am."[3]

Jack hears that an Albuquerque friend, Paul Bondi, has been jailed for refusing to register for the draft. So he does what any true friend would do: he gets himself tossed in prison so they can bust out together. Bondi—a graduate student in philosophy, no less—will have none of it. A meliorist, Bondi explains to Jack why he plans to do his time, to submit:

> Don't think for a moment that I imagine myself as some sort of anarchist hero. I don't intend to fight against Authority, at least not in the open. When they tell us to say, "I recant everything," I'll just mumble something out of the corner of my mouth. When they tell us to stand at attention and salute I'll cross the fingers of my left hand. When they install the dictaphones . . . and the wire-tapping apparatus and the two-way television I'll install defective fuses in the switchbox. When they ask me if I am now or ever have been an Untouchable I'll tell them that I'm just a plain old easy-going no-account Jeffersonian anarchist. That way I should be able to muddle along. . . .[4]

Jack escapes—alone—and flees on horseback to the mountains, pursued by the police, the army, and the weaponry of modern technology. Fans of Western literature have had a field day discussing what finally happens to Jack; in a twentieth-anniversary edition of the book, Abbey made a critical deletion that belied, for the hundredth time, the "smirking pessimist" tag. (Jack does not die in Abbey's revision—indeed, the "ghost cowboy" would return in *Hayduke Lives!*)*

Abbey's finest novel was his penultimate, *The Fool's Progress* (1988), an autobiographical wandering—"an honest novel," as Abbey called it—across America, a summing up of sorts. There

---

*Hollywood bought *The Brave Cowboy,* renamed it *Lonely Are the Brave* (1962), starring Kirk Douglas as Burns, and then, in an emblematic act of cowardice, the once-blacklisted screenwriter Dalton Trumbo *eliminated* the thematically crucial matter of draft resistance. Rubbing in the salt, he changed Paul's crime to the heartwarming act of harboring a family of adorable illegal aliens.

is a wonderful fictionalization of old Paul Revere Abbey in the character of Joe Lightcap:

> Joe Lightcap thought he was the only Wobbly east of the Mississippi River. The only freethinker in West Virginia. The only isolationist left in Shawnee County—a Republican county at that. Nobody paid him any attention and he knew it and the knowledge made him angry and lonely and sick in his heart. Joe Lightcap was not a philosopher; he took ideas seriously.[5]

Joe and his son Henry are blustery heretics, given to interrupting family picnics to complain about Roosevelt and bosses and the Good War. As Joe thunders,

> The majority of Americans never wanted to get into this rotten war. And when Roosevelt maneuvered us into it, even after Pearl Harbor, the majority still never wanted to go overseas to fight. That's why the government needs the draft, Holyoak. Because there was no other way they could get our boys into it. They have to force them to fight.[6]

Similarly, Ed Abbey and his dad were isolationists of the old American school. As Wayne Lutton put it in *Chronicles,* "Abbey was part Thoreau and [nineteenth-century anarchist] Lysander Spooner—with a heavy infusion of John T. Flynn and Charles Lindbergh."[7]

Abbey's most popular novel, *The Monkey Wrench Gang* (1975), became the Holy Writ of the Earth First! people, those tree-spiking apostles of ecotage. Abbey's monkey wrenchers roamed the Southwest, Nature's avengers, pulling up survey stakes, disabling bulldozers, blowing up bridges, dreaming and plotting that glorious day when the Glen Canyon Dam on the Utah-Arizona border is blasted to smithereens, right up to that big public works project in the sky.

In a posthumous novel, *Hayduke Lives!* (1990), with its epigraph "Down with Empire! Up with Spring," the monkey wrenchers are back at it. Though overly broad in humor, the book brims with Abbeyisms. He sings of the "blue-eyed, beetle-browed, ruddy-skinned, crude-featured, red-necked, basic native-American white male working-class chump, the only social stratum in America subject to legal and socially approved school, job, and advancement discrimination, accompanied by slurs and sneers."[8] The Paul Bunyan of ecotagers, George Washington Hayduke, is "the father of his country. Not of the America that was—keep it like it was?—but the America that will be. That will be like it was. Forward to anarchy. Don't tread on me. Death before dishonor. Live free or fucking die."[9]

Life does indeed imitate art: the Earth Firsters, who—before being taken over by the faddists in sensible shoes and fashionable causes—were living, breathing counterparts of Abbey's band of merry anarchists, were the targets of a massive FBI investigation in the late 1980s. As James Ridgeway and Bill Gifford perceptively noted in *The Village Voice,* "in the lexicon of the American secret police, anarchists are worse than Communists." Especially when the anarchists are gleeful saboteurs with no respect for government property. Abbey had foreseen this in *Hayduke Lives!* when Doc Sarvis said, "Like the I.W.W., they [Earth First!]'ll last until they become effective. Then the state moves in, railroads some of the leaders into prison, murders a few others for educational purposes, clubs and gasses and jails the followers and *voilà*!—peace and order are restored."[10]

Abbey dedicated *The Monkey Wrench Gang* to Ned Ludd, the mythical patron saint of the machine-smashing Englishmen of the early nineteenth century, borrowing his epigraph from Byron: "Down with all kings but King Ludd." Now, unabashed Luddites are as rare as Zoroastrians in America, at least on the public stage. One might expect them to be saturnine mopes, glum lamenters of modernity. Not these monkey wrenchers. They copulate and play cards and sleep under the stars, joyfully. Abbey's protagonists exult in life, live it with gusto and abandon. The sense of fun that courses through Abbey's prose is what really distinguishes him from Robinson Jeffers, with whom he is often coupled.

Jeffers, it must be admitted, was a deeply misanthropic man who once wrote,

I'd sooner, except the penalties, kill a man than a hawk.[11]

Abbey, in a cantankerous mood, might endorse that sentiment, but with a wink. For all his contempt for anthropocentrism, Edward Abbey enjoyed the company of people, and even in his harshest diatribes a certain . . . dare we call it love? . . . for his fellows shines through, leavening the bitterness.

Like most iconoclasts, Abbey enjoyed sniping, and occasionally his targets were kindred spirits. He caught all sorts of hell for mocking the theological nature writing of Annie Dillard: "I sat on a rock in New Mexico once," Abbey kidded, "trying to have a vision. The only vision I had was of baked chicken."[12] He loathed the Brooklyn-turned-Vermont anarchist Murray Bookchin, burlesquing him as Bernie Mushkin in *Hayduke Lives!*

Yet if he chided the famous, he exhorted and inspirited his lesser-known brethren. "Ignore the critics," Abby tells us in the preface to *Slumgullion Stew*. "Have faith in the evidence of your senses and in your common sense. Be loyal to your family, your clan, your friends, and your community. Let the nation-state go hang itself."[13]

Abbey practiced what he preached. When in 1987 the American Academy of Arts and Letters finally got around to recognizing the obstreperous Pride of Apppalachia, Ed Abbey told them he had plans to run a river in Idaho that week, and that trip was far more important than receiving the king's shilling.

Abbey died of circulatory problems in March 1989. With death imminent, his friends disconnected him from the life-support equipment, wheeled him out of the hospital, and drove him into the desert. They chose a remote spot for his grave, guarded by coyotes and vultures. As his friend Edward Hoagland wrote, "the last smile that crossed Abbey's face" was when a comrade told him where he was to be buried.[14]

At Abbey's raucous wake, a beery bacchanal in Utah's Arches National Park, Wendell Berry spoke of him as an intransigent patriot, an authentic American hero. Said Berry, "Patriotism is not the love of air conditioning or the interstate highway system or the government or the flag or power or money or munitions. It is the love of country."[15]

True fact, Wendell. As Abbey used to say, "America: Love it or Leave it Alone."

Edward Abbey's popular success—his elevation to folk hero, all those dog-eared copies of *Desert Solitaire* and *The Monkey Wrench Gang* getting read and reread—is a rebuke to the go-along-to-get-along crowd, the hankerers for government appointment.

Thoreau understood. "If one advances confidently in the direction of his dreams, and endeavors to live the life which he has imagined, he will meet with a success unexpected in common hours. He will put some things behind, will pass an invisible boundary; new, universal, and more liberal laws will begin to establish themselves . . . and he will live with the license of a higher order of beings."[16]

Edward Abbey did not speak in measured, cautious equivocations, in Heritage-Brookings weasel words. He spoke the truth. "I feel rage and outrage quite often," he told the *Los Angeles Times* shortly before his death. "I'd gleefully take part in a violent revolution—I'd love to go down to city hall in Tucson and tear it down. I'm getting more radical as I get older."[17]

As we all should.

"I write to entertain my friends and to exasperate our enemies," Abbey once stated. "To oppose, resist, and sabotage the contemporary drift toward a global technocratic police state, whatever its ideological coloration. . . . I write for the joy and exultation of writing itself. To tell my story."[18]

Edward Abbey told his story. And raised hell. And had

fun. He loved his five wives, his kids, his parents, his buddies, his literary ancestors, and his country. He lived an American life, and as long as the Spirit of '76 endures, so will he.

NOTES

1. Edward Abbey, *Desert Solitaire* (New York: McGraw Hill, 1968), p. 131.

2. Edward Abbey, "Immigration and Liberal Taboos," in *One Life at a Time, Please* (New York: Holt, 1988), p. 44.

3. Edward Abbey, *The Brave Cowboy* (Albuquerque: University of New Mexico Press, 1977/1956), pp. 69–73.

4. Ibid., pp. 104–105.

5. Edward Abbey, *The Fool's Progress* (New York: Holt, 1988), p. 150.

6. Ibid., p. 153.

7. Wayne Lutton, "Edward Abbey: R.I.P.," *Chronicles,* June 1990, p. 34.

8. Edward Abbey, *Hayduke Lives!* (Boston: Little, Brown, 1990), p. 72.

9. Ibid., p. 274.

10. Ibid., p. 230.

11. Robinson Jeffers, "Hurt Hawks," in *Rock and Hawk,* edited by Robert Hass (New York: Random House, 1987), p. 97.

12. Bob Sipchen, "Abbey: Rage on the Range," *Washington Post,* January 5, 1988, p. B2.

13. Edward Abbey, *Slumgullion Stew* (New York: Dutton, 1984), pp. xiii–xiv.

14. Edward Hoagland, "Edward Abbey: Standing Tough in the Desert," *New York Times Review of Books,* May 7, 1989, p. 45.

15. Bob Sipchen, "Edward Abbey Is Remembered," Rochester, N.Y., *Democrat & Chronicle,* May 23, 1989.

16. Henry David Thoreau, *Walden* (New York: Signet, 1960/1854), p. 215.

17. Sipchen, "Abbey: Rage on the Range," p. B2.

18. Edward Abbey, "A Writer's Credo," in *One Life at a Life, Please,* pp. 177–78.

9

Jack Kerouac: The Beat Goes Right

"When I pass to and fro, different latitudes, different seasons, beholding the crowds of the great cities, New York, Boston, Philadelphia, Cincinnati, Chicago, St. Louis, San Francisco, New Orleans, Baltimore—when I mix with these interminable swarms of alert, turbulent, good-natured, independent citizens, mechanicks, clerks, young persons—at the idea of this mass of men, so fresh and free, so loving and so proud, a singular awe falls upon me. I feel, with dejection and amazement, that among our geniuses and talented writers or speakers, few or none have yet really spoken to this people, created a single image-making work for them, or absorb'd the central spirit and the idiosyncrasies which are theirs—and which, thus, in highest ranges, so far remain entirely uncelebrated, unexpress'd."

—Walt Whitman, "Democratic Vistas" (1871)

Whitman's despair was premature. His earthy, rapturous poems collected in *Leaves of Grass* (first published in 1855) had refracted this spirit through one exuberant man's lens. Just fourteen years after the elegiac "Democratic Vistas" Mark Twain set a runaway slave named Jim and a runaway boy named Huckleberry Finn on a raft down the Mississippi River, redeeming John W. De Forest's call for a "great American novel" (which De Forest himself

165

almost wrote in *Miss Ravenel's Conversion* [1867]) and giving us the most enduring motif in our literature: the journey in search of freedom—and its frequent reward, self-discovery—played out against the backdrop of this vast and wondrous continent.

Whitman's lament was a common refrain in the music of the nineteenth century. It sprang from his conviction, fervently held and often frantically expressed, ragged but still right today, that there was a distinct American character: open, nobly coarse, free, accepting of ecstasy, virile. And just as the colonies had declared independence from Europe, with her accursed monarchies, despotisms, and aristocracies, so, too, should the American writer reject the chains and shackles of the Old World. Antebellum New England clergyman William Ellery Channing admonished his countrymen: "It were better to have no literature, than form ourselves unresistingly on a foreign one. . . . A country, like an individual, has dignity and power only in proportion as it is self-formed."[1]

The native rambunctiousness counseled by the preacher and the poet has found no better personification than Jack Kerouac. Few have demonstrated so well the political attitudes that issue from an Americanist aesthetic.

Jean-Louis Kerouac's life is happy proof that the writer need not be an effete *observer* of life, forever on the sidelines while the game goes on: he can live it with gusto. Born in 1922 into a devoutly Catholic French-Canadian family in the grimy old mill town of Lowell, Massachusetts, Kerouac had a boyhood devoted to that venerable trinity of football, girls, and books.

Yet this dashing, hard-drinking gridiron star adopted early in life a starkly simple, childlike moral philosophy from his saintly brother "Ti" Gerard, who died at age nine: "Never hurt any living being, all living beings whether it's just a little cat or squirrel or whatever, all are going to heaven straight into God's snowy arms so never hurt anything and if you see anybody hurt anything stop them as best you can."[2] From the wrong lips this may sound mawkish and infantile, but to Kerouac it was no joke.

He remained, to his dying day, that holy incongruity: a rugged pacifist.

Jack the nonviolent running back set off, football scholarship in hand, for Columbia University, where a broken leg promptly ended his athletic career. So he resolved, instead, to become "a great writer like Thomas Wolfe," and he soon fell in with a crowd of defiantly unkempt poets and wildmen who were in rebellion not against "Middle America," as is commonly supposed (Kerouac, for one, loved it dearly), but rather the sterile dissertation-writing, politics-playing, suffocating world of *Partisan Review* and Columbia professor Lionel Trilling (whom Allen Ginsberg had, and did not respect, as a teacher) and the whole generation of writers who were allowing the Cold War to misshape their work and concerns.

Kerouac and his new friends called themselves "Beats." San Francisco "humorist" Herb Caen renamed them "beatniks," a term Kerouac disavowed for its Soviet-stooge connotations. But the moniker caught on, fanned by sensationalist news coverage emphasizing the promiscuity of Beat girls, a myth punctured by Beat gal (and, briefly, Kerouac's wife) Edie Parker and others. By the mid-1950s a new cultural stock figure was born—the Beatnik, a sullen, goateed *artiste* with a black beret and a spacey girlfriend who recites, in a monotone, bad poetry blaming Dad and Mom for the atom bomb.

That image was a lie, lived only by the fools who gather like June bugs whenever the fickle spotlight of the media illumines the latest movement of the day. Kerouac took pains to distance himself from the faddists—a difficult task, since the precise meaning of Beat was always unclear. Some claimed that it meant liberation from the conformist straitjacket of the postwar era; others took it as affirmation of the wisdom of bums and hobos and other rascals. Novelist John Clellon Holmes and the self-professed thief-prostitute-raconteur Herbert Huncke said it meant "beat down," or tired of it all; the Catholic Kerouac asserted that it was an abbreviation of beatitude, a state of blessed happiness and cheerful acceptance of earthly suffering.

Whatever definition one prefers, the transcendent goal of the Beat movement—I use "movement" with some misgivings, for anarchy was its Polaris—was to revive American literature by infusing it with a mischief and glee that they saw vanishing from this land. Their model was Whitman; their method, an obsessively personal prose and poetry that was proudly, ebulliently American. As Kerouac later wrote: "Like my grandfather America was invested with wild self-believing individuality and this had begun to disappear around the end of World War II with so many great guys dead . . . when suddenly it began to emerge again, the hipsters began to appear gliding around saying, 'Crazy, man.' "[3]

The Beats called their technique "spontaneous bop prosody." Its essence can be gleaned from the first four of a list of Kerouac's own rules for composition:

1. Scribbled secret notebooks, and wild typewritten pages, for yr own joy
2. Submissive to everything, open, listening
3. Try never get drunk outside yr own house
4. Be in love with yr life

Critic Seymour Krim, a sympathetic explicator of the Beats, described spontaneous bop prosody this way:

> The bulk of highbrow young writers Kerouac's own age were strangling themselves, he believed, with grueling and ultra-sober notions of "wit," "tension," "density," and "complexity" in writing. . . . All this seemed falsely over-intellectual and forced to Kerouac and his band of guerrillas. Writing, they thought, loses all of its value to the individual if it has to be put through such a grotesquely convoluted process. . . . Thus Kerouac's "rhythm writing" —no censoring, no rationalizing, no tampering with the flow—was a most dramatic counterpart to the kind of statically intellectual work he felt was slowing down the literary scene. He wanted to tear open all the vents of being and let the actual thought at the moment it was conceived drop upon the page without apology.[4]

Hence the Ginsbergian dictum, "First thought, best thought," and while this begat reams of incoherent unstructured maunderings, at its best, Kerouac's prose is manic, mantic, joyously uninhibited. His purpose was to give voice to "the unspeakable visions of the individual." The result is long hyper-energetic sentence-paragraphs that carry the reader like a runaway train:

> The only people for me are the mad ones, the ones who are mad to live, mad to talk, mad to be saved, desirous of everything at the same time, the ones who never yawn or say a commonplace thing, but burn, burn, burn like fabulous yellow roman candles exploding like spiders across the stars and in the middle you can see the blue centerlight pop and everybody goes, "Awwww!"[5]

The mad yellow Roman candle who inspired this ejaculation was Kerouac's pal Neal Cassady, a strapping Kirk Douglas lookalike who seemed to the Beats to be some sort of cowboy prince. Born in the back seat of a jalopy in Salt Lake City, Cassady dazzled his friends with his expansive and generous nature, hell-bent lifestyle, voracious appetite for conversation, and prodigious sexual feats, leading Kerouac to immortalize him as Dean Moriarty in *On the Road* (1957).

Has there ever been a character as breathless as Dean Moriarty? Right at the beginning of the novel, fresh out of reform school, babbling nonstop about Nietzsche and fast cars and the meaning of life he enters the bookish New York world of Kerouac alter ego Sal Paradise, and leads Paradise and his friends on a series of wild trips across the country and into Mexico. Moriarty's reckless enthusiasm for life infects Paradise with the wanderlust, not as an expression of aimlessness but because there's just so damn much to see and feel in this country.

What is mundane and dreary to so many sad folks is, to Moriarty and his pupil Paradise, pure joy. A trip to the corner store becomes the occasion of an epiphany, a revelation of how rich and sweet our lives can be. Paradise walks into a Nebraska diner, haggard and hungry, and meets euphoria:

> I heard a great laugh, the greatest laugh in the world, and here came this rawhide old-timer Nebraska farmer with a bunch of other boys into the diner; you could hear his raspy cries clear across the plains, across the whole gray world of that day. Everybody else laughed with him. He didn't have a care in the world and had the hugest regard for everybody. I said to myself, Wham, listen to that man laugh. That's the West, here I am in the West. . . . It was the spirit of the West sitting right next to me. I wished I knew his whole raw life and what the hell he'd been doing all these years besides laughing and yelling like that. Whooee, I told my soul.[6]

The passage is typical of the book—a yelping, loving ode to America. The cowboy-deity Moriarty enters Paradise's slate-gray world, helps him to dig the spirit of the West, then takes his leave, walking, alone, into the dark American night. (Kerouac's canonization of Cassady is fully, if less compellingly, realized in his later *Visions of Cody* [1972].)

American men have forever set out for the frontier, fleeing the cozy coffin of domesticity. Sal and Dean were Huck and Jim, and in a few years they would be Wyatt and Billy on motorcycles racing through the barren beauty of the Southwest in *Easy Rider,* counseling strangers about the wisdom of "doing your own thing in your own time" and ultimately paying the price that postwar America exacts for dissent. "Always, in America, there remains from pioneer days a cheerful pariahdom of shabby young men who prowl causelessly from state to state, from gang to gang, in the power of the wanderlust," Sinclair Lewis wrote in *Arrowsmith,* and all the Beats were really doing is upholding the honor of tramps in a world run by Robert McNamara and his brethren in their gray flannel suits.

Kerouac claimed to have written *On the Road* on Benzedrine and booze over a three-week period in 1951. (The gestation was much longer.) It was rejected by publisher after publisher, until in 1957 Viking took a chance on the now despondent, penniless King of the Beats. The day after the novel's publication, the *New York Times* featured an effusive review by Gilbert Millstein, calling the book's appearance "a historic occasion." Fame and, for a time, fortune, followed.

Linked with "Howl," Allen Ginsberg's blow against the Moloch Empire,* *On the Road* was a cry for a revolutionary atavism, a return to the America of vagabonds and Indians and the fellow-feeling that flowed through Whitman's word-torrents. A handful of good young writers, notably Norman Mailer, recognized the Beats as kindred souls and rallied to their defense. Others, including Gore Vidal, admired their energy but disliked their literary output. As Truman Capote memorably said of Kerouac's prose, "That's not writing—that's typewriting."

Like Michael Myers in the *Halloween* series or the hockey-masked Jason in *Friday the 13th,* some villains keep regular hours. You can set your watch by their leaps from the shadows, rusty shivs in hand, ready to stick the knife in whatever is true or beautiful or American. Enter critic Norman Podhoretz, then doggedly climbing the ladder of success. The Beats are "hostile to civilization" he charged in 1958. The "suppressed cry" he detected in Kerouac was positively homicidal: "Kill the intellectuals who can talk coherently"—and these poet laureates of juvenile delinquency were poised to take over the country.[7]†

But what if the Beats *had* taken over the country? Most

---

*Moloch, a Canaanite fire god to whom children were sacrificed, is a favorite image of Ginsberg.

†Poddy loathed Jack and Elvis and James Dean: Middle American rebels unimpressed by parchment embossed with "City College of New York." ("So you people don't believe in God," Kerouac responded to his critics in *Playboy* in 1959. "So you're all big smart know-it-all Marxists and Freudians, hey? Why don't you come back in a million years and tell me all about it, angels?")

Podhoretz fancied himself one of "the guardians of our civilization." When in the 1980s Lowell was considering the long-overdue erection of a monument to its loving son, the columnist, uninvited, crashed the city's debate to argue against it.

shunned politics, unlike their patron saint Whitman, who began his career as a militantly free-trade newspaper editorialist aligned with the laissez-faire wing of the Jacksonian Democracy, the Loco-Focos. Allen Ginsberg, whose mother was a Communist, is a kind of leftist libertarian whose mantra is, "I don't like the government where I live." He is also part of the Jewish bohemian tradition that has enriched American anarchism. William S. Burroughs is a gun-toting anarchist whose favorite political writer is the Pat Buchanan of the 1940s, the dukes-up polemical brawler Westbrook Pegler. And Kerouac was, from the start, an antiwar Taft Republican.

"He believed in a conservative working-class America,"[8] writes Beat publisher John Montgomery. "He liked Ike, baseball, the Virgin Mary, Buddha and apple pie."[9] Indeed, he did like Ike but Kerouac preferred Robert Taft for the Republican presidential nomination. The collected letters of Allen Ginsberg and Neal Cassady are amusing on this point. Ginsberg is avid for liberal Illinois Senator Paul Douglas to receive the Democratic nomination in 1952, and he complains that Jack is solid for Taft. Kerouac also seems to have approved of Senator Joseph McCarthy: he regarded communism as un-American and, while his pacifist isolationism led him to oppose the Cold War and Vietnam, he wanted his America purged of this European impurity.

Montgomery, fictionalized as Henry Morley in Kerouac's *The Dharma Bums,* tells me that Kerouac even took a stab—unsuccessfully—at reading the libertarian novelist Ayn Rand. He did, however, enjoy *National Review.* When its editor, William F. Buckley, Jr., had him as a guest on his TV show, "Firing Line," the host was nasty and condescending and unable to understand how Kerouac could be, at once, against the Vietnam War, deeply respectful of American servicemen, contemptuous of literary communists, and of the opinion that "the hippies are good kids." These views are in perfect harmony, as any American understands, which is why the cosmopolitan Buckley didn't.

But to the Beats, politics was just so . . . soulless. The duty of the public man, after all, is to put reins on wild, self-believing individuals. There is no room in the Young Socialist League or the College Republicans for the Ti Gerards or the Dean Moriartys of this world.

Kerouac's faith reposed not in the men who pretended to shoot Liberty Valance but in men who actually did; in his beloved America, the land from which he drew his voice. Writer Jack McClintock sketches the gentle patriotism of a man supposedly "hostile to civilization itself":

> Kerouac told us once of a party of Ken Kesey's in New York, at which Ginsberg came up and wrapped Jack's shoulders with an American flag—with obvious satiric intent.
>
> "So I took it [he showed how he took it, and the movements were tender] and I folded it up the way you're supposed to, and I put it on the back of the sofa. The flag is not a rag."[10]

A couple of years after that party, on October 21, 1969, Jack Kerouac died. The pressures of sudden fame had sapped his vitality and driven him off the road long before. By the end of his life he was a bloated alcoholic, living in Florida with his wife and doting mother.

Kerouac had published nineteen books, relaying, with varying degrees of success, the unspeakable visions of one individual. His finest, *On the Road,* belongs in the canon of great American— and great Americanist—novels. Kerouac's body lies in a small Catholic cemetery in Lowell, visited now and then by those of us who cherish his memory and the America that was and can be again. His epitaph reads, "He Honored Life," and he did.

NOTES

1. Quoted in Van Wyck Brooks, *The Flowering of New England 1815–1865* (New York: Dutton, 1936), p. 110.

2. Jack Kerouac, "The Origins of the Beat Generation," *Playboy,* June 1959.

3. Ibid.

4. Seymour Krim, "King of the Beats," *Commonweal,* January 2, 1959, p. 360.

5. Jack Kerouac, *On the Road* (New York: Penguin, 1991/1957), p. 8.

6. Ibid., p. 21.

7. Norman Podhoretz, *Doings and Undoings* (New York: Farrar, Straus, 1964), pp. 147, 157.

8. John Montgomery, "Beat Generation without Haloes," in *Beat Indeed!* edited by Rudi Horemans (Antwerp: EXA, 1985), p. 44.

9. John Montgomery, "Helps to Reading Kerouac," in *Beat Indeed!* p. 68.

10. Jack McClintock, "This Is How the Ride Ends: Not with a Bang, with a Damn Hernia," *Esquire* (March 1970).

10

Autumn in New England:
The Last Jeffersonian

"To be a rebel is to court extinction"
—Louise Brooks, quoted in Barry Paris, *Louise Brooks* (1989)

The greatest gadfly in the American politics of our day, John McClaughry of Vermont, describes himself (with what he calls "a notorious Ozark accent"): "I am a 1700s Virginia republican, an 1800 Tertium Quid, an 1830s Loco Foco, an 1850s Republican, an 1890s western progressive, a 1930s agrarian distributist, and today a plain old decentralist agrarian Reaganaut."[1]

It makes perfect sense. Alas, no one gets it. McClaughry, who ought to have been a John Randolph, or at least a Burton K. Wheeler with a wicked sense of humor, is instead a relative unknown who laments that he is "branded a troglodyte by people who don't stop to listen to what I'm saying." The "trouble is," he wrote me in a desponding letter in 1991, "people try to fit pegs in holes. Most people have very few holes to work with: triangle, circle, square, rectangle, maybe pentagonal. When they get a peg the shape of the Mandelbrot set, they try to jam it unsuccessfully into one of their five holes, and then give up in confusion."

If McClaughry is right—and, given the evidence of the ballot box, he is—the bankruptcy of contemporary political discourse is to blame. An America in which Americanism thrived, or at least had a seat at the table, would find a place for John McClaughry.

John McClaughry was born in 1937 in Detroit to a mother who died shortly after his birth, and a father whom he has described as a "couch potato." He was raised by his grandmothers—one in Paris, Illinois, the other in Pontiac, Michigan. His family were border-state "petit bourgeois respectables" who "made the same pilgrimage that Lincoln's did." McClaughry hails from Vachel Lindsay country, and like that sad vagabond poet he knows that the American redemption must start in the small towns:

> O you who lose the art of hope,
> Whose temples seem to shrine a lie,
> Whose sidewalks are but stones of fear,
> Who weep that Liberty must die,
> Turn to the little prairie towns,
> Your higher hope shall yet begin.[2]

The wanderlust seized young McClaughry; like many tribunes of rootedness, he was itinerant for a time. He rode the rails west and picked up the hobo name of "Feather River John." In 1963 McClaughry moved to northern Vermont, bewitched by the gods of its hills. He built himself a log cabin on Kirby Mountain, raised a family, and plunged into politics, serving in the Vermont House and preaching a Jeffersonian gospel of dispersed power, strong communities, and civic responsibility. But far from finding the House a citizens' legislature painted by Norman Rockwell, McClaughry found timeservers who "sat around the card room, playing cribbage and tellin' stories about dogs that chase deer."[3]

This is not to say that McClaughry was a killjoy. He is

an expert crank letter writer. (His epistles from Nestle J. Frobish to California Congressman Jerome Waldie on behalf of the Worldwide Fair Play for Frogs Committee were published as *Fair Play for Frogs* in 1977 by Harcourt Brace Jovanovich.) He pulled off a neat prank in 1976 when he distributed a "Meet John Connally" pamphlet at the GOP convention. Ostensibly designed to promote the ex-Texas governor in the event of a stalemate between the Ford and Reagan forces, the document slyly skewered Connally as a "symbol of concentrated political and economic power." Nevertheless, it fooled several pundits, including the celebrated journalistic team of Germond and Witcover.

His circulars bristle with steely wit. Dunning supporters for contributions, he asks, "Won't you send me all the money you have been saving up to buy the Honus Wagner baseball card? Or pay for your chemotheraphy?" McClaughry's professed hero is Dr. Savannah of the Captain Marvel comics: "He had a mountain retreat and was always trying to find a way to blow up Des Moines. I spend my time writing and thinking and trying to get my message out to world leaders—but I can't seem to find a button to blow up Des Moines."

McClaughry did find a world leader, though. He wrote radio speeches for Ronald Reagan in the late 1970s, putting decentralist words in his client's mouth. McClaughry holds, with legendary Vermont Senator George Aiken, that "the rise and fall of a political party must depend on its ability to attract those who spin and those who toil"; bizarrely, McClaughry actually thought that Reagan did care for the sturdy folk on the Kirby Mountains of America. After the election, John McClaughry joined the White House policy staff.

But a Loco Foco is brave and true, and never slippery enough to slide through the corridors of power. McClaughry was almost fired from his White House job in March 1981 when he flew home in midweek to preside over the Kirby, Vermont, town meeting. He was a fount of fresh, unorthodox ideas, the kind that make ambitious careerists write you off as a kook. "My suggestion that we appoint America's most respected Indian elder as the U.S. representative on the UN Human Rights Commission, with no instructions but to speak plainly about justice for the oppressed nations throughout the world, was greeted in Foggy Bottom as evidence of advanced insanity on my part," McClaughry recalls.[4]

So he took the honorable route, the road less and less traveled: he quit. Yankee stubbornness, an intransigent loyalty to principle, motivated McClaughry. Thoreau's guidance is relevant: "If the tax-gatherer, or any other public officer, asks me, as one has done, 'But what shall I do?' my answer is, 'If you really wish to do anything, resign your office.' "[5]

McClaughry went home and got elected to the State Senate on an Old (circa 1798) Republican platform. Although initially pegged as a wild man, a troglodyte, an opponent of the twentieth century, he won grudging plaudits for his wit, hard work, and seriousness of purpose in defense of a political creed that elsewhere goes unchampioned. And McClaughry discovered just how hard a sell Jeffersonianism has become in an America in which jingo nationalism has eclipsed patriotism, and men care more about Madonna than the gal next door.

Vermont is a curious state politically. Frugal, flinty Yankees are scarce in Montpelier; "woodchucks," as natives are derisively called, are being overrun by those whom McClaughry terms the "Pretty People": affluent immigrants from New York City and Boston, transient Arcadians who have done deals and leveraged and arbitraged and still love the City—the Sunday *Times* in bed, the Museum of Modern Art in the aft, a stroll through the Village at dusk—and who want to make Vermont as pretty, quaint, and utterly lifeless as a picture postcard. (Over the New York border a similar conflict simmers in the Adirondack Mountains, where baseball-capped natives are losing their home ground to the Manhattan summer crowd, with their $400,000 condos and imperious citified demeanors.)

But unlike New York, Vermont hums with discourse. Dissidents are given a respectful hearing. Socialist Bernie Sanders won a seat in Congress in 1990. A Green party, gloriously disorganized, throws off a few sparks, inspired by the Burlington anarchist (and Edward Abbey *bête noire*) Murray Bookchin. And a populist political scientist named Frank Bryan, a scholar of rural governance, is the state's premier tub-thumping orator—if not kin to William Jennings, he's the state's nearest approximation.

Frank Bryan and John McClaughry are close, if contentious, friends, and they collaborated to write *The Vermont Papers* (1989), a blueprint for radically restructuring the state government. Proceeding from "values that are libertarian in the face of authority, decentralist in the face of giantism, and communal among our townspeople," they proposed to strip Montpelier of its accumulated powers, reducing it to the "protector of the environment and guarantor of basic civil rights and liberties."

Responsibility for welfare, education, and road maintenance would devolve to "shires," new units of government resembling counties. The shires would be small—with an average population of 10,000—and extremely democratic: "reeves," or shire legislators, would represent constituencies of about two hundred people. Shires would not be mere units of administration; they would actually *make* policy. A liberal Burlington shire, for example, might spend prodigally for welfare, while rural shires opted for Coolidgean parsimony.

With "geography as cocoon and history as memory," Vermont is an ideal site for the rebirth of grass-roots democracy. Its population is scattered among 246 small towns steeped in that grand New England tradition, the town meeting. Industrialism, and the dependence it breeds, passed Vermont by. The percentage of self-employed Vermonters is twice the national average; small, locally owned businesses and dairy farms predominate.

The Vermont Papers was radical and reactionary, as any

modern expression of the Spirit of '76 is bound to be. Its vision of men and women as *citizens*—rooted, community-minded people who enjoy their liberty but are ever mindful of their obligations to neighbors and the less fortunate—seems a charming anachronism in this feckless age. So, too, its celebration of local patriotism, of pride and healthy parochialism.

But populist anger also infuses the book: resentment against the "Pretty People" and those who disparage ordinary, undegreed Vermonters. McClaughry confesses to "a natural animosity toward urbanism" and that bias has led some reviewers to conclude, in McClaughry's words, that "these guys are living in a dreamworld of hobbits in the back country."[6] They do not address the maladies that the TV newsreaders tell us *really* matter: AIDS, African droughts, drug dealers bumping each other off. Serious problems, to be sure, but irrelevancies to the tens of millions of Americans who live in small towns and rural communities, who are fast becoming subjects of metropolitan rulers, serfs of large distant corporations.

Ironically, Vermont reviews of *The Vermont Papers* were generally less perceptive than notices in national publications. The problem, one suspects, was McClaughry's reputation. "The mere mention of this man's name brought foam to the mouths of liberals," a Vermont reporter has written.[7]

McClaughry's failure to reach leftist decentralists recalls the only other politician in memory to peddle such a thorough and plausible plan for reform: Norman Mailer. Brooklyn's favorite fugging son, in his 1969 Democratic primary campaign for New York's mayoralty, proposed the virtual abolition of the city's government and the devolution of power to the neighborhoods, along the lines of Jefferson's ward republic scheme. Mailer called himself a "left conservative," but no one to the right of Greenwich Village ever listened, and he tallied but 5 percent of the vote.

The McClaughry-Mailer parallel experiences are a sobering lesson to decentralists. Mailer was correct on every important issue—he even opposed fluoridation of the water supply—but

Manhattan's tuxedoed conservatives gave him nothing but sneers. (He wrote novels containing swear words, don't you know, and said nice things about the Black Panthers' demand for Harlem control of Harlem schools.)

McClaughry, despite his Green lifestyle, his communitarian language, his populist attacks on concentrated wealth, is a bugbear to the Vermont left. Like Mailer, his failure to break through the liberal-conservative gossamer is due to style. He likes Country and Western music. He used to call Eastern European countries "Captive Nations." He twits the gay rights movement.

Nevertheless, the man has something to say, and if Jeffersonianism is ever going to be resurgent in our America John McClaughry's the likeliest standard-bearer. He's a homespun populist but no demagogue; he's an intellectual fluent in the vernacular of American politics; he's a Northern agrarian, an admirer of both the Virginia planter-statesmen and the Vermonters who defied the Fugitive Slave Act. He loves history, lives and breathes it; Ethan Allen is very real to him.

McClaughry has portraits of his heroes on the wall: Jefferson, of course, and John Taylor of Caroline and Fighting Bob LaFollette and Robert Taft and his old boss, Reagan. He is a good friend of Green writer-activist Kirkpatrick Sale, and is undoubtably the only Reaganite ever to serve on the board of directors of the small-is-beautiful E. F. Schumacher Society. He knows who are the true wise but unsung men of twentieth-century politics: Amos Pinchot, Burton K. Wheeler, and the unheeded prophets who wrote *I'll Take My Stand* (1930) and *Who Owns America?* (1936).

McClaughry is also fond of ex-Oklahoma Senator Fred Harris, who with his classic motto, "No More Bullshit," enlivened the 1972 and 1976 Democratic presidential primaries. McClaughry's requiem for Harris's career serves, too, as a self-assessment: "Fred is an early 1900s Populist who's been propelled forward in time with all the talents that would have made him a contender in 1916, but now, no one gets what he's talking about."[8]

Harris never figured out how to get his message across. Neither has McClaughry. After McClaughry lost the primary campaign for the U.S. Senate in 1982, his friend Frank Bryan described what the candidate was up against: "How, with limited funds, to articulate his views to an electorate that does not possess the necessary concepts or language?"[9]

A decade later, McClaughry thought he'd learned. He entered the 1992 race for governor against the popular vanilla incumbent, Democrat Howard Dean. The Republican party, despairing of unseating Dean, thought it had nothing to lose.

McClaughry ran with vigor and wit. He had a catchy slogan—"For the People, for a Change"—and his campaign pose featured the candidate in workshirt and ballcap strumming a guitar. He was photographed presenting to a grinning Governor Dean the official McClaughry campaign attire: a pitch black T-shirt on which was a hooded executioner and an emblazoned "NEXT."

McClaughry campaigned on a "Prosperity-Accountability-Democracy" theme. While he was not overly vocal in advancing the radical reorganization embodied in *The Vermont Papers,* he did emphasize the need "to bring political power back home to our communities." McClaughry didn't have much money—$140,000—and at the top of the ticket was the hapless George Bush, who polled less than a third of the vote in "rock-ribbed Republican" Vermont. McClaughry wound up with just 23 percent of the vote—an embarrassment. (As Nixonian prankster Dick Tuck remarked upon losing a race, "The people have spoken—the bastards.")

What will John McClaughry do with the rest of his life? He dismisses suggestions that he write a memoir; the theme, he says, would be, "Jesus Christ, I tried to tell the dumb sumbitches [*sic*] how to do it and I might as well have been standing on the beach on Easter Island hollering uphill."[10] In his dejection McClaughry is like Edmund Wilson, Edgar Lee Masters, and John T. Flynn, the honor roll of America Firsters in a changed country. I leave Amos R. E. Pinchot off the list because, well, John McClaughry has the natural buoyancy without which any sane man would blow his brains out. (John corresponded with Pinchot's widow in 1975. On lavender note paper Mrs. Pinchot replied, "I know if Amos were alive, he would be standing at your side.")

A Jeffersonian renaissance in Vermont would be a wonderful way to usher out our Hamiltonian century. Yes, the Pretty People keep potting the woodchucks, and John McClaughry lost the governor's race by the largest margin in his state's history. The same thing had happened to Burton K. Wheeler in Montana in 1920. But he came back to win election to the Senate in 1922 and give America Firstism a foghorn voice. So don't give up on John McClaughry. He is, hands-down, the most interesting politician in America; it is his way, the Ethan Allen-Loco Foco-Prairie Populist way, wherein lies liberty, community, and the genius of the Old Republic.

NOTES

1. John McClaughry, interview with the author, June 27, 1990.
2. Vachel Lindsay, "A Gospel of Beauty," in *Collected Poems* (New York: Macmillan, 1925), p. 71.
3. Studs Terkel, *American Dreams: Found and Lost* (New York: Random House, 1980), p. 371.
4. John McClaughry, Letter to the Editor, *Reason* (October 1986), p. 9.
5. Henry David Thoreau, "On the Duty of Civil Disobedience," in *Walden and "Civil Disobedience"* (New York: Signet, 1960/1849), p. 231.
6. John McClaughry, interview with the author, June 27, 1990.
7. Tim Peek, "New Leaders for the 1990s," *Vanguard Press,* May 3–10, 1990.
8. McClaughry, interview with the author, June 27, 1990.
9. Frank M. Bryan, "The Loneliness of the Long-Distance Ideologue," *The Times-Argus* (Barre-Montpelier, Vt.), September 16, 1982, p. 5.
10. John McClaughry, letter to the author, December 12, 1992.

Part Three

America First Renewed

11

The New Party of the Old Republic

"Times change and men often change with them, but principles
never!"
 —Alexander Stephens, Vice President of the
  Confederate States of America,
  quoted in Rudolph von Abele, *Alexander H. Stephens*

In the fall of 1993 we glimpsed an alternative American political
landscape. The terrain was comfortably strange—the topographic
features looked familiar but everything had been moved, and
for one brilliant moment it seemed as if the natural order, the
one predating our contemporary helter-skelter, had been restored.

The window to this world was opened by the North American
Free Trade Agreement (NAFTA). Thanks to NAFTA the Democrats, Republicans, liberals, and conservatives split with a smooth,
clean break. The nominal leaders of the populist tendencies of
right, left, and angry center—Patrick J. Buchanan, Jerry Brown,
and Ross Perot—fit together like pieces of a jigsaw puzzle: the
true puzzle then became how it could have ever been otherwise.

Our ever loyal press, famously ignorant of history, panicked
at the prospect of revolt by the lowing herd of revenue cows,
and insisted that this queer coalition was a freakish thing, spec-
tacular but brief and (thank God) unstable. It had been whipped

187

into a frenzy by irresponsible demagogues, and once the dust cleared the kine would revert to kind. A little rebellion now and then isn't such a bad thing, after all, as long as the dissidents know that's it's just a game and when the morning dawns they've got to get up and go to work and do their eight-hour stint as cogs in the great wheel of the interdependent global economy.

NAFTA was the perfect bugbear for Americanists of all stripes: it sought to cede American jobs, American tax dollars, and American sovereignty to Mexico and multinational corporations and supranational bureaucracies. Its overweening ambition liberated (or exhumed?) a body of American nationalists who had been buried with the Bricker Amendment in the 1950s.* The Bricker Amendment, the last throaty roar of the Old Right, had sought to keep the provisions of any treaty from superseding the Constitution. Despite widespread support, the amendment was doomed by the opposition of President Eisenhower and the liberal Democrats who were, almost to a man, still in the giggling stage of infatuation with the siren Empire. The anti-NAFTA gang of autumn 1993 were the Brickerites with a strong left wing—a potential electoral majority.

Is the nightmare alliance of "the nativist right and isolationist left" against which William Safire once warned upon us?

There is ample precedent for the aborning America First coalition. Buchanan, Brown, Perot, and their harmonizing band of the bohemian right, patriotic left, and angry center are direct descendants of the old republican statesmen of the antimonopolist "Left" and voluntarist "Right" who came together in the 1930s to oppose the fascist thrust of the later New Deal: the National Recovery Administration, the court-packing plan, conscription, and the drift into war and the garrison state.

These old republicans—mistakenly deemed "progressives"

---

*The Bricker Amendment asserted national sovereignty in an age dominated by Cold War-driven internationalism. In 1994 the Republican "Contract with America" pledged to keep U.S. troops from serving under UN commanders, which was an echo of Bricker, however faint.

and lumped together with "race-improving" eugenicists and wealthy New England socialists and war-lusting magazine writers—included Senators Burton K. Wheeler, Gerald P. Nye, Thomas P. Gore, Hiram Johnson, William E. Borah, the junior and senior Robert La Follettes, and the maverick heroes Charles Lindbergh and Major General Smedley Butler.

They championed the small against the large, the parochial against the cosmopolitan: Nye made an early splash in North Dakota politics with his heated animadversions against not Wall Street but those financial centers of the upper Midwest, those havens of sin and usury—the Twin Cities.

Nye's side lost, the Kettle Hill-Hyde Park side won, and we got two world wars, endless dips into distant bloodlakes, the dispossession of once independent men, an engorged central government, ever-increasing concentrations of wealth and power, and wholesale violations of individual liberties. It has been, indeed, a rough ride.

This was more than just the age-old split between Jefferson and Hamilton, between a minimalist state pursuing a neutral foreign policy and a muscular central government engaged in world affairs. Alexander Hamilton, after all, ghosted a portion of Washington's farewell address, and he fully shared the first president's aversion to entanglements and alliances and "overgrown military establishments." The retroprogressives were up against something far more baneful and puissant than subsidy-seeking manufacturers. And though they are gone and forgotten, these desultorily organized defenders of an America that was too big for body bags and too small to fit into a gross national product left stakes that may guide us in redrawing, with sense and clarity, our own political map.

Historian Wayne S. Cole, whose lifework has been to understand these men, emphasizes that

> they feared and distrusted bigness of any sort—big business, big finance, big military, big government, big unions, and big

corporate farms. Their sympathies were with debtors rather than
creditors, with farmers rather than city people, with small businessmen rather than big business, with workers rather than employers, with producers rather than financiers and distributors,
with free competition within the country rather than monopoly,
with equality of opportunity rather than special privilege, with
limited constitutional government rather than monarchy or dictatorship, with legislative authority rather than presidential power,
with democracy rather than elitism, with faith in the common
man rather than experts, with domestic progress rather than
international expansion.[1]

Even though libertarians can find much here to admire, the
retroprogressives were not dogmatists; most favored government
provision of old-age pensions and emergency public jobs. They
viewed the progenitors (and, even more, the inheritors) of great
fortunes with suspicion, and they loathed plutocratic, anti-New
Deal front groups such as the American Liberty League. As
Nye scornfully observed, "the 'economy' leagues and the 'Liberty'
leagues . . . have not yet seen fit to protest the increased ap-
propriations for the Army and the Navy."[2]

The party line was healthy heterodoxy. As Tom Fleming
and Murray Rothbard have pointed out,[3] there were no com-
missars to enforce ideological regularity; no one was purged for
idiosyncrasy. Borah, for example, supported Prohibition; Wheeler
was committed to the Child Labor Amendment; Gerald Nye
thought FDR too miserly when it came to funding the Works
Progress Administration (WPA) and the Civilian Conservation
Corps (CCC). Many—Wheeler especially—were Roosevelt
enthusiasts in 1932, but then their FDR was the Hudson Valley
patroon with a demotic streak and a leveling hand, the Grover
Cleveland Democrat who, as governor, had decried "the tendency
to concentrate power at the top of a government structure" as
"alien to our system."[4]

The retroprogressives favored, in the words of novelist and
farmer Louis Bromfield, "free, dispersed, competitive and co-

operative capitalism."[5] The string of qualifying adjectives is crucial. Theirs was a somewhat wistful Jeffersonianism, befitting agrarians and antimilitarists in an increasingly industrial society harnessed to a chugging war economy. Lindbergh asked in 1939, "How long can men thrive between walls of brick, walking on asphalt pavements, breathing the fumes of coal and of oil, growing, working, dying, with hardly a thought of wind and sky, and fields of grain, seeing only machine-made beauty, the mineral-like quality of life?"[6]

Few actually lived on farms or Hamlin Garland's branch roads; most hailed from "towns from one thousand up to one hundred and fifty thousand," in which Herbert Hoover, a *sui generis* Progressive, saw "the very best results of all the forces in American life."[7] They were Sinclair Lewis hybrids, a lively mixture of Will Kennicott, the stolid and decent Gopher Prairie provincial, and Miles Bjornstam, the town Wobbly, a self-educated radical of unimpeachable character.

Lewis was a La Follette-Wheeler man in 1924, along with "a few sorehead farmers," as he wrote in "Main Street's Been Paved" in *The Nation*. (He did allow the possibility that "an honest-to-God Vermont schoolteacher like Cal Coolidge may understand America better than the average pants-maker who hasn't been over from Lithuania but six months.")

The present obscurity of Senator Wheeler, the most politically significant of the retroprogressives, is a shame, although it's not surprising since our national decision makers honor rather than jail Robert McNamara and Henry Kissinger. Wheeler was a Massachusetts Yankee with a law degree who wanted to see the West, so he took a train across the plains until he lost his stake in a Butte, Montana, poker game, and there he stayed. "If I could imagine Hell on earth, it would be Butte," said Wheeler's wife, a headstrong Illinois farm girl.

Wheeler won local renown as a U.S. district attorney who took on the Ananconda Copper octopus and refused to prosecute dissenters for sedition during the police state of President Wilson and Attorney General A. Mitchell Palmer in the late teens. Defeated in his race for governor in 1920—the Ananconda-controlled press dubbed him "Bolshevik Burt"—Wheeler was elected to the U.S. Senate two years later and quickly made headlines for his investigation into the corruption in Harding crony Harry Daugherty's Justice Department. In 1924, when Senator Robert La Follette raised the banner of republican populism, he chose Wheeler as his running mate (after Justice Louis Brandeis turned him down), later saluting his second as a "brilliant, incorruptible, courageous man."[8]

In the Senate, Wheeler emerged as a leading champion of the antimonopoly faction, defending small business, farmers, and the integrity of the hinterlands. He was, naturally, an anti-imperialist, outspoken in his support for Philippine independence and respect for Nicaraguan sovereignty. An early supporter of Franklin D. Roosevelt for the Democratic presidential nomination in 1932, Wheeler soured on the New Deal, which he came to see as fascist in its marriage of bureaucratic, corporate, and tamed labor interests. Like the other great Rockies progressive, William E. Borah, Wheeler regarded the price and production-fixing NRA as an iniquitous plan to cartelize the economy.

At his wife's prodding, Wheeler threw away his future in the Democratic party by spearheading Senate opposition to the president's 1937 court-packing proposal. "The liberal cause was never won by stacking a deck of cards, stuffing a ballot box or by packing a court,"[9] Wheeler averred with an anachronistic ardor that soon won him a meticulous income tax audit.

FDR referred to Mrs. Wheeler in private as Lady MacBeth; it was she, a proper woman imbued with a Zona Gale Midwestern spirit, who bolstered her husband as he committed political hara-kiri in the court battle. As Mrs. Wheeler's daughter Elizabeth W. Colman writes in a charming biography of her mother, "small midwestern towns . . . to her represented true democratic traditions. It had neither poverty nor great wealth. The residents were homogeneously middle-class; they believed in equality, plain living, and high thinking. Good-neighborliness was a cherished tradition."[10]

Mrs. Wheeler objected to the New Deal because it offended her human-scale sense of town life: "Dignity itself had been buried beneath a stack of government forms,"[11] she said. America was not an idea but a place, and the United States of Abstraction of the New Dealers had no place for the steel-spined Mrs. Wheeler or for a farmgirl like Belle Case La Follette, the wife, mother, and Wisconsin Progressive who schooled her children at home.

Anne Morrow Lindbergh described one America First dinner at which the Wheelers were present:

> I sit between Mrs. Wheeler and Mrs. [Alice Roosevelt] Long-worth. [Senator Wheeler] talks the whole time—a nice slow drawl. He just radiates a healthy American confidence, courage, and taking it in your stride. I like him very much and trust him. He has integrity, like Charles. He tells me I mustn't let it get under my skin and he tells me about all the things they've said of him in the different campaigns —how he was slandered, chased out of town, defeated, smeared. And of his wife sticking by him, urging him on, never minding. "If you can stand it, I can." There was a wonderful pride in him about his wife. American—American—American, I kept feeling as I talked to him.[12]

As an American of blood and sentiment, Wheeler hated peacetime conscription on the eve of America's entry into World War II. "No longer will this be a free land," he prophesied of this "greatest step toward regimentation and militarism ever undertaken." Ignoring the defamations, he insisted, "So long as this country remains at peace and so long as Congress has not declared war, so long as there is a remnant of democratic government, I will not be silenced."[13]

But he was. Wheeler's reference to the Lend-Lease Act of 1941 (by which the Roosevelt administration armed the allies) as "the New Deal's triple-A foreign policy—it will plow under every fourth American boy," effectively ended his career as a powerful senator. He had committed the unpardonable sin of *lèse-majesté*—and with wit, which only compounded the gravity of the offense.

British intelligence, working with the Roosevelt administration, sought to "destroy the credibility" of Senator Wheeler, according to William Stephenson in his spy memoir, *A Man Called Intrepid* (1976). Our lobster-backed former masters also regarded the antiwar populist John L. Lewis, one of the last labor leaders with guts, as "a menace to be liquidated." Lewis wanted Wheeler to get the 1940 Democratic presidential nomination, as did Borah, who shortly before his death was ready to cross party lines to endorse his friend. "He's a real liberal, not a phony one," the Lion of Idaho saluted his Montana neighbor.*

Borah, like Wheeler, was a green lawyer from Illinois who traveled westward until his money ran out in Boise. Often disparaged as a man who, when he hit a home run, stopped at first base, Borah was a liberal nationalist, a self-described Hamiltonian. His public stances, mocked at the time as crazy-quilt, had a sinewy consistency: he opposed the Wilson-Palmer censorship, the tariff, agriculture subsidies, and the cancellation of European war debts; he supported early recognition of the Soviet Union, the direct primary, and "a drastic immigration law, one which will prevent the country from being overrun with foreigners."

He was not an isolationist as that once-invidious term was understood: Borah broke with the Republican party to advance tariff reduction. But he was a jealous guardian of his country's autonomy, who foresaw with remarkable prevision a world tyrannized by "the gathered scum of the nations organized into

---

*The sheer decency of these men—who were politicians, after all—is also to be noted. Wheeler went out of his way to strike up a friendship with the reviled Senate outcast Huey Long. David McCullough, in his hagiographic *Truman*, admits that Wheeler and Borah were among the few senators to act kindly toward the new "senator from Pendergast."

a conglomerate international police force ordered hither and thither by the most heterogeneous and irresponsible body or court that ever confused or confounded the natural instincts and noble passions of a people."[14]

There was a day when professions of love of one's country did not begin and end with a recitation of its military might. Senator Hiram Johnson, the California Progressive, declared, "God put in every man's breast something besides a mere internationalism or a mere world vision beyond his country's confines. I may indeed have an admiration for another country, but after all God put in my heart, as he put in the hearts of most men, a love for my native land."[15]

Johnson was the son of a California railroad lawyer but he was an obstreperous cuss, similar in temperament to (if more garrulous than) the railroad's nemesis Annixter in Frank Norris's novel *The Octopus* (1901). He was windy and given to bombast; as Teddy Roosevelt's Bull Moose running mate in 1912 he held his own with that dynamo of bluster. Mencken was harsh: Johnson, he wrote, had "a conscience with almost as much stretch in it as a wad of chewing gum" and was "a great lover of the plain people, but always stopping short of a suicidal fondness."[16]

Well, maybe. But Mencken was a master of misjudgments, and even so prickly a Progressive as Harold Ickes, who abhorred Johnson's isolationism, conceded that Johnson, though an egotist, was honest and capable. A proud man who would be no one's second, he rejected Warren G. Harding's offer of the vice-presidential slot in 1920. If only Johnson "had known . . . what Warren Harding's blood pressure was," George Brennan famously conjectured.[17]

Yes, if only. We'd have been blessed with a ruddy, energetic president who proudly called himself "an American, a selfish, provincial, little American, for America first." G. K. Chesterton in *The Napoleon of Notting Hill* (1904) understood that "the patriot never under any circumstances boasts of the largeness of his country, but always, and of necessity, boasts of the smallness of it."[18] This is paradoxical only to those who have no such attachments. Is it any wonder that among the most vociferous advocates of a huge military establishment during the Cold War were immigrants who hadn't the time (or inclination) to develop a love of particular American places?

Another deep-dyed American contradiction is the martial antimilitarist. Ross Perot is a fine living example: an Annapolis man who has devoted countless hours and dollars to veterans' causes yet despised the Gulf War, opposed the invasion of Haiti, and denounces our meddling in Bosnia.

Perot's predecessor in the stormy autumn of the republic was Major General Smedley Butler (1881–1940). The beloved gimlet-eyed maverick marine and war hero was presidential hopeful Huey Long's choice for secretary of war. Upon his retirement in 1931, Butler barnstormed the country, vilifying an imperialism he viewed as profoundly un-American:

> I helped make Mexico and especially Tampico safe for American oil interests in 1914. I helped make Haiti and Cuba a decent place for the National City Bank boys to collect revenues in. I helped in the raping of a half dozen Central American republics for the benefit of Wall Street. . . . Looking back on it, I feel I might have given Al Capone a few hints. The best *he* could do was to operate his racket in three city districts. We Marines operated on three *continents*.[19] (Original italics)

General Butler was lionized by the virile left, but only until it became clear that Smedley was an American original, a cantankerous patriot. While he "wouldn't want to see a boy of mine march out with a Wall Street collar about his neck," he also decried the socialist call for U.S. intervention in the Spanish Civil War. "What in hell is it our business what's going on in Spain?"[20] he asked.

General Butler was an early and vocal supporter of the 1930s

Ludlow Amendment, which required a nationwide referendum to validate a congressional declaration of war. The Ludlow Amendment was a forerunner of Perot's electronic town hall and the Brown/ Buchanan demand for increased use of ballot initiatives. *Ramparts* editor and radical patriot Warren Hinckle saw the link; he hailed Perot's plebiscitary democracy as "part and parcel with the populist and La Follette progressive tradition."[21]

Like Perot, Butler was a practical dreamer, a stubborn man of action who thought things up on his own and then said them aloud, consternating the opinion referees. In 1936 he proposed to the readers of the *Woman's Home Companion* a constitutional amendment of his own to restrict American soldiers to the mainland and forbid our navy from venturing more than five hundred miles from the coastal United States.

General Butler told a Veterans of Foreign Wars convention in Buffalo, New York, in 1937, "It's your crowd that's going to do the dying and bleeding, not the Wall Street flag-wavers."[22] Two years later, incensed by the administration's bellicosity, Butler declaimed with typical bravado, "If there is another war I intend to make James Roosevelt go to the front line trenches. . . . I am not afraid! Let them shoot me! I'm all through. Let's get shot here at home if we're going to be shot."

Butler died peacefully in 1940. A destroyer was named for him, as was—in one of those sly ironies that suggest the Empire has a sense of humor—the marine base on Okinawa. His biographer Hans Schmidt hails the "personal integrity and populist candor that Butler achieved naturally as a straight-shooting loner"[23]; these same qualities virtually guarantee admission to the eccentric's wing of the national zoo.

The same mawkishness—or truly guileless sincerity—for which Perot is often ridiculed suffused Butler's speeches. It's not hard to imagine the bantam Texan making this radio broadcast in 1939:

Now—*you mothers,* particularly! The only way you can resist all this war hysteria and beating of tom-toms is by asserting the love you bear your boys. When you listen to some well-worded, some well-delivered *war* speech, just remember it's nothing but *sound.* No amount of sound can make up to you for the loss of your boy. . . . Look at him. Put your hand on that spot on the back of his neck. The place you used to love to kiss when he was a baby. Just rub it a little. You won't wake him up, he knows it's you. . . . Look at this splendid young creature who's part of yourself, then close your eyes for a moment and I'll tell you what can happen.

Somewhere—five thousand miles from home. Night. Darkness. Cold. A drizzling rain. The noise is terrific. All Hell has broken loose. A star shell bursts in the air. Its unearthly flare lights up the muddy field. There's a lot of tangled rusty barbed wires out there and a boy hanging over them—his stomach ripped out, and he's feebly calling for help and water. His lips are white and drawn. He's in agony. There's your boy.[24] (Original italics)

And there he is still, a bloody corpse being dragged through the sandy streets of Mogadishu.

There was a boy, born at West Point, raised in the shadows of the Capitol Dome and the Clover Adams monument in Rock Creek Cemetery, who links the retroprogressives, the Old Republicans, and the America Firsters with the revenants of the isolationist present. He admired Wheeler and Johnson, whom he saw while accompanying his blind grandfather on his daily Senate rounds. He appreciated Lindbergh because he was born to flight; his father, Eugene Vidal, was President Roosevelt's appointed director of the Bureau of Air Commerce. He was, naturally, a leader of America First at Exeter.

Senator Thomas P. Gore was a hater of war who had proposed a version of the Ludlow Amendment as early as 1917. Though FDR's henchmen engineered his defeat in 1936, his young cicerone, to the everlasting regret of the incumbent party, survived.

Gore Vidal, recalling his grandfather, wrote in 1992:

The so-called liberals—as they are always so-called—included Franklin Roosevelt. They were eager to go to war, once war came, on England's side. The so-called conservatives, like Senator Gore, were against war in general and any war to help the British Empire in particular. Today, when the meanings of so many words have been reversed, the conservatives speak fiercely against the, so-called by them, isolationists on the left, while the left (also known as Paleolithic conservatives) speaks of minding our own business and restoring a wrecked polity, thanks to forty years of profitless—for the people at large—imperialism.[25]

Vidal advised Jerry Brown throughout the 1992 primaries, during which the angular, slightly off-center former Jesuit seminarian metamorphosed into a fiery populist preacher. Brown stole much of his platform from Vidal, his opponent in the 1982 California Democratic Senate primary. (Vidal's version of Brown's controversial 13 percent flat tax was set at 5 percent—something you'd never have learned from reading the official conservative press.)

Jerry Brown really hit his stride with his slashing criticisms of NAFTA. He became the insurgent labor candidate, but this was no Walter Mondale cobbling together a hideous mosaic of featherbeds and union dues. Of NAFTA, Brown wrote, "Instead of democratic decisions made at the state and local level, under GATT [General Agreement on Tariffs and Trade] and the North American trade pact we would all be subjected to a supergovernment of unelected trade bureaucrats."[26]

This preference for localism against the centralized rule of experts helped define the retroprogressives, the Old Right, and certain strains of the New Left, and it is a standard feature of the new Americanists. It is the bond that links a Buchanan with a Brown, a New Hampshire libertarian with an Oregon hippie, and it is why SDS (Students for a Democratic Society) president and political theorist Carl Oglesby argued in the 1960s that "the Old Right and the New Left are morally and politically coordinate."[27]

The matters that occupied Burton K. Wheeler throughout his career—halting our slide into militarism; dismantling the empire; busting monopolies; preserving small-scale exchange and locally owned businesses; effecting a more equitable distribution of land and wealth without resorting to socialist tyranny; zealously guarding our sovereignty against internationalizing schemes; defending the rights of speakers to voice unpopular views; forging creative tools of direct democracy; challenging the party line as promulgated by the executive and his de facto press agent, big media—are the same concerns that animate the collateral movements led by Perot, Buchanan, and Brown.

Pat Buchanan's speech announcing his candidacy for the Republican presidential nomination in November 1991 featured jarringly archaic diction. George Bush, Buchanan thundered, "is a globalist and we are nationalists. He believes in some Pax Universalis; we believe in the old Republic. He would put America's wealth and power at the service of some vague New World Order; we will put America first."

(The Rockefeller-Nixon Republicans of the Bush administration hadn't even the geographic sense to put America last. Vice President Dan Quayle, responding to Buchanan in February 1992, opined, "During this presidential election year, you will hear voices from the left and right saying, 'Come home, America.' Well, Europe is our home."[28])

Like Nye deprecating the Liberty League, Buchanan insisted that "conservatism is about more than the constitutional right of big fishes to eat little fishes." Louis Bromfield understood, as does Jerry Brown, who condemned a system in which Washington, D.C., lawyers earn five hundred dollars an hour while a nurses's aide in Nashua is lucky to make six dollars, without benefits.

Buchanan's message struck a responsive chord in an empire-weary populace; he faded as a presidential candidate, of course, but then he lacked a solid target for his America First arrows. In 1993 Buchanan found one: NAFTA. Though dressed up in the pretty raiment of free trade, beneath the finery "NAFTA is about America and her future; and [Americans] do not want to see this republic married off to a Third World nation of eighty million whose average wage is 15 percent of our own."[29]

The pact "is about America's sovereignty, liberty, and destiny," argued Buchanan. "It is about whether we hand down to the next generation the same free and independent country [*sic*] handed down to us; or whether twenty-first-century America becomes but a subsidiary of the New International Economic Order."[30] This is high-octane populism of a potency unknown to the Republican party of William Simon and Richard Lugar. Buchanan was echoing Nye, who with plaintive futility demanded his GOP "separate itself from big business and take an aggressive attitude in support of the small businessman."[31]

Buchanan framed NAFTA with angles borrowed from the Bricker Amendment, but by this time enough people on the "left" had soured on internationalism that a mighty alliance was born, kicking and screaming, and if it's not smothered in the crib by the angels of death of official conservatism and liberalism— "nativist, xenophobic, anti-growth, protectionist know-nothing demagogues, and, most damning of all, *unproductive*," went the slur against NAFTA's would-be derailers—then we Americans will have a real debate, for the first time since Wheeler and Nye and Johnson and Gore went down in a plane piloted by Lucky Lindy and vanished, leaving fewer traces than Amelia Earhart.

"Sink NAFTA, and save the old republic,"[32] Buchanan ended one salvo, and while this salvage job may make raising the *Titanic* seem like plucking a toy boat from a bathtub, what patriot cannot heed the call?

"Don't follow leaders," advised Bob Dylan—who probably was not on Pat Buchanan's playlist in 1967 but should have been—and the counsel is sound. For all of Pat Buchanan's praiseworthy broadsides there is the problem of his background: I refer not only to his loyal service to two of our most internationalist presidents, Nixon and Reagan, but to his family, whose "trinity of political heroes," he wrote in his autobiography, *Right from the Beginning* (1988), "consisted of Douglas MacArthur, General Franco, and the junior senator from Wisconsin they called Tail Gunner Joe."33*

The 1950s Catholic Right—Buchanan's matrix—was less interested in this country than were socialist Jewish intellectuals such as Alfred Kazin and Irving Howe. To these Catholics "Americanism" was an essentially negative doctrine that placed communism at the center of American concerns, when in fact it belonged well beyond the margins. Middle Americans disliked communism, but in the same way they disdained escargot or cubism. I dare say that not a single member of my family was affected in any way by the mythically dark and horrific era of McCarthyism, and I seriously doubt that any of them gave a damn whether Joseph McCarthy or Edward R. Murrow prevailed in this whole silly, irrelevant episode in our history.†

---

*What are we to make of the the last two of this triad?

Joseph McCarthy defeated Senator Robert La Follette, Jr., in the 1946 Wisconsin Republican primary, an infamous moment in the history of Americanism's collapse. McCarthy was a sworn enemy of the retroprogressives, of whom young La Follette, despite his spotty voting record (he supported FDR's judicial reorganization), was a member in good standing. La Follette despised communism—it was a foreign ideology, after all—as well as the equally alien religion of anticommunism.

McCarthy, on the other hand, in addition to being a liar, was an interventionist whose foreign policy views were close to those of Harry Truman. He attacked La Follette as an isolationist who "oppos[ed] world cooperation." Young Bob La Follette killed himself in 1953, the same year that Robert A. Taft died and Joseph McCarthy, Roy Cohn, and William F. Buckley, Jr., were charting the course for the dreadnought of postwar conservatism.

Franco is even farther removed from the American realm. Smedley Butler's question—"What in hell is it our business what's going on in Spain?"—was on Main Street tongues in Xenia and Tulsa. Buchanan's father may have been a great guy but on this issue, at least, he had much in common with the starry-eyed reds who went to fight in Spain with the Abraham Lincoln Brigade.

†To Buchanan's credit, his favorite movie is *The Godfather*. You can tell a lot about a man by his taste in movies. (Or, in Ronald Reagan's case, by his roles. Defenders of small-town America who saw a friend in Reagan should have first checked out his finest performance, as the blithe blade Drake McHugh in the 1942 gem *Kings Row*. The village of Kings Row, tranquil on the surface, is beset by subterranean perversities and mental illnesses and even an amputation-happy sadistic

*   *   *

The official party has been roused; the clampdown of which the Clash warned is imminent. The leaders of the insurgent party are the easiest to dispose of. Perot is a paranoiac nut, Buchanan an anti-Semite, and Brown a sexually ambiguous goofball. Or so we are told. As for the writers and activists who are coming together under the rebel flag, call them names, cut off their grants, and they'll shut up. Or so it is believed.

For example, in March 1992 the *New York Times* informed us that Pat Buchanan, who gained three million votes in the Republican primaries, was all the rage among "the white-power and neo-Nazi groups at the darkest corner"[34] of our gloomy national psyche. Both Hollywood and the *Times* seem convinced that most working-class whites are violent racists who beat their wives and secretly assemble in huge Idaho conclaves to listen to the recorded speeches of Adolf Hitler.

This white racism charge is very strange, especially since opinion polls show that the single demographic group most favorable to America First attitudes toward foreign aid,

surgeon who removes Ronnie's legs to keep him from pursuing his lunatic but comely daughter. No wonder the Reagans prefer Bel Air to Dixon.)

Ross Perot asked a reporter several years ago, "You ever see that movie *Places in the Heart*? That's the town I knew." The film was written and directed by Robert Benton, who is from Waxahachie, twenty miles south of Dallas. It tells the story of a Texas widow of the 1930s who brings in a cotton crop with the help of an itinerant black handyman. Diligence and faith bring success; the widow and her hired man are models of cooperative individualism.

An epilogue, similar to that of *Our Town* but without Wilder's New England astringency, shows the generations, living and dead, taking communion together in the Waxahachie that will never die.

Places in the Heart is a beautiful film from which certain sentiments regarding family, faith, and community follow. So it came as no surprise to hear its fan Ross Perot, in one of his debates with Clinton and Bush, defend the virtues of small-scale schooling—despite his Navy background and the technocratic mania for hyper-efficiency one might expect of a business titan. The Clintons, on the other hand, wreaked consolidation all over Arkansas. (The president might enjoy Robert Benton's first movie, *Bad Company*, a picaresque tale of a scamp and a Methodist ducking conscription into the Army of the Potomac.)

immigration, military intervention, and protectionism is American blacks. Buchanan seems to understand this. "I don't doubt that one black worker in South Carolina making eight dollars an hour in a textile mill and supporting his family is probably not as efficient as, say, sixteen Chinese making fifty cents an hour," he told *Liberty* magazine during the 1992 primaries. "But the question is, why shouldn't we protect the job of that one black worker who is a fellow American, rather than opt for super-efficiency and buy the prison-made products of Deng Xio Peng?"[35]

The toughest nuts for our rulers to crack will be the ordinary Americans who are responding to the renegades. They are veterans, housewives, owners of small businesses, computer hackers, kids who like rock and roll, men on assembly lines—Robert Frost's insubordinate Americans.

Ordinary people have been unrepresented for half a century; North Dakota Representative Usher Burdick mourned in 1951, "We are without a party that will stand for this country. Both old parties want war and profits and the plain people like you and me have no means of bringing our vote to account. We will have to support one or the other of the great party candidates and when both are against us you can see how powerless we are."[36]

In 1992 they had an alternative, however imperfect, and despite a relentlessly hostile press Ross Perot got their votes. He won 23 percent of the vote in Burdick's North Dakota. He topped 25 percent in seven states, including Borah's Idaho and Wheeler's Montana.

Ross Perot must know that the Republican party—which Jack Kemp accurately describes as America's "new internationalist party"—will dissolve before it permits him to win the nomination fair and square. The same goes for Jerry Brown on the Democratic side—and as for Pat Buchanan, those devil's horns are there to stay.

With all that righteous anger, with rural and working and white-collar Americans dispossessed, with the pregnant realization that the game is rigged and it's time to clear the board, and with the appearance of tough and outspoken, even if sometimes eccentric, tribunes—the populist moment has arrived. After Maurice Bishop, Daniel Ortega, Manuel Noriega, Saddam Hussein, and Mohammed Farah Aidid, the good folk of Cedar Rapids and Youngstown and Syracuse are sick of sacrificing their sons and daughters and their money to the imperialist vanities of our rulers.

Superior men—Wheeler and Borah and Gore and Johnson and Butler—failed to brake the empire when it was just gathering steam, and the result is the runaway train we're riding, hurtling down the track, crimson-soaked, throwing off sparks and independents. The passengers have emerged from their separate compartments—after a very long sleep—and, milling around, have begun to realize just how much they have in common. Three pretty good engineers have already volunteered their services, and there will be more. Whether we crash before we retake the cab and hit the brakes is an open question.

NOTES

1. Wayne S. Cole, *Roosevelt and the Isolationists 1932–1945* (Lincoln: University of Nebraska Press, 1983), pp. 37–38.

2. Wayne S. Cole, *Senator Gerald P. Nye and American Foreign Relations* (Minneapolis: University of Minnesota Press, 1962), p. 174.

3. Murray Rothbard, "Life in the Old Right," *Chronicles,* August 1994, pp. 15–19.

4. Quoted in John T. Flynn, *Country Squire in the White House* (New York: Doubleday, Doran, 1940), p. 60.

5. Louis Bromfield, *A New Pattern for a Tired World* (New York: Harper, 1954), p. 306.

6. Quoted in Wayne S. Cole, *Charles A. Lindbergh and the Battle against American Intervention in World War II* (New York: Harcourt Brace Jovanovich, 1974), p. 165.

206 Part Three: America First Renewed

7. Quoted in Joan Hoff Wilson, *Herbert Hoover: Forgotten Progressive* (Boston: Little, Brown, 1975), pp. 70–71.

8. Quoted in Elizabeth Wheeler Colman, *Mrs. Wheeler Goes to Washington* (Hartland, Wis.: Elizabeth Wheeler Colman, 1989), p. 100.

9. Ibid., p. 163.

10. Ibid., p. 14.

11. Ibid., p. 147.

12. Ibid., p. 200.

13. Ibid., p. 205.

14. Quoted in John Chalmers Vinson, *William E. Borah and the Outlawry of War* (Athens: University of Georgia Press, 1957), p. 21.

15. Quoted in Peter J. Boyle, "The Roots of Isolationism: A Case Study," *Journal of American Studies,* April 6, 1972, p. 50.

16. H. L. Mencken, *A Carnival of Buncombe* (Chicago: University of Chicago Press, 1984/1956), p. 13.

17. Quoted in Harold L. Ickes, *The Autobiography of a Curmudgeon* (New York: Reynal & Hitchcock, 1943), p. 235.

18. G. K. Chesterton, *The Napoleon of Notting Hill* (Mineola, N.Y.: Dover, 1991/1904), p. 69.

19. Quoted in Hans Schmidt, *Maverick Marine* (Lexington: University of Kentucky, 1987), p. 231.

20. Ibid., p. 232.

21. Warren Hinckle, "Ross Perot, Hero of the Counterculture," *New York Times,* July 10, 1992, editorial page.

22. Schmidt, *Maverick Marine,* p. 243.

23. Ibid., p. 250.

24. Ibid., p. 244.

25. Gore Vidal, *Screening History* (Cambridge, Mass.: Harvard University Press, 1992), pp. 33–34.

26. Edmund G. Brown, "Free Trade's Huge Costs," *New York Times,* May 2, 1993, editorial page.

27. Carl Oglesby, "Vietnamese Crucible," in Carl Oglesby and Richard Schaull, *Containment and Change* (New York: Macmillan, 1967), p. 167.

28. *New York Times,* February 10, 1992, p. A3.

29. Patrick J. Buchanan, "NAFTA Surrenders U.S. Sovereignty," Rochester, N.Y., *Democrat & Chronicle,* August 22, 1993, editorial page.

30. Ibid.

31. Cole, *Senator Gerald P. Nye and American Foreign Relations,* p. 135.

32. Buchanan, "NAFTA Surrenders U.S. Sovereignty."

33. Patrick J. Buchanan, *Right from the Beginning* (Boston: Little, Brown, 1988), p. 14.

34. Peter Applebome, "Duke's Followers Lean to Buchanan," *New York Times,* March 8, 1992.

35. "Patrick A. Buchanan Interview," *Liberty,* March 1992, p. 18.

36. Quoted in Robert Griffith, "Old Progressives and the Cold War," *Journal of American History,* September 1979, p. 347.

12

The Devil Thumbs a Ride: Buchanan, Perot, and the Middle American Revolt

"We have America to win; we have nothing to lose but our chains!"

    —Murray N. Rothbard, "A New Strategy for Liberty" (1994)

If Edgar Lee Masters could be proved wrong, and the world did make sense, and the good guys won once in a while, President Gore Vidal and his vice president, John McClaughry, would be presenting the Amos R. E. Pinchot medal of patriotic insubordination to Clarke Abbey, Edward's widow, in America's answer to the Athenian agora, the Sauk Centre, Minnesota, lyceum.

Dream on.

One encouraging sign of the 1990s is that for the first time in forty years, mainstream—well, significant tributary—politicians are mouthing Americanist slogans. Middle Americans have responded: witness our rulers scrambling to man the parapets, training their guns on the milling Dakota Goths outside the gates.

Virginia Governor Douglas Wilder was the first major politician of the decade to brandish "America First" as a campaign shibboleth. "We cannot focus all our energies on the international arena at the expense of America's finances and economic health," Wilder stated. "If jobs are going to be found, why not for Americans? If schools are going to be built, why not schools for Americans?"[1]

Once upon a time in America this was an innocuous truism; today, it is a revolutionary murmur that sets off the alarm at the thought police station. The governor was lectured, with a kind of stern bemusement, as if he were a little boy who had been caught swearing. The unspoken assumption was that Wilder, a proud black son of Virginia, was an intellectual discredit to his race, who probably didn't understand the connotations of those two incendiary words "America First." *Nazi! Pacifist naif! Fever swamp dweller!* But just in case the governor knew whereof he spoke, he was scolded by a *New York Times* editorial and warned not to utter these inflammatory words again. Wilder quietly dropped the slogan. Themeless, his campaign collapsed into the muck of intrastate politics after he and LBJ's son-in-law, Virginia Senator Charles Robb, had a nasty row over illegal taping, sex scandals, et al. that spilled onto the gossip pages.

PAT BUCHANAN

Pugnacious columnist Patrick J. Buchanan, for a variety of reasons, was the wrong man for the job in 1992, but we play the hand we're dealt and the America Firsters, by and large, rallied to his banner.

Buchanan is by all accounts a kind and decent man. He has a ready Irish wit and is the best stylist in the pontificating business. He handled the ritual crucifixion of Americanists with the humor and fortitude displayed so charmingly in his autobiography, *Right from the Beginning*. He showed real guts in taking on George Bush, the sanguinary invader of Panama and attacker of Iraq. Still, Buchanan was an unsatisfactory candidate.

First, he had a "Jewish problem." The immediate cause of Buchanan's woes was a remark made in August 1990 on the television show "The McLaughlin Group" (of which he was a regular member) that "there are only two groups that are beating the drums for war [against Iraq]—the Israeli Defense Ministry and its amen corner in the United States."[2]

This was a vast overstatement, of course, but then hyberbole is a tool of the trade. Senators Richard Lugar and Alfonse D'Amato and the globalist WASPs buzzing around in the Bush White House were just as avid for war as belligerent Zionists, and far more powerful to boot. The tetchy columnist A. M. Rosenthal unloaded on Buchanan in the *New York Times,* and to his credit Pat, his Irish up, refused to make the craven apology that is de rigeur for those accused of insensitivity. "Well, there goes the B'Nai B'rith Man of the Year award," Buchanan joked in a blistering reply, and the mutual enmity was cast in stone. There were the usual petty acts of censorship and intimidation— the Anti-Defamation League bombarded newspapers with requests to pull Buchanan from their pages and replace him with ardently pro-Israel right-wingers like syndicated columnists George Will and Charles Krauthammer, who called Buchanan "a woolly mammoth, frozen in Siberian ice as a perfectly preserved specimen of 1930s isolationism and nativism"[3]—but Buchanan survived, bloodied but unbowed, to fight on.

Compounding his sins, Buchanan made the quite correct observation that the body bags coming back from the Kuwaiti desert would be filled with "kids with names like McAllister, Murphy, Gonzales, and Leroy Brown."[4] The inference was that there wouldn't be many Rosenthals or Foxmans on the slab in that Delaware warehouse: the Jewish intellectuals shrieking for war were playing with the lives of working-class and rural Catholic and Protestant whites, blacks, and Hispanics.

With respect to the ethnic composition of the U.S. Army and the U.S. intelligentsia, this was indisputably true, but as Galileo could tell you, truth is seldom a convincing defense in heresy trials. Several of Buchanan's Jewish friends—Murray Rothbard, Michael Kinsley of *The New Republic,* historian Paul Gottfried, and Allan Ryskind of the conservative weekly *Human Events*—offered personal testimony to his unbigoted, if un-varnished, character. Rothbard ascribed the anti-Semite smear to the Establishment fear of renascent antiwar sentiment on the Right; so did Gore Vidal, who otherwise has little respect for Buchanan.

The high-water mark of the Buchanan campaign was his announcement speech in November 1991, discussed in the previous chapter, in which the candidate articulated a Wheeler-Nye Middle Americanism of a high order. It sounded so unlike the old Buchanan, who had been in favor of any and all U.S. interventions—in Vietnam, Nicaragua, Angola, and a host of impoverished Third World nations most Americans have never heard of. Amazingly, the import of the November 1991 speech was ignored by the entire working press: it was as if the pope had denied the virgin birth and yet the headlines read "Pontiff Reaffirms Faith." The king of the hard-right polemicists—a man who had lionized Ollie North; who had, since childhood, sup-ported even those interventions we never made (the Suez, Dien Bien Phu, Hungary)—had declared himself a Little American opposed to war, and the dolts in the newsroom never blinked an eye. Buchanan, almost alone among national figures, had actually rethought everything in the wake of the Soviet disinte-gration—and he had the intellectual courage to discard the interventionist assumptions that had shaped his politics for three decades.

Buchanan's speech bore the unmistakable imprint of *Chron-icles* editor Thomas Fleming—not as ghost but as guiding in-spiration. Buchanan's astonishing transmutation from screech-ing warhawk to neo-isolationist nationalist dove seems to have been greatly aided by his reading of *Chronicles.* This magazine, published by the Rockford Institute in Illinois's second-largest city ("midway between Chicago and Galena," its boosters boast), has a circulation of less than twenty thousand; but it has, since Fleming's accession to the editorship in 1986, become the best-written, most provocative, and certainly most latitudinarian magazine in America.

Fleming is an unreconstructed Confederate intellectual, a Ph.D. in classics who spent the 1960s listening to the Velvet Underground and reading with the kind of intense catholicity characteristic of independent souls. He remains sympathetic to the New Left, or at least that prairie power wing of it that sought to break down overgrown institutions and restore the intimate, small-scale life of prewar America. He is a brilliant essayist, an acid wit, a raconteur—in short, the finest American editor since Mencken. And more than anyone else, Fleming is responsible for the reflowering of America First simply because he has given Americanist writers a forum. (Need I add that Fleming has been accused of xenophobia, anti-Semitism, and racism?)

Buchanan acknowledges his debt to Fleming, and though Fleming is too much the maverick to fall in behind a politician (he's also a far more radical decentralist than Buchanan), he tendered advice when asked.

The other outlaw who made Buchanan's conversion possible was the Happy Warrior of the libertarian movement, Murray N. Rothbard (his parents named him Murray because they thought it sounded Scottish), a delightfully idiosyncratic econo-mist and vivid polemicist* who had been (1) a right-wing Re-publican Jew who earned a Ph.D. at Columbia in the 1950s; (2) a supporter of both the 1948 Thurmond-Wright States' Rights ticket and the 1968 Peace and Freedom party; (3) a movie critic, heir to laissez-faire economist Ludwig von Mises, and exposer of the Ayn Rand cult; and (4) an encomiast, at various times, of Robert A. Taft, the Black Panthers, tax renegade Gordon Kahl, New York City mayoral candidate Norman Mailer, Senator

---

*As this book was being readied for publication, Murray N. Rothbard died of cardiac arrest at the age of sixty-eight. The world has lost some of its color.

Mark Hatfield, the Students for a Democratic Society, and Pat Buchanan.

Though short in stature (and thus a longtime semi-serious proponent of "Short People's Lib"), Rothbard cast a long shadow. Almost alone, he kept the flame of America First isolationism burning during the dark night that set in with Senator Taft's death and the *National Review*'s birth in the early 1950s. Though primarily an economist, Rothbard wrote with great panache about the isolationist tradition and succeeded in infusing (through such fans as SDS president Carl Oglesby) the New Left with the insights of the Old Right. In the 1960s especially, he and his friends, libertarian scholars Joseph Peden and Leonard Liggio, sought a new linkage between the good people of Left and Right, and if they failed at least they failed nobly.

As Rothbard wrote a quarter-century ago in *Ramparts*:

Twenty years ago I was an extreme right-wing Republican, a young and lone "Neanderthal" (as the liberals used to call us) who believed, as one friend pungently put it, that "Senator Taft had sold out to the socialists." Today, I am most likely to be called an extreme leftist, since I favor immediate withdrawal from Vietnam, denounce U.S. imperialism, advocate Black Power and have just joined the new Peace and Freedom party. And yet my basic political views have not changed by a single iota in these two decades![5]

This is an irresistible hook, and hundreds of curious young people took it, giving anarchism an exposure it had not had in this country since being discredited by Leon Czolgosz, who assassinated William McKinley. It also foreshadowed the confusion engendered by Buchanan's antiwar activities. The Quaker who wore a "McGovern/Buchanan: The Peace Ticket for '92" button would have loved the Jewish Taftite Murray Rothbard-Black Panther Eldridge Cleaver axis.

Rothbard was an inveterate strategist, and from his perch

as co-president of the Old Right John Randolph Club he advised the Buchananites to engage in "right-wing populism: exciting, dynamic, confrontational, rousing, and inspiring."[6] The Buchanan race, Rothbard believed, "created a new radical, or Hard Right, very much like the original Right before *National Review*."[7]

Rothbard's *bête noire* was William F. Buckley, Jr., and the *National Review*, which he blamed for perverting the American Right. (The preponderance of ex-CIA operatives within *National Review* has given rise to speculation by Rothbard, Garry Wills, and others that the transformation of the Right was not the result of [to use a favored libertarian term] spontaneous evolution.)

National Review, according to Rothbard, was at its inception "pro-war, pro-militarist, and theocratic, gathering about itself a scintillating group of older pro-war, ex-Communist and ex-leftist intellectuals of the 1930s dedicated to destroying the 'God that had failed' them—the Soviet Union and the Communist movement. To this group of ex-Communists were gathered a group of younger, theocratic anti-Communist Catholics,"[8] fond of Franco and Joe McCarthy, and convinced that it was the providentially decreed duty of the United States to patrol the world.

To his great credit, Buchanan did break free of Catholic Right fetters. With the ascent of Mikhail Gorbachev he began to wonder if a mutual Soviet-American pullout from militarized Europe was indeed possible. By 1990 Buchanan was demanding a complete withdrawal of U.S. troops from Europe: "by bringing the boys home," he wrote, the savings would permit us "to invigorate U.S. industry, to recapture markets our allies took away from us as we defended them."[9]

Even at the height of the Cold War, a significant minority of Americans wanted the boys (and their tax dollars) to stay home. Yet this chorus of voices added up to not even a whisper in the corridors of power. The tremendous "disjunction between elites and the public" which Murray Rothbard identified is nowhere more evident than in the conduct of foreign affairs.

"America First" seeks to bridge the enormous gap between public opinion and public policy—which is why it invites a vituperative hailstorm from the guardians of "respectable opinion."

Buchanan made a game attempt to connect with Middle America, but his campaign rapidly took on the negative tone that one would expect of a McCarthyite. The Bush-bashing was fun, and profitable, too; but rather than sketch the contours of the restored republic he extolled in his announcement speech, the candidate sank to gay-baiting and portentous warnings about "liberalism," a pretty exhausted bogeyman after a dozen years of Republican rule.

Nevertheless, Buchanan livened up a dull campaign. Exit polls in the kickoff New Hampshire primary showed a shockingly close race, and in the early evening hours an upset did not appear impossible. Most Americans went to bed believing that Bush and Buchanan were neck and neck, and though Buchanan ended up with only 37 percent of the vote (Bush got 53 percent), it was a splendid shot across the Rockefeller Republican bow.

The campaign fell apart after New Hampshire, however. Buchanan miscalculated badly, shifting his emphasis from the very popular themes of low taxes and America First to attacks on nipple rings and coprophilia. He ran ads ad nausem on Georgia television featuring grainy snippets from a film about gay black men that was funded, in part, by the National Endowment for the Arts. (The grant, ironically, had been given during the puritanical Reagan presidency.) The tawdriness of the Buchanan campaign suggested that its candidate—a lifelong Washingtonian—knew a lot less about America than he claimed to. Also hobbling the effort was his sister Bay, who, in an admirable act of family loyalty, had been put in charge by her brother of his operation. On television Bay comes off as only slightly less frantic than Laverne and Shirley. (She reportedly fumbled the ball when Hollywood heartthrob Mel Gibson, a Catholic traditionalist, offered to raise money for Pat.)

The reaction to Buchanan spoke volumes about the fears

of the ruling class. The solemn bores at the *New York Times* deemed him "primitive and vague," "dangerously naive and ill-timed," and, of course, packed to the gills with "resentment."[10] The same shorthand appeared in all the corporate media pieces about Buchanan: he was reviving hatreds with his simplistic and ominous America First program, which was tapping hidden wells of "resentment." He was angry: as a boy he'd been in several fistfights, and seemed still to take a pubescent pride in beating up his rivals.

Not since George Wallace's working-class insurgency in 1968 has a major candidate received such uniformly bad press. And like Wallace—who was far more of a dove than Nixon or Humphrey on Vietnam, a fact dutifully unreported, lest it blunt the demonization—Buchanan was boxed into a snug little corner marked "Far Right" and nothing he said could get him out of it.

The Cerberus-like guardians of responsible opinion— William Bennett; William F. Buckley, Jr.; even Ellen Goodman— barked up a storm. Bennett—who, by virtue of his tactics as the nation's drug czar and his efforts to nationalize education policy, even to the point of forcing a Washington-written curriculum on schools from Fresno to Fort Lauderdale, has become a virtual fascist—charged that Buchanan "sounds like George McGovern in foreign policy, sounds like Richard Gephardt in trade policy, and sounds like Jackson in policy toward Israel— not Scoop Jackson, but Jesse Jackson."[11]

Bennett had stumbled onto something. Buchananism, seen through the spectacles of orthodox Left and Right, *is* something of a smorgasbord. So is America Firstism. The protectionism that Congressman Gephardt preached in his unsuccessful 1988 race for the White House, the explicitly isolationist "Come Home, America" theme of McGovern's 1972 campaign, and Jesse Jackson's unwillingness to give Israel the key to the American exchequer—these amount to a logical, coherent worldview that strikes a responsive chord in Middle American hearts even as it sparks fear in our rulers.

Samuel Francis, *Chronicles* columnist, theorist of the new nationalism, and a close Buchanan advisor, argues that

> for the first time since the Depression perhaps, there loomed the prospect of a unified people transcending the artificial and obsolete framework of right and left and militantly intent on dislodging the reigning elites to take power back to their own bosoms for their own purposes. Today this is known as "fascism"; it used to be called "democracy," which is the real reason the left-right establishment is so frightened by it.[12]

No construct is more holy to the priests of the establishment than the comfy seesaw of Left and Right, with its utterly predictable motions. Those who sit astride the planks can be sure of a pleasant ride; they need never fear being thrown. Bullies who threaten the playground, such as Huey Long, Malcolm X, and George Wallace, are disposed of with impressive dispatch.

For a time, before he reverted to his Right-Wing atavistic gay-baiting and Congress-bashing, Pat Buchanan started to resemble one of the more unsavory outsiders, Father Charles Coughlin (1891–1979), the radio priest who founded the 1930s' National Union for Social Justice. Although remembered today, if at all, as a rabid ultrarightist, Father Coughlin actually espoused an economic program that was cooperativist, antimonopolistic, and pro-labor. He detested banks and financiers, and the uneven distribution of wealth in a land of both DuPonts and Roosevelts and John Does who couldn't pay the rent. Under White House pressure the Church ordered Father Coughlin to mute his pro-labor rhetoric and concentrate instead on ministering to the Shrine of the Little Flower parish in Royal Oak, Michigan. While it is true that by the late 1930s Father Coughlin was a raving anti-Semite he also had a feeling for working-class America, and he never forgot that war is a racket. He lived to a Methuselan age; during the Vietnam War Father Coughlin said, "I have sympathy for the young people of this nation. . . . Why should our young men go over there? If I were forty years younger I would be out there leading today's youth." Father Coughlin even dipped a toe into the inhospitable waters of presidential politics, launching the ill-fated Union party, which sought an Old Right-Western Progressive alliance. However, the party's thoroughly honorable candidate, North Dakota Congressman William Lemke, polled only 892,000 votes in the 1936 election and the union dissolved. Two years later Philip La Follette tried to do the same thing with his National Progressive party, but this met with even less success.

Buchanan sounded positively Coughlinite when he denounced "vulture capitalists" and insisted that "conservatism is about more than the constitutional right of big fishes to eat little fishes."[14] He fell afoul of Rothbardian libertarians when he said in New England, "Some of my friends in the conservative movement are thoroughly cerebral. They don't address the issues of the heart. They say free trade, that's it. These are our people who are losing their homes, losing their jobs, losing their way of life. Unbridled capitalism—if you will, free trade theory— can be a very, very brutal force. It's a nice thing to sit in a think tank and say it's all for the best. But in the short term let them come to New Hampshire."[15]

This was the voice of a Pat Buchanan who just might have fulfilled William Safire's prophecy that he would someday lead an alliance of "the nativist right and isolationist left," who might have forced the first real debate over the wisdom of empire since the days of Norman Thomas, Burton K. Wheeler, and Gerald P. Nye.

Buchanan failed, and what is most remarkable is how little short-term success he had in putting the republic back in Republican. In the heady wake of New Hampshire, the novelist Chilton Williamson, Jr., hailed the emergence of "a new conservative agenda devised by Little Americans whom the imperialist conservatives will ignore at their peril"[16]; but when the dust had cleared the party was as monolithic as ever in support of a New

World Order overseen by vaguely American mandarins. George Bush's parting shot at an ungrateful nation, the pouring of troops and tax dollars down a bottomless hole named Somalia, encountered no significant opposition from the party of Borah and Taft.

"When the legend becomes fact, print the legend," said the editor in John Ford's *The Man Who Shot Liberty Valance.* The legend in this case is that an Irish bully named Buchanan tried to tap into the racism that is never far from the American surface and he was finally shot down, but not before delivering a noxious nationwide address that was a virtual incitement to a "white riot" against the government.

The notorious 1992 Republican Convention speech in Houston, when read by the clear light of day, is pretty tame partisan mush. Buchanan salutes the "liberation" of Grenada and the bullying of Nicaragua (both of which true Little Americans abhorred), and tips his hat to George Bush, leader of the greatest party in the history of the world. He needles Hillary Clinton and the gay rights movement and concludes with a call to "take back our cities, and take back our culture, and take back our country." Jerry Brown and Ross Perot had said the same thing, and the earth kept spinning. Telejournalist David Brinkley praised the speech immediately upon its conclusion; not until the arbiters of acceptable opinion weighed in was Buchanan's harmless tubthumper transmogrified into a clarion call for holy war.

This is not to say that Buchanan wants to live and let live. His writings before 1989 betrayed a libertarian streak about as narrow as J. Edgar Hoover's. He did, in fact, suggest that AIDS was nature's retribution against homosexuals, and he is not punctilious about protecting the rights of pornographers to vend their wares.

Nor does he subscribe to the "open borders" doctrine that much of the Right, influenced by Julian Simon and Ben Wattenberg, embraced at the dawn of the Reagan era. The candidate was widely mocked for proposing that a "Buchanan Ditch" be dug along the U.S.-Mexican border to keep Mexicans on their side of the Rio Grande. Most Americans want to make the border less porous, but the Buchananites, unlike inland Americans, view immigration as a critical, perhaps the paramount, issue. The impulse is the same that drives the anti-immigration parties of Western Europe: whatever is distinct about American culture will be obliterated by the hordes of unassimilables.*

Race, contrary to conservative plaints, is *not* the great unmentionable in American politics. If anything, we obsess too much about it. "Racist" has lost its sting as an epithet because of its indiscriminate use, but it is especially inaccurate when applied to the Buchananites, who are guilty of nothing more than loyalty to their own.

"Why are we more shocked when a dozen people are killed in Vilnius than [by] a massacre in Burundi?"[17] Buchanan asked the London *Sunday Telegraph.* "Because they are white people. That's who we are. That's where we come from." The candidate was reviled for this remark, though no one really refuted it; nor did they credit the corollary: that a Kenyan properly cares more about the affairs—including massacres—of Liberia and Rwanda than of Canada. Of course these sentiments are not tied exclusively, or even usually, to race or blood. I grieved far more for the black man down the street who died of a heart attack than for any of a thousand white people who died that same day. The decedent was my neighbor, and as such occupied a larger place in my heart than a stranger. If this disturbs you, you are a strange bird indeed.

Pat Buchanan fell short, and though he continues the long march, now under the banner of his front group, The American

---

*Those who wish to understand how deeply felt this fear is should read French novelist Jean Raspail's futuristic *Camp of the Saints* (1975), in which France disappears under the onrush of millions of low-caste Indian refugees. To call Raspail and the Buchananites "racist," as the stenographers of the corporate media do, is cheap and shoddy. This is a legitimate worry, one shared even by many advocates of open borders.

Cause, he will never get the Republican presidential nomination. He has been so completely demonized by the corporate media that the best he can hope for is to play the quadrennial dog in the manger, pulling 15–20 percent of the Republican primary vote and giving the *New York Times* something to stew about.

Rather than bolt to Perot, as a gutsy populist would have done, Buchanan played the "good loser," making pro-Bush speeches in small towns. He spent 1993 in a conciliatory mood, even saying in his column that "in foreign policy . . . a consensus is emerging [on the Right]." (He bases this incredible claim on the neoconservative strategist Irving Kristol's call to pull U.S. troops out of Europe. Kristol was an anti-NATO unilateralist well before America First poked its head back out of the ground, and to claim that he speaks for most movement conservatives is preposterous.)

Buchanan ought to have sought the advice of Gore Vidal on matters American, but that would have put a dent in the old "The Fags Are Coming! The Fags Are Coming!" fund-raisings. The flat tax did lead some of the more adventurous supply-side Republicans, notably gadfly economic journalist Jude Wanniski, into the Brown camp, but for the most part the Brown campaign was composed of engaged left-wing environmentalists and union dissidents. It had spirit and spunk, however, and as the weeks flew by Brown found the populist cadence the most congenial. His attacks on our one-party system were cogent, even brave—they made Buchanan, ever the loyal Republican, seem timorous by comparison—and when Brown won the Connecticut primary in March he appeared to be on the verge of a stunning resurrection. Alas, New York was next, and the old Brown, the calculating son of Pat, resurfaced. He hinted that Jesse Jackson would make a fine running mate, and then and there he lost the Jewish vote because of the remark Jackson had made in 1984 about "Hymietown." Brown faded to black, partly because of the Jackson gambit but also as a result of a story on ABC's "Nightline" alleging visitors had smoked marijuana in Brown's house while he was governor. The proper response to which is: So what?

In any event, Brown promises to stick around, a Harold Stassen with something to say, and he may very well challenge Clinton in the 1996 primaries. However, the "Citizen Moonbeam" image so sedulously painted for Brown by the corporate media will be as impossible to shed as that of the angry, resentful, sweaty-browed, Catholic authoritarian will be for Pat Buchanan, and like many fine men who fight the law, they will learn that the law usually wins.

ROSS PEROT

If the Americanist cause is to capture the presidential flag before the millennium it will be with Ross Perot astride the white horse. (How hostile journalists hated to let go of that prefatory H.; it is as if they had in mind Edward Abbey's belief that you can always spot an asshole by the initial before his name.)

Perot received terrible press during his on-again, off-again 1992 presidential campaign. At first he was considered a charming oddity, like a one-legged football player or blind beauty queen, and as long as he spoke in vague generalities on talk shows and showed off his Norman Rockwell collection to visiting TV celebrities he was perfectly harmless. But Perot turned out to be a Texarkana patriot who knew where the bodies were buried. He knew a great deal about the national security state and its sordid doings—the Nixon-Kissinger abandonment of American POWs in Laos, the Reagan-Bush skullduggery in the Middle East—and didn't hesitate to talk about them.

For this breach of empire etiquette Perot was slammed mercilessly by journalists and distinguished senior fellows with an eye for the main chance. Typically, *The New Republic*—house organ of callow Clintonism—called Perot "deeply disturbed," "paranoid," and given to "relentless bizarreness."[18]

The journalistic herd mooed on about how Perot was not addressing "the issues," when in fact he was an informed and courageous opponent of the Gulf War, an advocate of education reform of the sort enacted under his leadership in Texas—notably a toughening of eligibility requirements for high-school athletes—and he broached the subject of entitlement cuts, a hitherto off-limits topic. No, he didn't have a stable of rent-a-scholars cranking out legislative sausage, promising to push for full funding of Head Start; but he had what the hapless Bush derided as "the vision thing," which was of "America as a nation with discrete national, political, and economic interests" and a middle class that was "the political, economic, and cultural core of the nation."[19]

The description is Samuel Francis's; he used it to define the Buchanan agenda, but I think Perot did it better. Perot—the bantam billionaire, the sentimental populist, the patriot and champion of veterans who stood squarely in opposition to the (at the time) tremendously popular Gulf War—is an American original. He comes not from some ideological lagoon but from Texarkana and Dallas in the heart of Texas. Perot is an iconic figure, the Western individualist who does things his own way and gives cohesion to the community he comes to treasure. People like him, they understand right off the bat that he is an American. Perot's phenomenal popularity declined in 1992 only after he ceded control of his persona to the monopolistic networks and their insecure newsreaders. He's a nut! A conspiracy fanatic! A control freak! Or so the information-molders told us day in and day out, and after a while even the less credulous started to believe. (Of course, his impetuous withdrawal from the race in July didn't help.)

Perot's passion is direct democracy; no Perotism quite so frightened our rulers as his proposed "electronic town hall" by which citizens would give their representatives an earful of *vox populi*. Campaign manager Ed Rollins and the other mercenaries who hopped on and off the Perot gravy train reportedly were aghast that their wagonmaster actually *believed* in that direct democracy stuff.

The details of the electronic town hall were always sketchy, and Perot's efforts since the 1992 election to refine the idea have been halting. The referenda he envisions seem to be advisory, although votes on taxation may be binding. Even foreign policy is to be reviewed by the people. This really invites derisive snorts: imagine, a working stiff in Iowa having a say in the momentous questions of war or peace.

A national referendum on war was in fact a staple of Middle American populism in the final days of the old republic. In the early twentieth century, the Anti-Imperialist League demanded a nationwide vote on the annexation of the Philippines. As anti-Hun propaganda heated up between 1914 and 1917, William Jennings Bryan and Senators Robert La Follette and Thomas Gore advanced variations on the referendum model.

The Great Commoner declaimed: "I so believe in the right of the people to have what they want that I admit the right of the people to go to war if they really want it. There should be a referendum vote about it, however, and those who voted for war should enlist first, together with the jingo newspaper editors."[20]

The people never did get the vote, but they sure got the war(s).

The war referendum's most famous incarnation was in the 1930s as the Ludlow Amendment, namesake of Louis Ludlow, an Indianapolis Democrat who, as a cub reporter, visited his city's first citizen, ex-President Benjamin Harrison. The old general, rocking on his front porch, lectured young Ludlow, "We have no commission from God to police the world." The lad never forgot.

Ludlow's amendment stated that

except in the event of an invasion of the United States or its Territorial possessions and attack upon its citizens residing

therein, the authority of Congress to declare war shall not become effective until confirmed by a majority of all votes cast
thereon in a nationwide referendum. Congress, when it deems
a national crisis to exist, may by concurrent resolution refer
the question of war or peace to the citizens of the States, the
question to be voted on being, Shall the United States declare
war on ———?[21]

Like Perot, Ludlow claimed that technology (in his case,
radio) made feasible a national vote. Americans would listen
to debates between interventionists and isolationists; an informed
citizenry would then march to the polls (or drop a postcard
in the mailbox) to determine if Johnny should go marching off
to war. In an uncanny (and no doubt unconscious) echo of
Ludlow, Perot told *TV Guide* that until American homes are
equipped with interactive televisions, postcards will serve as
ballots. And, sure enough, in March 1993 Perot's United We
Stand organization placed tear-off questionnaires in sixteen million copies of *TV Guide*. (Unfortunately, the questions were on
the order of "Do you favor finding a cure for cancer?" Oh well,
there is a down side to amateurism.)

Ludlow's amendment reached the House floor only once,
in December 1937, and was defeated in a procedural vote of
209 to 188. The irony is that Ludlow enjoyed widespread popular
support (68 percent in a 1938 Gallup Poll) and he would have
won in a national referendum.

The Establishment was not amused. The *New York Times*'s
Arthur Krock (now played by the *Washington Post* pundit David
Broder) huffed, "No more fantastic proposal has ever had serious
consideration in Congress."[22] Elsewhere the *New York Times*,
in the best Larchmont-lord-dismissing-the-uppity-Irish-maid fashion, editorialized, "The consensus of well-informed opinion is
strongly against this plan."[23]

George Bush's hero Henry L. Stimson, the Republican who
would serve as FDR's secretary of war throughout World War II,

presented the establishment case against the Ludlow amendment. "When we come to the important question of whether we shall submit to a major surgical operation we do not hold a popular referendum among our friends and count noses." No, we defer to "chosen experts" to whom we have "entrusted the determining factors of our fate." They are "extremely conservative in deciding [to] fight," Stimson assured readers.[24]

Perot's radical but inchoate plan for an electronic town hall rests on a different premise. Its elevated view of the people recalls that of Senator Gore, who once said, "The voice of the people is the nearest approach to the voice of God."

Perot told Americans that they are "the owners of the country," a formula alarming to our rulers, who regard anyone west of the Hudson and the Beltway as a halfwit. "The people" are now a rude beast who must be taxed and disciplined and regimented and placated with mildly titillating TV shows. Their involvement in lawmaking would run afoul of the Constitution! scream our legion of Arthur Krocks, who remain unruffled when presidents—without a declaration of war by Congress—send American troops to Panama or Grenada or Somalia.

"Congress cannot be counted on to check the Administration in any war crisis": the National Council for the Prevention of War understood this five decades ago. And things have gotten worse.

But I digress. The point is, Ross Perot's radical proposal for an electronic town hall, which he seems to have more or less thought up on his own, has an America First lineage. It's also one of those ideological agenda-benders that cut across Left and Right and unite good people on all sides. (Talk about strange bedfellows. The Ludlow Amendment has slept soundly for over fifty years, awakened only on April Fools Day of 1971, when it was reintroduced, verbatim, as the People Power over War Amendment by the unlikely duo of segregationist John Rarick of Louisiana and black leftist Parren Mitchell of Maryland.)

Murray Rothbard was a great enthusiast for Perot's town

hall. Indeed, the Happy Warrior of the Old Right endorsed Perot before the latter withdrew from the 1992 presidential race in July. (Thereafter Rothbard regarded Perot as "a nut."[25]) The Old Right never got behind Perot as it had Buchanan, although Tom Fleming told me that almost every editor and contributor to *Chronicles* owned up to voting for the real Texan in November.

The Perot campaign was the most stentorian roar yet from MARs, the "Middle-American Radicals" whom political sociologist Donald Warren identified in the 1970s as those middle-class whites who flocked to the George Wallace campaigns. A Middle-American Radical, according to Warren, is anyone "who views his own well-being as threatened by a combination of economic elites on the one hand and governmental favoritism directed toward ethnic minorities on the other."[26] To MARs, the Republicans represent the former interest and the Democrats the latter. Warren thinks that Perot, in his helter-skelter way, has become the most powerful MARs voice of our age.

Ross Perot spoke to Middle Americans, radicals and otherwise, in a way that Pat Buchanan, Washington-bred and nurtured by the conservative movement, never could. He is folksy and blunt, and if he relies too often on fusty apothegms, well, what uncle doesn't? While Buchanan drifted off into the netherworld of cavorting black men kissing on federally funded celluloid, Perot zeroed in on matters of real concern to Americans in Boise and Cleveland: the North American Free Trade Agreement, which Perot predicted would make "a giant sucking sound" as faithless manufacturers deserted American cities for cheap Mexican labor; the influence of lobbyists, especially those who toil so profitably on behalf of foreign governments and firms; and the prodigious waste in the Department of Defense, which still subsidizes the defense of Western Europe, Korea, and Japan (which, contrary to popular understanding, has the third-largest war budget in the world) to the tune of one hundred billion dollars annually.

Perot's America is stoutly inclusionist. He has steered clear of anything remotely resembling a racialist appeal. Though he dismisses affirmative action as silly, Perot has ignored the issue's vote-getting appeal, and in 1992 he explicitly repudiated the support of "haters," including any and all associated with Louisiana's David Duke, a former Klan member who ran well-publicized races for the governorship and the U.S. senate. Unlike George Wallace, previous tribune of MARs, Perot's appeal is nationalist without being racist, and—in keeping with his Southwestern, Rockwellian dreams—generally cheerful, sanguine, and positive.

How stingingly unfair that the last straw in Perot's decision to drop out of the race in July 1992 was the misrepresentation of a speech he had given to the NAACP in Nashville, at which he addressed the assemblage, on one or two occasions, as "you people." Never mind that Perot's message was a plea for mutual aid and community concern; the corporate media flayed him for his awkward locution, and that was that: the insurgent said to hell with it.

But he returned, and the nineteen million votes cast for Perot and his dignified, if laconic, running mate, Admiral James Stockdale, betoken a potentially lethal blow to empire. For one thing, Perot was the first national candidate in memory to break on through to the other side of the paralyzing Left-Right divide. Besides the aforementioned Warren Hinckle, the eccentric but occasionally coruscant leftist-Democrat political guru Pat Caddell was excited about Perot. Hollywood stood solidly behind Clinton, although actor-director Clint Eastwood and young political satirist Dennis Miller, formerly of TV's "Saturday Night Live," were Perotistas.

About half of all young voters today call themselves "independent," and pollster Gordon Black finds that 57 percent of Americans want a new third party. (Black tried to fill the bill himself with his Independence party [IP], launched in early 1993, but few citizens wanted to jump aboard a ship captained by washed-up politicians like John Anderson, who ran unsuccessfully for president as an independent in 1980, and Hawaii's

Cecil Heftel. The IP was resolutely upper middle-class, worlds removed from the gray-collar Perotist base.)

Donald Warren argues that Perot has destroyed "the dichotomy of liberal and conservative movements as the defining reality of American politics. He has created a unifying theme for a new political alignment: one centered on the populist yearnings of Middle America."[27] This is why the corrupt conservative movement, dedicated to the wealthy and the defense contractors, hates Perot. Militantly globalist, conservatism sees America First populism as its antithesis—and for once, it's right. As for the liberals, the very phrase "populist yearnings of Middle America" calls up visions of Klan rallies.

The lineaments of a Perotist third party platform are visible: it features an array of citizen-politician measures, including term limits and restrictions on lobbying; deep spending cuts and modest entitlement reforms; the withdrawal of most, if not all, U.S. troops and subsidies from Europe and Asia; and a Main Street can-do civic responsibility ethic that is the healthiest face of Babbittry. The Perotists recognize that there is more to being American than simply acting as a docile allegiant consumerist of the New World Order: they are likely to resist globalist schemes such as multilateral trade agreements and UN-sponsored military actions; also they may want to crack down on immigration, legal and illegal.

The Perotists miss the boat, from my point of view, on the biggest "issue" of all: how to return education, government, charity, and everything else to a manageable scale. Nevertheless, this is a potent brew, with nothing in it that the Buchananites will gag on.

The new Americanists have no choice but to create a third party. Buchananites can point to Republican right turns in 1964 and 1980, but Goldwater's foreign policy was squarely behind the empire (his speechwriters were just more honest in their bellicosity); Ronald Reagan was an old Cold War Democrat who wanted to cut taxes on the rich, which, after a seemly fight, the rich allowed him to do. If either of these men had so much as uttered "America First" in a drunken aside they'd have forfeited the crown, as Robert Taft did, or been slandered, as was Burton K. Wheeler, or been shot dead, as was Huey Long.

Buchanan's brain trust knows this. Thomas Fleming of *Chronicles* speaks of a "trick shot" in which Americanists "shoot the elephant in such a way that he falls on the donkey and crushes it."[28] The mass defection of Republican voters to Perot in 1996 would be the first stage of this process.

The potshots by the corporate media will not cease, at least not until Ross Perot keels over or bows out of politics. The *New York Times* never runs a story on Perot without a demeaning adjective or two and the suggestion that those in his audience are not "the right kind of people." After all, they voted for a man whom not a single sitting member of Congress endorsed.

There is an enormous gulf between those who live in America and those who run it. If the new America First political movement is to be more than just another con job, it must close that gulf.

Who should "run" America? No one. Or 250 million single individuals. Every man a king, every woman a queen, as the martyr Huey Long once sang. Ross Perot is, to borrow his favorite word, fascinating. For my money he'd be the first good president we've had since Grover Cleveland, but only fools place their trust in white knights. Perot is a man, and as such is deeply flawed; besides, as Americans from Emerson to Mencken have known, following leaders is a fool's game; the top-notch man goes his own way, to the beat of his own drummer. Only when we restore to Americans their birthright—local self-government in prideful communities that respect the liberties of every dentist and Baptist and socialist and lesbian and hermit and auto parts dealer—will we remember what it means to be an American, first.

NOTES

1. Quoted in Thomas Fleming, "America First 1941/1991," *Chronicles,* December 1991, p. 12.

2. Quoted in Howard Kurtz, "Pugnacious Pat," Rochester, N.Y., *Times Union,* September 25, 1990, p. C12.

3. Quoted in Eric Alterman, *Sound and Fury* (New York: HarperCollins, 1992), p. 288.

4. Quoted in "Where's the Rest of Him?" *New York Times,* February 21, 1992, editorial page.

5. Murray N. Rothbard, "Confessions of a Right-Wing Liberal," *Ramparts,* June 15, 1968, p. 48.

6. Murray N. Rothbard, "A New Strategy for the Right," *Rothbard-Rockwell Report,* March 1992, p. 8.

7. Ibid., p. 15.

8. Murray N. Rothbard, "Toward a Strategy for Libertarian Social Change" (unpublished manuscript), p. 139.

9. Patrick J. Buchanan, "Disbelievers in Pax Americana," *San Jose Mercury News,* November 16, 1990.

10. "Pat Buchanan's Small World," *New York Times,* January 13, 1992, editorial page.

11. Quoted in Fred Barnes, "War Footing," *The New Republic,* March 16, 1992.

12. Samuel Francis, "The Buchanan Revolution, Part I," *Chronicles,* July 1992, p. 12.

13. Quoted in *Profiles in Populism,* edited by Willis A. Carto (Old Greenwich, Conn.: Flag Press, 1982), p. 169.

14. Quoted in "Pat Buchanan's Politics of Pain," *New York Times,* February 16, 1992, editorial page.

15. Quoted in "Buchanan Watch," *Libertarian Party News,* April 1992, p. 14.

16. Chilton Williamson, "Striking Back at the Empire," *Arizona Republic,* February 23, 1992, p. C3.

17. "Where's the Rest of Him?"

18. "Cuckoo's Nest," *The New Republic,* November 16, 1992, p. 7.

19. Francis, "The Buchanan Revolution, Part I," p. 11.

20. Quoted in Ernest C. Bolt, Jr., *Ballots before Bullets* (Charlottesville: University Press of Virginia, 1977), p. 22.

21. Arthur Krock, "In the Nation," *New York Times*, December 14, 1937, p. 26.

22. Ibid.

23. *New York Times*, January 10, 1938, p. 16.

24. Henry L. Stimson, letter to the editor, *New York Times*, December 22, 1937, p. 14.

25. Murray N. Rothbard, interview with the author, May 16, 1993.

26. Donald Warren, "Ross Perot and Middle-American Radicalism," *Chronicles*, April 1993, p. 49.

27. Ibid., p. 50.

28. Fleming, "America First 1941/1991," p. 14.

13

The Coiled Rattlesnake:
An America First Foreign Policy
for the 1990s

"Whatever we owe elsewhere, our first and highest obligation
is here in America, our first concern is our own people."
—Senator William E. Borah, 1925

The dissolution of the Soviet Union and its empire—in the blink
of an eye, red disappeared from the political spectrum—set off
in the precincts of the military-industrial complex a frantic
scramble for new enemies. Swarthy Latino drug dealers with
five o'clock shadows . . . Green pacifists in heavy sweaters . . .
crazed Muslims . . . jackbooted Russian nationalists carrying
suspicious-looking icons . . . many were presented, but few
scared anyone.

In 1952 a cheeky young polemicist named William F.
Buckley, Jr., had argued that the menace of a worldwide Communist revolution required conservatives to set aside for the
moment their scruples about the leviathan state. "We have to
accept Big Government for the duration—for neither an offensive

nor a defensive war can be waged . . . except through the instrument of a totalitarian bureaucracy within our shores."[1] The implicit promise was that once the red threat had been vanquished, America would return to being "a normal country," as Reagan's U.N. Ambassador, Jeane Kirkpatrick, has put it.

Nothing of the sort happened. Instead, our conservative and liberal mandarins devised a new series of tasks for what they ominously called the world's only remaining superpower. Henceforth, the armed forces of the United States are to plant, with trowel and bayonet, the seeds of capitalist democracy in all the countries of the world, even those whose native customs and traditions are inimical to Western democracy. We are to enforce the existing boundaries of such nations as Kuwait, no matter how unjustly they may have been drawn in the past. We are to intervene in civil wars and arbitrate disputed elections. If it suits our purpose, as in Haiti in 1993–94, when trying to restore our client president, Jean-Bertrande Aristide, we speak reverently of the sacredness of the polls; when we seek to dislodge the duly elected government of a nation, as with Nicaragua in the mid-1980s, we scoff that elections in such a benighted land are, perforce, "illegitimate." Our troops ladle out porridge to hungry Somalis and mow down Panamanians loyal to their corrupt president (and erstwhile CIA collaborator), Manuel Noriega. We are not coming home.

William Graham Sumner, the celebrant of the "forgotten man" and Jeremiah of the Spanish-American War, saw the future written on the waters of Manila Bay. "The conservative elements in this country are making a great mistake to allow all this militarism and imperialism to go on without protest,"[2] Sumner said, never dreaming that by the mid-twentieth century the "conservative elements" would look askance at anyone intrepid enough even to utter the word "imperialism," let alone condemn it.

As the idol of communism crumbled, Murray N. Rothbard wondered, "The Cold War is over, so why don't we go back to America First? It's pretty clear that most of the Cold War people are liars."[3]

Still, the glorious sight of communist tyrants slinking away as shaggy students, barrel-chested workers, and bemused intellectuals marched and sang with comradely gusto kick-started the America First renewal. Steadfast conservatives, libertarians, old republic leftists, decentralists, and a veritable mélange of patriots and dissidents began constructing an America First platform for the post-Soviet world. It was much more than an exercise in forbidden nostalgia.

The timing was propitious. Even at the peak of the Cold War, public opinion surveys had found that up to one-third of Americans favored bringing our troops home from Europe and Asia. A pessimistic view of our ability to maintain an empire abroad while prospering at home enjoyed a vogue in the latter years of the Reagan presidency, boosting to best-seller status Paul Kennedy's *The Rise and Fall of the Great Powers* (1987). In 1991–92, President Bush's evident lack of interest in American affairs triggered the America First-inflected presidential campaigns of Douglas Wilder, Tom Harkin, Jerry Brown, Pat Buchanan, and Ross Perot.

Thomas Mann of the Brookings Institution told *Time* magazine in December 1991, "Only a bipartisan consensus among elites kept the country's latent isolationism at bay." The consensus at elite levels holds, but isolationism has finally broken the surface of the water after its forty-year submergence.

No formal platform exists, nor is one likely to: this is far too versicolored and contentiously American a lot to swear collective allegiance to a single document. There are, across this broad band, differences in emphasis, focus, and sometimes policy. An America First third party led by Pat Buchanan—a distinct possibility after Buchanan fails, as he must, in the 1996 Republican primaries—will resemble in shape but differ in shading from a Middle American party organized by Ross Perot. The old republic left of Gore Vidal and, should he exhibit unwonted constancy,

Jerry Brown, largely shares the foreign policy of the Buchananites, though a vast gulf separates them on such matters as legal abortion and the limits of social tolerance.

This gulf is not an unbridgeable one: a common commitment to decentralism might lead us back to the virtues of local option. Let San Francisco be San Francisco, and Utah be Utah, and permit the people of each locality to make the rules under which they live. All we need are visionaries who break the left-right leg irons and light out for the high country. Burton K. Wheeler saw himself as a "left-wing Coolidge"; Gore Vidal accepts the twin labels of "left-wing isolationist" and "paleolithic conservative." Norman Mailer's ambidextrousness—being to the left of the liberals and to the right of the conservatives—has been previously noted. Tom Fleming digs Lou Reed and the Southern agrarians. The way is out there, and it can be found.

Witness the late godfather of revisionist history, William Appleman Williams: Naval Academy graduate and New Leftist; unpretentious scholar who appropriated an Andy Kim pop song lyric from "Rock Me Gently" as an epigraph; and lover of seaside poolhall towns who jilted Madison, Wisconsin, for the clover of Oregon State. In *America Confronts a Revolutionary World* (1976) Williams urged a return to the loose association of self-governing states provided for in the Articles of Confederation. In this Williams was echoing the retroprogressive ideological kin of Amos Pinchot, Justice Louis Brandeis, who recommended, "The United States should go back to the federation idea, letting each state evolve a policy and develop itself. There are enough good men in Alabama, for example, to make Alabama a good state."[4]

"God gave us two great oceans," Hiram Johnson was fond of saying. He waved off the prospect of a Nazi Germany attack on the United States: "We could stand on our shores, with our airplanes and carriers, and a vastly superior navy, and laugh at [Hitler's] efforts."[5]

The oceans remain our ramparts, and despite the development of intercontinental ballistic missiles no nation in the world poses a credible threat to invade or occupy these United States. America Firsters of right-wing persuasion are generally supportive of missile defense such as that proposed by President Reagan in his Strategic Defense Initiative (SDI), although the Reaganites regarded SDI not as an isolationist guarantor but as a means of achieving incontestable nuclear superiority over the Soviet Union.

The staunchest advocate of SDI within the Reagan administration was Defense Secretary Caspar Weinberger, who, despite his hawkish pronouncements, presaged the America First reappearance. Reagan himself was a thoroughgoing Cold Warrior in the Harry Truman-John F. Kennedy tradition. "There is isolationist sentiment buried deep in this country," he wrote unhappily in his diary after 241 Marines were blown up by suicide car-bombers in Beirut in October 1983. Secretary Weinberger had opposed the Lebanon mission, and while he may never have met a weapons system he didn't like, from the MX missile to SDI, Weinberger evinced a wariness of foreign involvements that had not been seen in a defense secretary since Charles Wilson of the Eisenhower administration.

In remarks to the National Press Club on November 28, 1984, Weinberger laid out the following six criteria for intervention:

1. The United States should not commit forces to combat overseas unless the particular engagement or occasion is deemed vital to our national interest or that of our allies.

2. If we decide it is necessary to commit combat troops into a given situation, we should do so wholeheartedly and with the clear intention of winning.

3. If we do decide to commit forces to combat overseas, we should have clearly defined political and military objectives.

4. The relationship between our objectives and the forces we have committed—their size, composition and disposition—must be continually reassessed and adjusted if necessary.

5. Before the United States commits combat forces abroad, there must be some reasonable assurance we will have the support of the American people and their elected representatives in Congress.

6. The commitment of U.S. forces to combat should be a last resort.[6]

Alas, like the man who signs a temperance pledge and then defines abstemiousness as drinking fewer than a dozen beers a day, Weinberger adduced but one example of an intervention that did not fulfill these criteria with ease: the "peacekeepers" (a classic Newspeak term our complaisant press has dutifully adopted) sent to Lebanon in 1982. The defense secretary also took obligatory swipes at "people . . . advocating a return to post-World War I isolationism"[7] and those demented peaceniks who doubted that a Soviet Union rendered decrepit by seven decades of communism actually threatened American security.

Still, Weinberger refrained from extolling the most extravagant goals of global messianism, e.g., imposing Western-style systems and industrial mixed economies on Asian and African societies. And he acted as the Reagan administration's solitary (and generally unpersuasive) voice against such despicable acts as the 1986 U.S. bombing of Libya.

Weinberger's speech was roundly criticized at the time by *The New Republic.* Yet how tepid the secretary's address appears in retrospect, especially when compared with the more recent programmatic manifestos of Samuel Francis and Pat Buchanan.

Francis, a Tennessean who earned a Ph.D. in British history and is now a columnist for *Chronicles* and the *Washington Times,* blueprinted an America First foreign policy as his friend Buchanan launched his 1992 campaign.

Samuel Francis's version of America First involves "a radical dismantling of the Cold War state . . . abrogating most of the mutual defense treaties of the 1950s, withdrawing most of the troops and military bases from Europe and Asia, and terminating almost all foreign aid"[8]—and Francis is the house hawk. He calls for a U.S. sphere of influence encompassing our entire hemisphere, whereas Buchanan restricts this to "Central America, the Caribbean, and the northern littoral of South America." Going beyond Weinberger and back to conservative nationalists such as Senator Taft, who emphasized the primacy of the legislative over the executive branch, Francis writes that "no U.S. troops should be committed to combat in the absence of congressional approval and unless military victory is the stated goal."[9] (In his provocative contribution to the 1982 symposium *The New Right Papers,* Francis urged an "activist and expansionist nationalism"; his subsequent evolution makes for an illuminating study in the intellectual history of the modern Right.)

Francis abjures imperialist ambitions, as do other America Firsters. Most go so far as to insist that Puerto Rico, Guam, the Virgin Islands, and other territories be granted their independence. (At the cutting edge, several call for freeing Hawaii and Alaska.) Thomas Fleming writes, "We should treat the nations of Central America with diplomatic dignity, as befits their status as sovereign states, and should not trouble ourselves with the form of government the peoples of El Salvador, Nicaragua, and Panama are willing to endure. At the same time, the United States should give them not a penny of loans or credits."[10] If, however, "they begin to intervene directly in the affairs of their neighbors," the U.S. shall unsheath the rod.

Whether Pat Buchanan is sincerely anti-imperialist is still an open question. He fairly trembled with pride over Reagan's 1983 "liberation of Grenada." As White House communications director he flayed foes of U.S. aid to the Nicaraguan contras as traitors who stood with "Daniel Ortega and the communists." This traducement, redolent of such guttersnipes as *The Nation*'s

Freda Kirchwey and Joe McCarthy, should serve as a warning to isolationists in the Buchanan camp that the army might yet stray from the true Americanist path into the millenarian, convert 'em or kill 'em Right.

America First is diametrically opposed to Reaganism, especially that policy known as the "Reagan Doctrine" under which assistance, sometimes covert, was funneled to ostensibly anticommunist factions in civil wars in Angola, Mozambique, Nicaragua, Cambodia, and other equatorial and subtropical outposts. Reagan, a marrowy Cold War liberal who had once been a member of the World Federalists, told an audience at Oxford University in 1992 that "it is not only right, but morally imperative, that the UN military intervene in Somalia." He called for "a standing UN force—an army of conscience" as part of "a humanitarian velvet glove backed by a steel fist of military force." More than one hundred Somalis—including women and children—were murdered by these steel fists over which Mr. Reagan waxes encomiastic. Somalis loyal to the popular clan leader ("fugitive warlord" in Newspeak), Mohammed Farah Aidid, burned the United Nations flag, to loud cheers from America Firsters.

The public's lingering uneasiness over foreign wars is seldom echoed in the corridors of power, unless by such odd men out as West Virginia Democratic Senator Robert Byrd, leader of the congressional opposition to U.S. participation in the United Nations occupation of Somalia. As Byrd stated, "I do not see in front of this chamber the UN flag. I never saluted the UN flag. I saluted Old Glory, the American flag."

Despite the Reaganite charge that the post-McGovern Democratic party is chockablock with quasi-pacifists, Byrd is the exception. The heaviest congressional support for U.S. bombing of Bosnian Serbs in 1993–94 came from Democrats (few of them veterans, by the way). Even Berkeley, California, Congressman Ron Dellums, who for years fought on the leftmost flank of the House of Representatives, discovered the joys of empire when he became chairman of the House Armed Services Committee in 1993. Dellums, the antimilitarist conscience of the Congress, agitated for U.S. action to restore Aristide in Haiti; indeed, most members of the erstwhile peace movement adjunct known as the Congressional Black Caucus were gung-ho for gunboat diplomacy on Hispaniola. White legislators who came of age during the days of anti-Vietnam activism—Congressman David Obey of Wisconsin and Senator John Kerry of Massachusetts—also waved the bloody flag for a Haitian invasion.

Yet a poll taken by ICR Survey Research in June 1994, at the height of the media clamor to plant Old Glory in Port-au-Prince, found just 28 percent of Americans in favor of such an intervention; meanwhile, a solid majority (62 percent) wanted their country to admit fewer Haitian refugees.

Which leads us to what Edward Abbey called the strongest liberal taboo: closing the damned door.

Pat Buchanan was excoriated in 1992 for espousing an immigration policy that mainstream California politicians such as Governor Pete Wilson and Senator Dianne Feinstein had largely adopted just one year later. Buchanan demanded "a closing of our southern frontier to invading illegals, by troops if necessary, a toughening of our asylum laws, [and] a cutback on legal immigration to spouses and minor children of those already here," a position prefiguring the passage of California's Proposition 187 in 1994.[11] His notorious "Buchanan ditch," to be dug along the U.S.-Mexico border, was derided as a wacky xenophobic fantasy, though by century's end it, too, may seem reasonable.

Sam Francis goes even further. He writes, "Immigration from countries and cultures that are incompatible with and indigestible to the Euro-American cultural core of the United States should be generally prohibited, current border controls should be rigorously enforced, illegal aliens already here should be rounded up and deported, and employers who hire them should be prosecuted and punished."[12]

This sounds draconian, but more and more Americans are

feeling the frustrations voiced by Robert Byrd in a candid moment on the Senate floor: "I pick up the telephone and call the local garage. I can't understand the person on the other side of the line. I'm not sure he can understand me. They're all over the place, and they don't speak English. Do we want more of this?"[13]

Apparently not. A periodic *New York Times*/CBS poll asks "Should immigration into the United States be kept at its present level or decreased?" Those replying "be decreased" shot from 33 percent in 1965—the year of the last major liberalization of immigration laws—to 61 percent in 1993. By a 50 to 30 percent margin, respondents said that new immigrants "cause problems" rather than "contribute to this country." A *Newsweek* poll of July 1993 found that while 59 percent of respondents believed that immigration was "a good thing for this country in the past," only 29 percent thought it was "a good thing for this country today."

Immigration as an issue has yet to spread beyond the flood plain of Southern California, Southern Florida, Texas, and, to a lesser extent, New York City. (Harlem Congressman Charles Rangel, who is, arguably, the most powerful and savvy black politician in America, cosponsored a constitutional amendment denying citizenship to the American-born offspring of illegal aliens.)*

A large proportion of immigrants between 1981 and 1990 were from Asia (37.3 percent); Mexicans, Central, and South Americans accounted for an additional 35 percent. Barely 10 percent of the new immigrants were of European origin; they

---

*This is a non-issue in my rural Genesee County, New York, home, although for the last decade the valedictorian of Batavia High School has typically been the son or daughter of a foreign doctor, native physicians being reluctant to practice in the hinterlands. These kids do well in school—their faces are prominent in the newspaper photos of Batavia's top ten seniors—but I have noticed that they depart for college and never return. Perhaps hometown loyalties are weak among all immigrants, but I wonder if these successful children of the Korean and Pakistani and Chinese diasporas aren't forming a class of prosperous, well-educated, rootless nomads who live everywhere and are at home nowhere.

were even outnumbered by newcomers from the Caribbean. An infamous *Time* magazine cover story of April 9, 1990, predicted that "by 2056, when someone born today will be sixty-six years old, the 'average' U.S. resident, as defined by Census statistics, will trace his or her descent to Africa, Asia, the Hispanic world, the Pacific Islands, Arabia—almost anywhere but white Europe." This is a best (or worst) case scenario: by the second generation immigrant birthrates tend to drop, and a reversal of U.S. immigration policy may yet forestall this multiracialist trend. But to America Firsters the stakes are nothing less than the survival of a predominantly white America.

The *Camp of the Saints* nightmare foreseen by America Firsters is a polychromatic nation speaking a babble of tongues, an America in which Islam, voodoo, and bullfighting supplant baseball, Methodism, and Thoreau. As Edward Abbey drily asked, "How many of us, truthfully, would *prefer* to be submerged in the Caribbean-Latin version of civilization?" (original italics)[14]

America Firsters of libertarian sympathies often favor fairly open borders, provided that immigrants are ineligible for government social services.* The anti-immigration cast of this movement has earned it the usual objurgatory taunts of "racist" and "xenophobe"—epithets whose purpose is to silence dissent. Nativism is a kind of Demogorgon, a monstrous spirit the very mention of whose name causes instant death to those who hear it.

Yet *Chronicles'* Tom Fleming, for one, explicitly rejects racially motivated immigration policy: he points out that descendants of African slaves have deeper American roots than the vast majority of public intellectuals, and that it is folly to welcome German immigrants while rejecting Haitians. Fleming and his magazine also expressly reject such police-state measures as "identity cards, routine searches, and the English Language Amendment."

America Firsters of all stripes, however, agree to a man

---

*This is the position I take, though I am sorely tempted by the moat.

that foreign aid to *all* nations, from Germany to Thailand, must be eliminated or drastically reduced, not only for budgetary reasons but because our sponsorship of client states and Westernized elites embroils us in the snares of ancient blood rivalries.

Even as Yassir Arafat was being canonized in American newspapers as a combination of Gandhian pacifism and Metternichian shrewdness, a CNN/*USA Today* poll found 65 percent of Americans opposed to any aid to the fledgling Palestinian state. The *New York Times* dismissed similar public hostility to internationalism (namely, opposition to U.S. involvement in UN occupation forces) as the result of "simple nativism, a cultural distrust of government and a visceral hatred of bureaucracy"[15]— which is to say, old-fashioned American sense.

Contemporary America Firsters base their ideal of a Little America which refrains from foreign involvements on the awareness expressed by Wendell Berry:

> My love must be discriminate
> or fail to bear its weight.[16]

We can neither think nor act globally, in this view. (Or as Berry would have it, our works must not extend beyond the range of our love.) It is practical as well as morally incumbent upon us to help the penniless family down the street; we can do so directly, without any bureaucratic intermediary, and the object of our benefaction is known to us. Not so with the massive government-to-government transfers that characterize our foreign aid programs.

The general bias of America Firsters toward freedom of enterprise and trade spurs a deep skepticism about the worth of embargoes. The U.S. embargo of Haiti in 1994 was widely denounced by America Firsters, as has been the three-decades-old U.S. embargo of Cuba.

America Firsters do *not* wish to disengage from the world. Travel, cultural exchanges, and the like would go on much as before; indeed, the libertarian contingent would repeal the 1952 McCarran-Walter Act, which has permitted the State Department to bar entry to "subversive" foreigners ranging from Canadian naturalist author Farley Mowatt to the late Salvadoran would-be caudillo Roberto d'Aubuisson.

The caricature of America Firsters as ostriches, collective heads stuck in the sand, indifferent to life's passing procession, is sheer nonsense. They are, in general, catholic in interests, and the demilitarized and decentralized state they envision would lead to a flowering of the humane arts.

A Mohican elder, Senator Eugene McCarthy, based his historic 1968 defiance of the bipartisan Cold War consensus on the belief that "America's contribution to world civilization must be more than a continuous performance demonstration that we can police the planet."[17] McCarthy was—and is—a decent poet, and as such he understands the debilitating effect of empire on art. Perhaps the last Midwestern progressive bearing Wheeler-Borah stripes, McCarthy has of late brooded over the effects of unlimited immigration: in his old age he has shucked off left and right and has settled into his natural political role as, simply, an American. Eugene McCarthy was his era's pre-eminent isolationist politician, while Richard Nixon was the age's chief internationalist—an inconvenience for those who like their history in black and white.

Buchanan advisors joked in 1988 that their man Pat might campaign under the banner "Let the Bloodbath Begin." The tangy irony is that Buchanan is far less likely than any other national Republican figure to ship American men and women to foreign shores.

His 1992 effort was the most radically antiwar campaign since Henry Wallace's 1948 Progressive party race; in fact, candidate Buchanan made George McGovern look like General Curtis "bomb them back into the Stone Ages" LeMay. Buchanan endorsed, with qualifications, the Cato Institute's Ted Carpenter's

248 Part Three: America First Renewed

proposal to reduce the U.S. soldiery from 2.1 million to under one million.

While the Clintons and Doles dither over whether to keep 100,000 or 200,000 troops guarding Europe, America Firsters, including Buchanan, would have the United States withdraw all remaining troops from Europe. Indeed, we would bid leave to NATO itself, enabling that elephantine entity to become a military arm of the European Community. (NATO's engorgement of Russia through the Partnership for Peace Program, which provides for NATO-Russia joint military exercises, reminds us that an institution, once deprived of its raison d'être, seldom expires quietly.)

Defense analyst Earl C. Ravenal estimates the annual U.S. budget expenditure on NATO at upwards of one hundred billion dollars, but Republican conservatives, putative penny-pinchers, are loath to give up the ghost. The party's 1994 "Contract with America" actually pledged to strengthen the alliance. This hazy universalism, this woolly dream of an integrated world in which we are Europe and Europe is us, comes dangerously close to John Lennon's injunction to "imagine there's no country," and it was smashingly appropriate that this anthem provided the score for Roland Joffe's film *The Killing Fields,* based on Dith Pran's account of Pol Pot's earnest effort to institute Lennonism in Cambodia.*

Our transatlantic garrisons were never intended to be permanent. When Senator Bourke Hickenlooper of Iowa asked Secretary of State Dean Acheson in a 1949 Foreign Relations Committee hearing on the proposed North Atlantic Treaty Organization if the United States was "going to be expected to send substantial numbers of troops over there as a more or less

---

*The British may have lost their empire but they have redoubled their chutzpah. "You Can't Go Home," *The Economist* instructed its American readers as the voices of Buchanan and Harkin grew more clamant. The tone was that of a solicitous hostess asking a favorite party guest to stay a while—never mind that the beggared guest is shelling out one hundred billion dollars for the privilege.

permanent contribution to the development of these countries' capacity to resist," the urbane diplomat replied, "The answer to that question, Senator, is a clear and absolute 'No.' "[18] Given Foggy Bottom's usually degraded standards of veracity, that is an answer of some precision.

The seeming inextricability of the NATO bond was vividly illustrated during a 1986 PBS forum of former presidential aides. Moderator John Chancellor asked the gathering, "Sometimes presidents want to do damn fool things they have to be talked out of, and so my question to all of you . . . is: How do you talk a president out of a damn fool idea?" Former Eisenhower aide General Andrew Goodpaster recalled:

> [Ike] came over one morning rather exasperated and said, "I've said that I want to start reducing our forces in Europe. You know that's our policy, and I want action to be initiated on that." I said, "Well, Mr. President, it isn't quite our policy."
>
> "What do you mean?"
>
> I said, "Well, that's the goal that's stated—to work down to long-term strength—but it's conditioned on the ability of the Europeans to fill the gap that's there, the gap we created."
>
> "No," he said, "that's not right. Our policy is to make that reduction and I want to get that started."
>
> I said, "Well, Mr. President, that really isn't the policy. It's conditioned in this way." He glared at me, and he said, "I've got Foster Dulles coming over here today, and I'm going to have him straighten you out on this."
>
> Well, I didn't say a word to Secretary Dulles when he came over. We went in together, and the president looked up and he said, "Foster, I want you to straighten Andy out on this once and for all. It *is* our policy to reduce those forces in Europe." And Foster Dulles, bless him, said, "Well, Mr. President, it isn't quite that clear. We always have put that condition on it, that the Europeans have to be able to fill that gap." The president looked up at Foster Dulles and he said, "Foster, I've lost my last friend."[19]

Goodpaster's fellow panelists chuckled politely and the conversation moved on, with nary a nod to the trillions of American tax dollars subsequently spilled on the European continent as a result of Goodpaster's placing fidelity in a globalist ideal above loyalty to his boss, his president, his commander in chief.

America Firsters also demand the withdrawal of the forty thousand or so U.S. Army and Air Force troops currently guarding South Korea, thereby entrusting the prosperous South—with a population twice as large and a GNP ten times as large as that of the suffocatingly centralized North—with its own defense. Should North Korea need defanging, this is a task eminently achievable by China and Japan. Doug Bandow of the Cato Institute, an ex-Reagan aide who quit the administration when Reagan reneged on a promise to end draft registration, has written extensively on the benefits of a U.S. decampment from the Korean peninsula: potential budgetary savings would exceed ten billion dollars.*

Ex-president Jimmy Carter, who negotiated an end to the brief flareup in mid-1994 over North Korea's burgeoning nuclear program, had proposed seventeen years earlier to remove all U.S. ground troops from South Korea over several years. Carter's zeppelin was blown out of the sky by Cold Warriors of both parties; the Clinton administration, staffed almost exclusively by multilateralists and hawks, has given no indication that the boys will be coming home any time soon.

America Firsters were nearly unanimous in condemning the 1991 war against Iraq; Tom Fleming called it "a genocidal slaughter of a primitive people who happened to get in the way of Mr. Bush's rhetoric."[20] Similarly, America Firsters have stood foursquare against any intervention in the civil war currently raging in Bosnia.

---

*Bandow's outspokenness on this matter got him released from a project at the Heritage Foundation, which, like many Washington, D.C., conservative organizations, has unfathomably deep South Korean ties. See Paul Gottfried's *The Conservative Movement* (1993) for details of the Korea First sentiment of various Washington operatives.

In Bosnia as elsewhere, the corporate media cheerlead for war. *Newsweek* stated in May 1993 that U.S. bombs ought to kill Bosnian Serbs "because to enjoy the benefits of global leadership, we have to bear the costs, too."[21] The pronoun is choice: "we"—that is, the Nebraska and Watts and Louisiana parents of 19-year-old boys and girls who will be shipped home in body bags—are decidedly *not* the sorts who edit *Newsweek*.

And yet the martial drumbeat has turned a large segment of a people whose motto used to be "don't tread on me" into embodiments of an "I'll tread on you" ethos. The ease with which public opinion is manipulated by a univocal media is frightening. An ABC News poll of August 9, 1990, shortly after Iraq's invasion of Kuwait, asked Americans if they favored assassinating Saddam Hussein: an astonishing 42 percent answered yes—astonishing because just two weeks earlier probably not one in ten Americans knew who Saddam Hussein was.

There are enough case studies in the folly of dissent to dissuade political timeservers from advertising America First views. Senator Robert Dole (R-Kansas), though he has compiled a typically interventionist Republican voting record ever since his early career as a Vietnam hawk, nevertheless stirred Old Right hearts when in his October 1976 vice-presidential debate with Walter Mondale he referred to the Vietnam, Korean, and two world wars as "Democrat wars." To the gasps of those who understand imperial etiquette, the first rule of which is never to badmouth the empire, Dole continued, "I figured up the other day, if we added up the killed and wounded in Democrat wars in this century, it would be about 1.6 million Americans, enough to fill the city of Detroit."[22]

Mondale checkmated the incautious Kansan by asking, "Does he really mean to suggest to the American people that there was a partisan difference over involvement in the [Second World] war?" Never again would Dole speak candidly about "Democrat wars." His second wife, Elizabeth, head of the unimpeachable Red Cross, has smoothed whatever serrated edges the once jagged Dole had, and as he cranks up his campaign for the 1996 Republican presidential nomination the softer Bob Dole is battering President Clinton for his timorousness in aiding, with men and materiel, the Bosnian Muslims in their religious war against the Bosnian Serbs. Do not, however, expect Bill Clinton to grin at the camera should he debate Senator Dole in 1996 and say, "I was counting up the dark-skinned people killed in Republican wars in Iraq, Nicaragua, Panama, Grenada. . . ."

When in February 1994 U.S. planes attacked Bosnian Serbs, virtually the only dissentient voice or pen was that of Pat Buchanan, who asked the anachronistic question, "Exactly where does President Clinton get the right to issue ultimata, to immerse America in the Bosnian bloodbath, or to bomb a nation, Serbia, that has not attacked the United States?"[23]

America Firsters insist on congressional primacy in warmaking. This puts them at odds with those Washington, D.C., conservatives who, under the assumption that Republicans have a long-term lease on the White House (despite the occasional sublets to Southern Democrats like Carter or Clinton), assert executive possession of virtually unlimited powers in the conduct of foreign affairs. Republicans blithely invade sovereign nations without a declaration of war from the Congress (as in Panama) or ignore congressional strictures on abetting foreign disputants (as in the Ronald Reagan-Robert McFarlane-Oliver North secret funding of the Nicaraguan contras in defiance of the Boland Amendment, which forbade such aid). America Firsters would revive in some form the Bricker Amendment, discussed in chapter 11, and would demand congressional approval of any dispatch of American soldiers to non-American seas or soil. (That the latter is even an issue suggests just how dead a letter our Constitution is.)

The Republican landslide of 1994 changed little beyond who got the coveted office hideaways in the Capitol. The new Speaker of the House, the voluble Newt Gingrich, is a dedicated internationalist: indeed, as minority whip he helped secure congressional passage of NAFTA and GATT, and as Speaker he abetted President Clinton in handing twenty billion dollars in loans and loan guarantees to Mexico in the winter of 1995. Opposition to those loans came from populist quarters: Ross Perot, Pat Buchanan, and the anti-corporate left—one more stitch binding the new America First coalition.

Gingrich's bizarre fusion of futurism and Reagan Republicanism will bring him into conflict again and again with the America Firsters. The Speaker envisions a twenty-first century in which "every American will have a cellular phone, which will probably be a fax, which will probably be a modem, which will probably tie them into a world—whether they want to or not, frankly, every American will be competing in the world market with Germany and China and Japan."[24] A world, in other words, in which global commerce acts as the great homogenizer, erasing our differences and throwing us all into the same competitive pot. A world in which regional and ethnic particularities disappear in the chase for the almighty dollar (or whatever Esperanto term is used for a global currency).

"I'm from nowhere,"[25] Gingrich is said to have remarked in graduate school: a fitting Speaker for the New World Order. His House lieutenants are nearly as avidly globalist as Gingrich, and Senate Republican Majority Leader Dole, light years removed from his impolitic "Democrat wars" crack of 1976, was a staunch supporter of the Gulf War, NAFTA, GATT, and the Mexican loan guarantees. Early in the new Republican congressional reign backbenchers forced minor reductions in the foreign aid budget, but such sops to the populists are unlikely to coopt even the mildest America Firsters.

At its core, America First is the descendant of Hamlin Garland's regionalism, of his belief that each locality must write and paint and keep its own record; must tend its own affairs; must grow in the way that is peculiarly Wisconsin, or Dakota, or New York. Tom Fleming locates the America First bedrock in the Catholic principle of subsidiarity: "let every competent level of society—individual, family, neighborhood, town, county, state, and nation—manage its own affairs. America First also means my family first, Charleston first, South Carolina first."[26]

As our bloody century winds down, the loudest arguments throughout the world are between the apostles of local autonomy and the panjandrums of the New World Order. In this dispute the government of the United States is the most powerful and implacable foe of the America First—or Québec First, or Basque First, or Zulu First—idea. Secretary of State Warren Christopher, at his 1993 confirmation hearing before the Senate Foreign Relations Committee, greeted the proliferation of newly independent nations with horror. "We'll have five thousand countries rather than the hundred plus we now have." To which America Firsters reply: marvelous!

Wendell Berry says, "The great threat in the world now is the placelessness of powerful people—people who have no allegiance to any community and therefore no reason . . . not to destroy any community that gets in their way."[27]

George Bush, whose official residence was a hotel room, ordered the slaughter of more than two hundred thousand Iraqis who posed no threat whatsoever to Americans or our territory. Bill Clinton, the boy from Hope (via Georgetown and Yale and Oxford), oversaw the holocaust in Waco, Texas. Ronald Reagan, originally from Dixon, Illinois, lives among the clouds in Bel Air, and the farther Richard Nixon roamed from Whittier, California, the more his moral compass went haywire. The only rooted president of the last quarter century, Georgia farmer Jimmy Carter, is the only elected chief executive of our era who has not ordered the killing of human beings. However ineffectual, he kept the Fifth Commandment. (Gerald Ford of Grand Rapids, now an errant golfer in Palm Springs, also did little harm during his brief tenure in the Oval Office.)

Contrast the destructive and unconstitutional acts of these worthies with the promise of America First: an America of distinct regions, flavorful localities, self-governing neighborhoods, and the foreign policy of the coiled rattlesnake, defending its nest but letting the outside world go its own way, unmolested.

Do we really want the cityless and countryless world that Henry Olerich foresaw? Do we want to live in an America in which the flickering image of a starving Rwandan on CNN is more immediate to us than the plaintive cries of the hungry girl down the road; a world in which young Americans don blue helmets and travel halfway around the globe to enforce the resolutions of the United Nations, while in small towns across America volunteer fire departments are undermanned?

It takes a worried man to sing a worried song, as the old folk tune goes, and by the urgency in their voices Americanists are clearly convinced that the hour is getting late. How much longer will there even be an America to place first?

NOTES

1. Quoted in Murray N. Rothbard, "Confessions of a Right-Wing Liberal," *Ramparts,* June 15, 1968, p. 50.

2. William Graham Sumner, "The Conquest of the United States by Spain," in *On Liberty, Society, and Politics* (Indianapolis: Liberty Fund, 1992/1899), p. 282.

3. Murray N. Rothbard, interview with the author, May 16, 1993.

4. Quoted in Otis L. Graham, Jr., *An Encore to Reform: The Old Progressives and the New Deal* (New York: Oxford University Press, 1967), p. 124.

5. Quoted in Peter G. Boyle, "The Roots of Isolationism: A Case Study," *Journal of American Studies* 6 (April 1972): 42.

6. Caspar W. Weinberger, "The Uses of Military Power," *Defense 85,* January 1985, p. 10.

7. Ibid., p. 5.

8. Samuel Francis, "Principalities and Powers," *Chronicles,* December 1991, p. 10.

9. Ibid., p. 11.

10. Thomas Fleming, "Banana Republicans," *Chronicles,* January 1990, p. 13.

11. Patrick J. Buchanan, "American Melting Pot Is Not Melting," Rochester, N.Y., *Democrat & Chronicle,* June 8, 1993, editorial page.

12. Samuel Francis, "Principalities and Powers," *Chronicles,* December 1991, p. 11.

13. Quoted in Deborah Sontag, "Calls to Restrict Immigration Come from Many Quarters," *New York Times,* December 13, 1992, p. E5.

14. Edward Abbey, "Immigration and Liberal Taboos," in *One Life at a Time, Please* (New York: Holt, 1988), p. 43.

15. Brian Hall, "Blue Helmets, Empty Guns," *New York Times Magazine,* January 2, 1994, p. 43.

16. Wendell Berry, "The Mad Farmer Manifesto: The First Amendment," in *Collected Poems* (San Francisco: North Point, 1985), p. 154.

17. Eugene J. McCarthy, *The Limits of Power* (New York: Holt, Rinehart, and Winston, 1967), p. 238.

18. *Congressional Record,* January 5, 1951, p. 59.

19. "Tales from the Top," *The Washington Monthly,* April 1987, p. 24.

20. Thomas Fleming, "America First 1941/1991," *Chronicles,* December 1991, p. 13.

21. Mark Whitaker, "Getting Tough at Last," *Newsweek,* May 10, 1993, p. 22.

22. "Dole and Mondale Clash over Inflation and U.S. Foreign Policy," *New York Times,* October 16, 1976.

23. Patrick J. Buchanan, "Who Approved U.S. Bombing Serbs?" Rochester, N.Y., *Democrat & Chronicle,* February 16, 1994, editorial page.

24. Quoted in David E. Rosenbaum, "Republicans Like Both Previews and Reruns," *New York Times,* December 11, 1994, p. D1.

25. Quoted in Howard Fineman, "The Warrior," *Newsweek,* January 9, 1995, p. 28.

26. Fleming, "America First 1941/1991," p. 13.

27. "Interview with Wendell Berry," *Safe Food News,* Winter 1994, pp. 9–10.

Epilogue: The Road to Trump

After this book's publication in 1995, the renascent America First isolationist sentiment took a nice long nap. (Surely there was no connection!)

Ross Perot failed to build upon his remarkable 1992 insurgency. His polite army of hopeful Middle Americans scattered; he ran again in 1996 on the Reform Party line, though his campaign was inchoate, even pointless. His primary motivation seemed to be the denial of the party's nomination to ex-Colorado Governor Richard Lamm, a Democratic Malthusian best known for his musings on the rationing of healthcare for the elderly.[1] (Lamm would have polled in nursing homes about as well as Perot did at Harvard.)

No longer the avuncular dispenser of folksy cracker-barrel wisdom, Perot was consistently mocked as "crazy" by the media. His skepticism of the Gulf War and the US/UN interventions in Somalia, Haiti, and Bosnia were sedulously ignored, lest they complicate the narrative. He selected as his running mate the protectionist policy maven Pat Choate, but discussion of the tariff held little interest for the press. As in 1992, Perot's campaign was stoutly inclusionist; his brand of nationalism was blessedly free of any trace of racial animosity.

Pat Buchanan ran for the GOP nomination again in 1996, this time as the tribune of a populism no longer rooted in the increasingly irrelevant Goldwater and New Right movements but instead retooled for the late twentieth century. He denounced NAFTA and

GATT, questioned the growing inequities of wealth in America, and, anticipating the ideological purges of the next millennium, he took on "those who despise America's past, assault her monuments, trash her history, and mock our traditions and beliefs."[2]

Buchanan prefigured Trump, albeit in a far more articulate and sophisticated, if less electorally successful, way.

He proposed tariffs of 10 percent on goods from Japan, 20 percent on those from China, and a "social tariff" on imports from Mexico and the Third World, as well as a five-year immigration freeze. His "conservatism of the heart"[3] combined economic nationalism, a defense of the federal-government-woven safety net, and the abstention of the US military from most if not all overseas wars.

"If we can send an army halfway around the world to defend the border of Kuwait I don't see why we can't secure our border with Mexico," said Buchanan.[4] He called for a "double-linked security fence," a less-grandiose version of the Trump wall, and not as earthy as the "Buchanan ditch" he had pledged to dig along the US–Mexico border in 1992.[5]

The former Nixon speechwriter had become a harsh critic of capitalism—which, unlike timorous Democrats, he called out by name: "I think a lot of modern corporate capitalists, the managerial class basically has no loyalty to any country anymore, or any particular values other than the bottom line."[6]

Buchanan, for the first time, sounded agrarian themes otherwise wholly absent from the policy dialogue of the time: "We have to ask ourselves as conservatives what it is we want to conserve in America. . . . I don't worship at the altar of efficiency as I believe some so-called conservatives do. To prefer a 100,000-hog confinement to hundreds of family farms, it seems to me, is not conservatism. I mean, that's to worship at a supermarket civilization."[7] (Buchanan even borrowed a couple of lines from this book, for instance calling Phil Gramm the "bellhop of Wall Street," as Amos Pinchot had Teddy Roosevelt.[8])

Pat Buchanan shocked the political media by winning the 1996 New

Hampshire primary, whereupon he was subjected to a vitriolic onslaught in the mainstream press in which he came off as Lucifer's black-sheep brother. *Newsweek* said his "appeal is built on fear,"[9] the *New Republic* called him "Evil,"[10] and the *New York Times* (in an article, not an editorial) said he was "speaking in code, using xenophobic images . . . or anti-Semitic references to excite bigots without alienating mainstream voters."[11] As evidence the *Times*man breathlessly reported that in a speech Buchanan had "lingered with great relish on each of the syllables in Justice Ruth Bader Ginsburg's three names," an anti-Semitic slur of surpassing subtlety.[12] Would he not have done the same with John Pierpont Morgan or Franklin Delano Roosevelt?

Lacking Ross Perot's wealth and Donald Trump's reality-show-honed ability to bypass the gatekeepers of Acceptable Opinion and speak directly to viewers, Buchanan's campaign flamed out. The Two Minutes Hate worked. On the bright side, it probably kept him from an appointment with his own Arthur Bremer.

Buchanan was bested for the nomination by Kansas Senator Bob Dole, who had long since repented of his "Democrat wars" crack in the 1976 vice presidential debate. By 1996, Senator Dole had taken to carrying in his pocket a copy of the Tenth Amendment to the Constitution, which reserves to the states and the people those powers not expressly delegated to the national government.[13] This was rich: rather like Teddy Kennedy brandishing a copy of the Sixth Commandment. Alas, no enterprising reporter ever asked Dole about his second—and trophy—wife Elizabeth's crowning accomplishment as Ronald Reagan's Secretary of Transportation: the imposition of a nationwide drinking age of twenty-one, which effectively nationalized what had theretofore been, since the repeal of Prohibition, a state matter. (Senator Dole, in defeat, transmogrified into a pitchman for Pfizer and its erectile dysfunction pills.)

Dole, once a piquant and even witty hatchet man, had come to embody the permanent political class. In resigning from the Senate to run this last race, he declared—in a speech reportedly ghosted by novelist Mark Helprin—"I will seek the presidency with nothing to fall back on but the judgment of the people of the United States and nowhere to go but the White House or home."[14] By "home" Helprin sought to conjure golden wheat fields and dusty roads and the sun setting on Russell, Kansas, as Bob and Liddy sipped lemonade on the front porch, serenaded by crickets, serene in the bosom of home sweet home. But what "home" really meant to Dole was his apartment in the Watergate or an occasional private-plane hop down to his condo in Bal Harbour, Florida. Like most of the political class of our age, he had forsaken home for power and never batted an eyelash.

Among the few to really ken Buchanan was Norman Mailer, the pugilistic novelist and author of the radically decentralist 1969 campaign for the New York City mayoralty, with its twin slogans of "Power to the Neighborhoods!" and "No More Bullshit." Mailer, who said he had long dreamt of a "left-right coalition" and in fact called himself a "left conservative," saw in Buchanan the possibility of a populist tribune who might seriously challenge what he regarded as the corporate stranglehold on the country. (Mailer's musings, wrapped around an entertaining interview with the candidate, appeared in the August 1996 *Esquire*.)

Buchanan made one more run for the Rose Garden, but not before he had published *A Republic, Not an Empire* (1999), an instructive tour of American foreign policy and diplomatic history in which the author's antiwar sympathies were made more explicit than ever. The book was denounced by the usual Beltway gasbags, perhaps aghast that a politician had actually written his own book. Buchanan's suggestion, in the section on the Second World War, that the United States might have been better off staying out of the fray and allowing Hitler and Stalin to destroy each other was willfully misinterpreted by hostile critics who were unaware that pre–Pearl Harbor opinion polls showed overwhelming support for avoiding the transatlantic bloodbath.

In a way, the traducing of Buchanan for this book made historical sense. After all, the debate over intervention in 1940–41 set a pattern for smearing antiwar movements. Buchanan's libelers, smug denizens of what Gore Vidal called the "United States of

Amnesia," had no idea that the America First Committee was the largest antiwar organization in American history, with eight hundred thousand members and a Main Street Republican base but wings taking in prairie populists and libertarian intellectuals and patriotic socialists. They'd have been astounded to learn that it was founded at Yale Law School by students who went on to distinguished careers in the American establishment—Sargent Shriver, first head of the Peace Corps and George McGovern's running mate in 1972; Potter Stewart, US Supreme Court Justice; Robert D. Stuart Jr., CEO of Quaker Oats and ambassador to Norway; and Kingman Brewster, later president of Yale. If they'd bothered to pick up the standard scholarly works on the AFC by Wayne S. Cole and Justus Doenecke, they'd have discovered that the committee took great pains to exclude anti-Semites, including the followers of Father Coughlin, the radio priest. The America First Committee was as American as Bob Dylan and tax revolts.

The America Firsters opposed involvement in the European War because they feared a replay of the disastrous First World War. They were in no wise pro-Nazi; their oft-expressed opinion and desire was that Nazi Germany and Soviet Russia would bleed each other dry, and that absent US intervention on the side of Joseph Stalin, Stalin and Hitler would destroy each other, surely a blessing to the world.

No one knows what would have happened had the United States sat out the war. Possibly catastrophe, possibly the mutual and devoutly to be wished destruction of the Hitler and Stalin governments, possibly something else. But why is what actually *did* happen—the deaths of six million Jews, tens of millions of Russians and Poles and Germans and Japanese and others; half a million American deaths and an unprecedented uprooting of our population and the hypertrophying of the American state; the deliverance of half of Europe to Stalin and Soviet tyranny—why is this, "the Good War," thought to be the best possible outcome of that bloody lustrum, and why are we essentially forbidden to ask if other paths and policies might have produced a better outcome?

Seventy-five years after Pearl Harbor, the question remains unaskable. As Pat Buchanan learned the hard way.

Buchanan realized early on that the path to the 2000 GOP nomination was of Donner Party–level impassability, so he sought instead the mantle of the remnant of Ross Perot's Reform Party. A bitter struggle ensued in which Perot kept his distance from Buchanan, the presumptive front-runner, and a series of anti-Buchanan pretenders came and went, among them none other than the New York real-estate baron Donald Trump. Alluding to *A Republic, Not an Empire*, which Trump had obviously not cracked, the New Yorker called Buchanan "a Hitler lover" and "an anti-Semite" before leaving a race he never formally entered.[15] (Sixteen years later, Pat Buchanan was one of Donald Trump's only boosters in the commentariat, which shows either an extraordinary capacity for forgiveness or a faulty memory.[16])

After a bitter factional struggle, Buchanan claimed the nomination. Illness and a lack of money prevented him from ever hitting his stride, though he delivered a powerful acceptance speech in which he thundered:

> Friends, I am called many names. Isolationist is one of the sweeter ones. But the truth is: We are not isolationists. We do not want to isolate America from the world. We Americans come from all countries and continents, and want to trade with and travel to all countries, and have commercial, cultural, and diplomatic contact with every nation on Earth. But we will no longer squander the blood of our soldiers fighting other countries' wars or the wealth of our people paying other countries' bills. The Cold War is over; it is time to bring America's troops home to the United States where they belong—and end foreign aid. And when I step out on that inaugural stand to take the oath—when my hand goes up, the New World Order comes crashing down.[17]

This was no mere boilerplate. Shattering the calcified right-wing orthodoxy, Buchanan called during that campaign for ending the Cuban embargo and forswearing economic sanctions against Iran, Iraq, and other nations, arguing that "our sanctions are sowing seeds of hatred that will one day flower in acts of terrorism against us."[18] ("Pat, you were right; we should have listened to you," said no Republican panjandrum on September 12, 2001.)

The first time I met Pat Buchanan, in the early 1990s, I urged him to make a third-party presidential bid with Gore Vidal as his running mate. He laughed, incredulous, and looked at me as if I had just introduced myself as Bill from Neptune's outermost moon. When I interviewed him in 1998, he told me how much he had enjoyed reading Vidal's work. And when I interviewed him one more time, in 2000, as his Reform Party race was foundering, victim of sandbagging by Perot's henchmen and his own serious health problems, he was hopeful in the face of overwhelming odds.

"I'm very sanguine that we're going to win this battle one day," he told me. "'America First' as a foreign policy is the only foreign policy that the American people will support over the long haul. You can get them ginned up for a crusade against the latest Hitler—Saddam Hussein in the Gulf—and you can even get them, though they were not enthusiastic, to support smashing a little country like Serbia that they don't know a thing about except what they read in the papers about them all being horrible people. But I'll tell you, if you start taking casualties in great numbers, Americans will balk and resist."[19]

They haven't yet. Not really. The interminable war in the Middle East that has been waged, to the indifference of most Americans, for nigh unto fifteen years has cost perhaps half a million Iraqis and Afghans their lives, but American deaths are still under ten thousand, not anywhere near Vietnam territory. The war is out of sight and out of mind—except for those who fit veterans for prosthetic limbs or clean the bedpans of twenty-one-year-old men with traumatic brain injuries.

As for Jerry Brown, the third member of that 1992 triad, the protean politico grew even more radical, but only for a brief time. In a 1995 interview with the *Progressive* he praised both the "right-wing" militias (a corporate media hobgoblin of Bill Clinton's first term) and the Black Panthers for "calling attention to the dangerous power-grab of the state."[20] He denounced the Clinton anti-terrorism measures as providing for "unlimited detention, for roving wiretaps, for trials based on secret evidence, for eliminating the capacity to confront witnesses, for blacklisting organizations, for punishing people based on guilt by association, restricting habeas corpus"— substantially the same critique civil libertarians made of the USA PATRIOT Act six years later.[21] Jerry Brown sounded as libertarian as his erstwhile foe and later ally Gore Vidal.

But genes will tell. Brown was elected to a third term as California governor in 2010. There he sits still. He has governed as a mainstream liberal, no more adventurous than his hack father Governor Pat Brown. Before the June 2016 California primary, in which the insurgent socialist Bernie Sanders had a last shot to derail Hillary Clinton's Wall Street–funded campaign, Brown endorsed the pro-Iraq War, pro-PATRIOT Act, pro–Wall Street bailout, pro–Trans-Pacific Partnership Clinton. She won California and the nomination, setting up as the most hawkish Democratic nominee since at least 1964. Jerry Brown, sadly, shed his heterodoxy as he entered his dotage. (Then again, the sempiternal and changeable Brown may have another act in him—perhaps as an ascetic back-to-the-land nonagenarian?)

Ralph Nader, theretofore known as a consumer activist, was a more thoughtful and less mercurial carrier of the America First banner on the populist left.

Nader made explicit appeals to conservatives in his campaigns of 2000, 2004, and 2008. He scored the PATRIOT Act as a threat to "domestic liberty," he defended the "precious traditions of local self-rule" in public schools against George W. Bush's centralizing No Child Left Behind Act, he castigated the entertainment industry for its "subversion of family values, parental discipline and winsome childhoods," and he sounded the Perot-Buchanan alarm that our "local, state and national sovereignties" were being undermined by NAFTA, the World Trade Organization, and putatively American corporations that flaunted their disloyalty to American workers.[22]

Nader, whom party-line Democrats would blame for draining

votes from the neocon-tutored Democratic nominee Albert Gore in 2000, also asserted what has now become an almost charmingly anachronistic conviction: "We may not agree with others, but we will defend their right to free speech as strongly as we do for ourselves."[23] The spectacle in 2016 of social-justice fascists and paid agitators beating up Americans who have the effrontery to exercise their right to attend Trump rallies—and the despicable if predictable failure of corporate liberals to condemn such behavior and defend the right of Trump to speak and people to hear him—sets one to wondering if, after Nader, we have reached the nadir.

Antiwar and isolationist sentiments were severely eroded at the dawn of the twenty-first century, when nineteen radical Muslims hijacked four airliners and crashed them into the World Trade Center, the Pentagon, and a Pennsylvania field, killing over three thousand innocents.

Only six Republican members of the House of Representatives voted against the 2002 Authorization for the Use of Military Force against Iraq and, by extension, the subsequent US invasion of that country, which the administration of President George W. Bush sold to the nation as a condign response to Iraq's alleged possession of (nonexistent) "weapons of mass destruction." (In *America's War for the Greater Middle East*, the percipient and mournfully wise army veteran and historian Andrew Bacevich discerns the real reasons for this catastrophic act of aggression: "First, the United States was intent on establishing the efficacy of preventive war. Second, it was going to assert the prerogative, permitted to no one other country, of removing regimes that Washington deemed odious. And finally, it was seeking to reverse the practice of exempting the Islamic world from neoliberal standards."[24] Conform to the shifting standards of the Indispensable Nation—or else.)

One of the six Republican dissentients, Ron Paul, was a Texas backbencher who represented in almost-pure form the Old Right hypothesized and hymned by Murray Rothbard. (Another of that noble sextet, Rep. John "Jimmy" Duncan of Tennessee, has distinguished himself as the preeminent congressional tribune of America First in the new century.)

When, in the run-up to Iraq War II in 2003, Rep. Paul proposed that Congress at least observe Article 1, Section 8 of the Constitution and make a formal declaration of war, House International Relations Committee chairman Henry Hyde (R–IL) responded, "There are things in the Constitution that have been overtaken by events, by time. Declaration of war is one of them. There are things no longer relevant to a modern society. We are saying to the president, use your judgment. [What you have proposed is] inappropriate, anachronistic; it isn't done anymore."[25]

Hyde was laureled by his party; Paul was libeled. Paul must have felt sometimes like Charlton Heston being mocked and snorted over by the jeering simians of *Planet of the Apes*.

Ron Paul, who had made a quixotic run for the presidency as the 1988 candidate of the Libertarian Party, was antiwar to the point of quasi pacifism. (Is there another American politico whose favorite song is Buffy Sainte-Marie's "Universal Soldier"?[26]) He also favored scrapping the Federal Reserve, the drug war, most Cabinet departments, and virtually every outgrowth of the leviathan state. His announcement that he would seek the 2008 GOP presidential nomination was relegated to single-paragraph stories buried deep in the newspaper, surrounded and suffocated by mattress and auto-parts ads.

The Republican machine resisted Paul at first, seeking even to bar him from debates because of his insufficient enthusiasm for the slaughter of Middle Easterners. But he attracted enthusiastic, wildly diverse crowds who cheered his message of peace and civil liberties.

Paul's campaign achieved liftoff in a shower of boos and catcalls, when at a May 2007 Republican debate in South Carolina he asked, referring to Osama bin Laden and al Qaeda: "Have you ever read about the reasons they attacked us? They attack us because we've been over there."

Former New York City mayor Rudy Giuliani, competing with

Arizona Senator John McCain for the backing of the neoconservatives, demanded an apology of Paul. The Texan stuck to his (pacific)
guns. Overnight, donations to his campaign poured in from Republicans, Democrats, libertarians, leftists, and those just sick of the
martial sanctimony saturating American discourse.

Paul's solution to the Iraq quagmire—"Just leave"—was derided
as unpatriotic and simplistic, though in retrospect it would have saved
hundreds of thousands of lives and trillions of taxpayer dollars.[27]

Paul ran gamely in both 2008 and 2012, though the respective
nominations went to the most bellicose (McCain in 2008) and pro–
Wall Street (Mitt Romney in 2012) candidates. He was smeared with
the usual epithets for his forthright and across-the-board opposition
to foreign wars, foreign aid, and the surveillance state constructed
in the aftermath of 9/11. When his young supporters chanted "Bring
them home!" at rallies in Iowa and New Hampshire, the echoes of
George McGovern's marvelous slogan, "Come Home, America,"
were unmistakable. The dove of peace, which had found a brief
Democratic home in 1972 thanks to the patriotic South Dakotan,
was flapping her wings at the GOP. But not to worry: the neocons
had hired guns ready to blast the poor bird to feathers and guts.

I spoke at Congressman Paul's 2008 Rally for the Republic
in Minneapolis, a Labor Day weekend counter-convention to the
zombie dance the Republicans were sponsoring for John McCain's
coronation in St. Paul. Ten thousand people, mostly young, showed
up: homeschoolers, home brewers, punk rockers, evangelical Chris-
tians, radical Kansans, and reactionary New Englanders—American
girls and boys, beautifully stained in the American grain, hip to
Republican lies and Democratic statism. Hell no, they said: we
won't go. Their lives are too precious to serve as cannon fodder for
the wars of Bush-Cheney or Obama-Biden or Hillary Clinton or, if it
comes to that, Donald Trump. They demanded honesty, liberty, and
respect for all things small and smaller: they had nothing but scorn
for the liars and whores who run the Empire. I tell you, it did my
hick American anarchist heart good.

In the other Twin City, the Republicans were nominating Senator John "Bomb, Bomb, Bomb, Bomb, Bomb Iran" McCain, a carpetbagging ex-Vietnam POW who, after wisely opposing the deployment of US troops to Lebanon in 1982 (241 were killed by a truck-bombing a year later[28]), became a bullying, seemingly unhinged supporter of US intervention and escalation of every conflict under the sun, reserving a special animus for Iran and post-Soviet Russia. He expressed a willingness to keep US troops in Iraq for "a hundred years,"[29] though that is, perhaps, not surprising when one considers McCain's utter placelessness: having attended twenty schools and lived a deracinated life even by the nomadic standards of the military, his loyalty is not to any particular place but rather to a bureaucratic institution (the military) and an abstraction (the American Empire).[30]

McCain's nomination marked a historic low (or high) of Republican war lust: the party once home to Gerald Nye, Robert Taft, and the president who warned his countrymen against the military-industrial complex had chosen as its standard-bearer the most hawkish figure in American public life.

McCain lost to a man almost as placeless as he. Senator Barack Obama (D–IL), lauded as the "world candidate," was born in Hawaii, a state that is only in the union because of its military significance. He has never advertised his Hawaii connection; perhaps it seems too exotic. Raised also in Indonesia and at various times resident in Los Angeles, New York City, and finally Chicago, Obama is a "cosmopolitan," which by some lights means a sophisticate but which a character in Henry James's *Portrait of a Lady* defined as "a little of everything and not much of any. I must say I think patriotism is like charity—it begins at home."[31]

"Isolationist!" shriek the Thought Police if confronted by a James-like opinion. And in fact in 2008 candidate Obama asseverated that "we cannot afford to be a country of isolationists right now."[32] Then again, cosmopolitans think we can *never* afford to leave other countries alone and mind our own business. Because their business *is* our business. Or as Obama says, American security is "inextricably linked to the security of all people."[33] That is a prescription for limitless internationalism. It is a recipe for blundering into numberless wars—which are fought, disproportionately, by those God & Guns small-town Americans pitied by Mr. Obama's upper-middle-class supporters. The views of Obama and McCain were redolent of the biblical assurance that not even a sparrow can fall to the earth unnoticed by God. This congruence of the roles of the deity and US foreign policy is not reassuring to those who desire peace and a modest role for the US military.

While President Obama has been deservedly praised for restoring relations with Cuba (as Pat Buchanan and Ron Paul had urged years earlier) and engaging with, rather than demonizing, Iran, he rejected the Paulist tack of "just leave." At this writing, several thousand US troops are in Iraq.[34]

Ron Paul's spirited campaigns demonstrated that a not insubstantial minority of Americans, Republicans and otherwise, hungered for a country that minded its own business and let its citizens pursue their lives in peace. There might even be an opening for the America First program described earlier in connection with Senator Burton K. Wheeler and the retroprogressives of the 1930s: "halting our slide into militarism; dismantling the empire; busting monopolies; preserving small-scale exchange and locally owned businesses; effecting a more equitable distribution of land and wealth without resorting to socialist tyranny; zealously guarding our sovereignty against internationalizing schemes; defending the rights of speakers to voice unpopular views; forging creative tools of direct democracy; challenging the party line as promulgated by the executive and his de facto press agent, big media."

And then along came Donald Trump.

I considered mentioning Trump in this book the first time around. I had kept a file on him when I was an editor at the libertarian monthly *Reason*, for when he dipped his toe in the political waters in 1987 as a prospective candidate for the Republican presidential nomination, the real-estate mogul had advocated "burden-sharing," or requiring the NATO allies to pay more for their own defense.[35] This policy prescription was associated with foreign-policy realists on the Right, among them economist Melvyn Krauss and Irving Kristol, the godfather of neoconservatism. (First-generation neocons like Kristol were not bloodthirsty war hawks but, more typically, social democrats appalled by the New Left. Though Cold Warriors, they tended not to be belligerent chicken hawks: that role was left to the next generation, whose most visible spokesman is Irving's son, Bill Kristol, bumbling marplot of the Never Trump movement.)

Trump kicked off his campaign in June 2015 with a speech that almost immediately galvanized supporters who had never heard a celebrity candidate speak in anything but anodyne platitudes.

"The US," Trump said, "has become a dumping ground for everybody else's problems. . . . When Mexico sends its people, they're not sending their best. They're not sending you. They're sending people that have lots of problems, and they're bringing those problems with us. They're bringing drugs. They're bringing crime. They're rapists. And some, I assume, are good people."[36]

Trump pledged to build a "great, great wall on our southern border" and make Mexico pay for its construction.[37] He would erect even higher walls against imported goods in the form of tariffs and taxes.

"Sadly, the American Dream is dead," announced Trump, who pledged to "make America great again."[38]

Lost in the breathless press accounts of the announcement was Trump's statement that we gained "nothing" from the Iraq War and lost trillions of dollars and thousands of lives. In the coming weeks he would amplify that critique, albeit in his rambling and fragmentary way. Like Ron Paul, he denounced the Iraq War in a South Carolina GOP debate, charging that George W. Bush had "lied" the nation into war. He criticized US intervention in Syria and Libya. He refused to rattle sabers against Russia and its president, Vladimir Putin, and, in an echo of his burden-sharing opinions of the 1980s, he complained that "the United States bears far too much of the cost of NATO."[39]

In what was billed as a major foreign-policy address in April 2016, Trump vowed to put "America First" and borrowed from John Quincy Adams's classic formulation of American noninterventionism when he said, "The world must know that we do not go abroad in search of enemies, that we are always happy when old enemies become friends and when old friends become allies. That's what we want: We want to bring peace to the world."

Trump's was, in sum, an audacious challenge to the reigning martial internationalism of the Republican Party, but outside the precincts of a revivified realist school of foreign policy on the moderate Right, no one paid much attention. Smug pundits were too busy tweeting and having attacks of the vapors over Trump's uncouthness. How dare an unscripted candidate interrupt the quadrennial snoozefest!

Donald Trump is and is not in the tradition of the men and women profiled in this book.

I am conflicted about Trump, but I love as countrymen the Trump supporters, drawn from that narrowing swath of Americans who remain patriotic, desperately so, their naiveté laced with cynicism (or is it the other way around?), scorned by their (our) country's enemies (chicken hawks; social-justice warriors; Conservatism, Inc.), so hungry for someone in authority (or on television) who seems to give a damn that they have latched onto the titan of American Bombast.

A Mexican wall? I'm afraid that my public-works fantasies are limited to painting a splashy "LOVE" in the road where Exit 48 of the New York State Thruway meets Oak Street, an homage to John Gardner's 1972 novel *The Sunlight Dialogues*. But then I dream small.

Trump's base overlaps with that of the last let's-roll-up-our-sleeves-and-fix-this-thing businessman-candidate, Ross Perot, whose bantam deportment concealed a relatively peaceful, mildly isolationist outlook, skeptical of foreign interventions and openly hostile to such managed trade deals as NAFTA.

The more intriguing Trump parallel is with the much-demonized press baron William Randolph Hearst, remembered today as the target of Orson Welles's *Citizen Kane* and as the laird of Hearst Castle, which makes Trump Tower look like the Little House on the Prairie.

Hearst, reviled by the ruling element of both parties, steered a populist course, supporting William Jennings Bryan, denouncing the "hyenas" of Wall Street and their preening bellhop Teddy Roosevelt (who "sold himself to the devil and will live up to the bargain"[40]), and unsuccessfully pursuing the Democratic presidential nomination in 1904, only to be bested by Judge Alton B. Parker, the candidate of Wall Street.

Hearst earned a lasting reputation as a jingo jackass during the Spanish-American War, though it is unlikely he actually wired Frederic Remington in Cuba, "You furnish the pictures and I'll furnish the war."[41] Thereafter Hearst inclined to neutrality, suspicious of foreign entanglements but ever ready to respond to real or perceived slights. His newspapers were blazoned with the declaration "America First Should Be Every American's Motto."[42]

Like Trump, who rejects the Russophobia of the globalists in favor of peaceful coexistence, Hearst was soft on Russia, boldly advocating recognition of the Bolshevik government in the 1920s. Hearst was also a full-throated immigration restrictionist, both on racist anti-Asian grounds and also because he saw hardworking immigrants as undermining the standard of living of the American workingman.

Neither appreciated the Little America or contented himself with homely pleasures and republican simplicity. Trump, with his ridiculous boast that "I'm the most militaristic person there is,"[43] surely would assent to this Hearstian sonority: "We want big Americans, in a big America, guarded by a big navy, fearing nobody, bullying nobody, insulted by nobody and sitting in peace and honor, ringed with her hundred ships of battle, ready and able to face the world in a just struggle."[44] But for all this bluster, Hearst stood with the peace party before both world wars.

Trump is especially popular among veterans[45]; the scriveners of the Hearst empire wasted no shade of purple in plumping for an endless infusion of cash and benefits to ex-soldiers, whether in establishment-friendly (the GI Bill) or menacingly populist (the Bonus Army) form. Hearst was downright radical in championing the Bonus Army, that aggregation of twenty thousand threadbare veterans of Mr. Wilson's War to End All Wars who camped in Washington during the summer of 1932 before Douglas MacArthur routed them. (Trump and Bernie Sanders were the only 2016 candidates one could imagine supporting the Bonus marchers.)

As Ian Mugridge writes in his perceptive *The View from Xanadu: William Randolph Hearst and American Foreign Policy*, "like all effective demagogues he had a knack of putting his finger on the real resentments and grievances of the people to whom he catered and on whom he depended."[46]

Too much can be made of the parallels—Melania Trump is no Marion Davies, and Hearst had a much better grasp of current affairs—but these two singular plutocrats do share nationalist, anti-elitist impulses, and are, to their credit, hated by our rulers.

'Tis bizarre that the hopes of so many decent American patriots repose in a celebrity deal-maker, but this is what we were left with after the collapse of the mystifying campaigns of Senators Jim Webb (D–VA) and Rand Paul (R–KY)—the men who ought to have been appealing to those Trump voters. (Rand, son of Ron, ran an astonishingly limp campaign in which he downplayed his skepticism of foreign involvements and sang from the trite psalter of Reagan Republicanism. His father must have been appalled.)

The phrase "America First" was suggested to Trump not by a close reading of old Hearst papers but by a *New York Times* interviewer in March 2016. Trump, taking the bait, replied, "I'm not isolationist, but I am 'America First.'"[47]

Unlike Buchanan and Perot, who contemplated reductions in the "defense" budget, Trump has said that the military should be "funded beautifully,"[48] whatever that means, though his aversion to nation-building and insistence that the other nations of NATO pull their weight imply certain economies. (I put *defense* in quotes not as a puerile punctuative gesture but in recognition of the unintentionally illuminating remark of Indiana Republican Dan Burton, former chair of the House Government Reform Committee, who in 2002 called the Department of Homeland Security "a Defense Department for the United States, if you will."[49] Think on that for a moment.)

Donald Trump fits into none of the dichotomies that I hoped might redefine American politics: centralist-decentralist, globalist-Little American, imperialist-republican.

He has no apparent objection to close cooperation between the state and big business, though he is certainly not a fascist, as his more hysterical detractors charge. He is not an expansionist, an imperialist, or an idolater of the central state über alles. He is a nationalist, to be sure, and as such views with meet suspicion the economic and bureaucratic edifices of internationalism, which he believes to be inimical to the best interests of the American people (if not their rulers).

There is nothing of the agrarian in Trump, no trace of localism (though he is unmistakably a Gothamite). If Perot was oblivious to matters of scale, preferring nationwide direct democracy to the radical devolution of political, economic, and cultural power (my preference), Trump is in love with grandiosity, with hugeness, with a bigger-is-better philosophy that is the antithesis of the humane and human scale Little American numen which is the best angel of America First.

Trump's stand on what once were called "social issues" are essentially those of a liberal Republican. He is friendly to gay rights and obviously comfortable with gay people, and while his feints toward religiosity are risible, he does not hold religious people in contempt. His name has become a talisman to those who chafe under the univocal and monocultural hegemony of political correctness. To them, Trump has the appeal of Ulysses S. Grant to Abraham Lincoln: "I can't spare this man. He fights."

And he slights, too, especially Muslims and Mexicans who are in this country illegally.

I largely ignored immigration in this book. I suppose that's because I was then and am today of two, or two thousand, minds on the subject. As a Christian and a believer in the right of migration, I incline to open borders, yet I agree with the libertarian economist Milton Friedman's contention that free and open immigration is only desirable in the absence of a welfare state; otherwise the native population will simply be overwhelmed.

My experience with Mexican immigrants in our agricultural town has been only positive, and I suppose the example of my wife's parents further fuddles my mind on the subject: her father was an Armenian immigrant from Syria, and her mother's parents fled Germany in the 1930s. They were welcome in America, as is anyone who's not looking for a handout or a grievance card.

Donald Trump has offered a more detailed plan on immigration than he has on any other subject. Stating that "a nation without borders is not a nation," he calls not only for a Mexican wall and a moratorium on the admission of Muslims to the United States but also for stricter enforcement of immigration laws, ending birthright citizenship, and, in an America First flourish, directing the monies spent on refugee resettlement to finding parents for American orphans.[50]

I am reminded of Senator Borah's line: "Whatever we owe elsewhere, our first and highest obligation is here in America, our first concern is our own people." This fell then and falls now upon the ears of the placeless as offensively parochial, petty, and small-minded. Not knowing their neighbors, playing no role in the lives of their communities, they deny that the mere fact of proximity entails any claim on their loyalty. Many don't even bother to hide their disdain for the working-class folk who are Trump's most ardent and vocal supporters.

Trump sells his restrictionism as a defense of the American worker: a populist line with tremendous popular appeal, which is perhaps why the gatekeepers of acceptable opinion have done their best to exclude it from national conversation in recent decades. Strikingly, African Americans remain the demographic disposed most favorably toward America First attitudes on foreign wars, immigration, and protectionism; if Trump could win even one-third of their votes he'd be gaudying up the White House in January 2017.

Like Trump, Bernie Sanders, the Brooklyn-bred socialist and US Senator from Vermont who ran a vigorous campaign for the 2016 Democratic nomination against Wall Street's candidate, Hillary Clinton, understood the appeal of solidarity.

Sanders was a more consistent, if less vocal, noninterventionist than Trump. He emphasized economic issues almost to the exclusion of matters of empire. Early in the campaign he dismissed open borders as a capitalist ruse to drive down the wages of working people, but he muted such opinions as the weeks went by, eventually adopting a pro-immigration position largely indistinguishable from that of Secretary Clinton.

John McClaughry did not join the Sanders bandwagon. "I have watched Bernie in Vermont for the past thirty-five years," he told me in 2015, "since he and his radical hippie pals took over the tiny dirt-poor town of Stannard. To his credit, Bernie has defiantly called himself a socialist from the beginning, even under pressure to 'tone it down.' He remains fully committed to 1960s (if not 1860s) Marxism, and every morning he sets out to advance the Socialist Movement and defeat its enemies."[51]

Not McClaughry's mug of cider, to say the least. University of Vermont professor of political science emeritus Frank Bryan, coauthor with McClaughry of *The Vermont Papers* and author of *Real Democracy* (2004), the classic study of Vermont town meeting, was ambivalent. Bryan did TV and radio ads for Sanders in previous campaigns, but he considers Sanders an "intense partisan . . . imprisoned by his own ideology"[52]—a centralized leftism that is antipodal from the humane, anarchist-tinged left of Mailer, Paul Goodman, Dorothy Day, and other American originals.

The enthusiasm generated by Sanders's grass-roots campaign suggests that a political market exists for an egalitarian, antiwar candidate of the Left—a prospect not pleasing to the mandarins and financiers of a modern Democratic Party that seems more interested in nationalizing public-restroom policy than it is in the decimation of the American working class.

Sanders was treated by much of the press as an endearingly dotty uncle, rather like Perot had been in the early stage of his 1992 campaign. Had the Vermonter posed a serious challenge to Hillary Clinton, that dottiness would have been shown in a much darker light.

Still, he'd have been a media darling compared to Donald Trump. Once he shot to the top of the polls, Trump was subjected to a full-bore campaign of media vilification unrivaled in American history for its comprehensiveness.

But then we might have predicted that. When *haven't* populists or foes, however eccentric and irregular, of America's endless wars been covered in libelous muck? Just ask Bob La Follette the Hun-lover, Charles Lindbergh the Nazi, Martin Luther King Jr. the communist, or any of those slandered as "unpatriotic conservatives" or "anti-American leftists" for opposing the US invasion of Iraq.

The hard truth is that anyone standing against the American war machine will be smeared by the *New York Times* and the court stenographers of the Empire. The calumnies hurled at Buchanan and Perot are being tossed with even greater velocity—and panicky desperation—at Trump, whose critique is far less sophisticated than Buchanan's and lacks Perot's generous heart.

The silent partner in the anti-Trump hysteria is Conservatism, Inc., headquartered inside the Beltway and over the sprawling nothingness of Occupied Northern Virginia. This more or less permanent array of scholars-for-hire, fundraising wizards, and Republican fronts is slavering over the prospect of a Hillary Clinton presidency.

It would be Powerball and the Clampetts' oil strike rolled into one. The resultant direct-mail gusher would rain widows' mites all over the mailrooms of the Beltway Right. President Hillary Clinton would be a windfall, the most lucrative bogeyman since Teddy Kennedy waddled off this mortal coil.

Is Trump a fluke? Will he lose in November 2016 and dissipate like a bad dream in the morning light, as the Republican Party resumes its role as agent for Wall Street, the military-industrial complex, the Fortune 500, and those "libertarians" who prize a reduction in the capital gains tax over the tatters and shreds of the Bill of Rights? Or is Trump a bell in the night pealing for an America that minds its own business, that tends to its own, that goes not abroad in search of enemies to destroy, that believes that there was and is a country some-where underneath the carapace of Empire, and that just maybe that country, its people (of all colors), and its many distinctive cultures are worth preserving from the hideous and homogenizing maw of global monoculture and the full-on paranoiac state of perpetual war?

Damned if I know.

"Make America Great Again"? Nah. Let's make America good. We do that by reinvigorating the dormant traditions of local self-government, of neighborly liberty, of charity and love, and that wonderful indigenous blend of don't-tread-on-me defiance of remote arrogant rule with I'll-give-you-the-shirt-off-my-back communitarianism.

We do it, in other words, by remembering how to be American.

NOTES

1. Associated Press, "Gov. Lamm Asserts Elderly, if Very Ill, Have 'Duty to Die,'" *New York Times*, March 29, 1984.

2. Patrick Buchanan, "If I Don't Run, the Older Party Wins, by Default," Rochester *Democrat & Chronicle*, February 19, 1995.

3. See John Judis, "Taking Buchananomics Seriously," *New Republic* (March 18, 1996): 18–20.

4. Joe Klein, "A Plausible Hothead?" *Newsweek* (May 29, 1995): 45.

5. Marianne Means, "The Barbed Wire Solution," *Observer-Reporter*, March 3, 1996.

6. Samuel Francis, "Buchanan Taps a Populist Vein," *Washington Times*, September 12, 1995.

7. Ernest Tollerson, "In Iowa, Buchanan Tries to Convince Conservatives That He's Their Man," *New York Times*, December 3, 1995.

8. "Pat Buchanan's Happy Days," *Economist* (September 9, 1995): 37.

9. Howard Fineman, "Extreme Measures," *Newsweek* (March 4, 1996): 20.

10. "See No Evil, Speak No Evil, and Evil," *New Republic* (March 11, 1996), cover.

11. James Bennet, "Candidate's Speech Is Called Code for Controversy," *New York Times*, February 29, 1996.

12. Ibid.

13. Ralph Z. Hallow, "New Dole Pushes 10th Amendment," *Washington Times*, April 7, 1995.

14. William Safire, "White House or Home," *New York Times*, May 16, 1996.

15. Francis X. Clines, "Trump Quits Grand Old Party for New," *New York Times*, October 24, 1999.

16. Chris Cillizza, "Pat Buchanan Says Donald Trump Is the Future of the Republican Party," *Washington Post*, January 12, 2016.

17. Patrick J. Buchanan, Reform Party Nomination Acceptance, press release, August 13, 2000.

18. Francis X. Clines, "Buchanan, in a Change, Calls for End to Sanctions," *New York Times*, December 17, 1999.

19. Bill Kauffman, "'I'm Liberated; Free at Last!' A Talk with Pat Buchanan," *Chronicles* (November 2000): 14.

20. "The *Progressive* Interview: Jerry Brown," *Progressive* (September 1995): 36.

21. Ibid.

22. Ralph Nader, "Dear Conservatives Upset with the Policies of the Bush Administration," archived at https://web.archive.org/web/20040702033113/http://www.votenader.org/why_ralph/index.php?cid=14 (accessed July 20, 2016).

23. Justin Raimondo, "The Nader Moment," antiwar.com, November 1, 2000.

24. Andrew Bacevich, *America's War for the Greater Middle East* (New York: Random House, 2016), p. 238.

25. Ron Paul, *The Revolution: A Manifesto* (New York: Grand Central Publishing, 2008), p. 54.

26. Lew Rockwell, "Ron Paul's Foreign Policy of Peace Is Central to the Message of Freedom," *Mises Daily*, mises.org, August 6, 2015.

27. "Costs of War," Watson Institute of International and Public Affairs," www.watson.brown.edu (accessed July 19, 2016).

28. Ted Galen Carpenter, "John McCain on Foreign Policy," *Chronicles* (July 2008): 14.

29. Justin Raimondo, "The Madness of John McCain," *American Conservative* (February 11, 2008): 10.

30. Bill Kauffman, "The Candidates from Nowhere," *Counterpunch*, April 16, 2008, www.counterpunch.com.

31. Henry James, *The Portrait of a Lady* (New York: Penguin, 2011/1881), p. 97.

32. Brendan O'Neill, "Make the World Safe for Hope," *American Conservative* (February 25, 2008): 7.

33. Ibid., p. 8.

34. Mark Thompson, "Number of U.S. Troops in Iraq Keeps Creeping Upward," *Time*, April 18, 2016, www.time.com.

35. Michael Oreskes, "Trump, the Noncandidate, Sounding Presidential," *New York Times*, September 2, 1987.

36. "Here's Donald Trump's Presidential Announcement Speech," *Time*, June 16, 2015, www.time.com.

37. Ibid.

38. Ibid.

39. "Transcript: Donald Trump Expounds on His Foreign Policy Views," *New York Times*, March 26, 2016.

40. Ian Mugridge, *The View from Xanadu: William Randolph Hearst and American Foreign Policy* (Montreal: McGill-Queen's Press, 1995), p. 26.

41. Ibid., p. 10.

42. Ibid., p. 113.

43. Gene Healy, "Trump's Biggest Lie: 'I'm the Most Militaristic Person' in This Race," *Federalist*, August 17, 2015, www.thefederalist.com.

44. Mugridge, *View from Xanadu*, p. 102.

45. Cameron Easley, "Poll: Veterans Much Prefer Trump to Clinton," *Morning Consult*, May 26, 2016, www.morningconsult.com.

46. Mugridge, *View from Xanadu*, p. 27.

47. "Transcript: Donald Trump Expounds."

48. "Transcript: Donald Trump's Foreign Policy Speech," *New York Times*, April 27, 2016.

49. Hearing of the House Government Reform Committee, June 20, 2002, p. 6.

50. "Immigration Reform That Will Make America Great Again," www.donaldjtrump.com (accessed July 19, 2016).

51. Bill Kauffman, "Bernie Sanders—Yes or No?" *American Conservative* (September/October 2015): 43.

52. Ibid.

Bibliography

Abbey, Edward. *The Brave Cowboy.* Albuquerque: University of New Mexico, 1977/1956.

———. *Desert Solitaire.* New York: McGraw-Hill, 1968.

———. *Down the River.* New York: Dutton, 1982.

———. *The Fool's Progress.* New York: Holt, 1988.

———. *Hayduke Lives!* Boston: Little, Brown, 1990.

———. *The Monkey Wrench Gang.* Philadelphia: Lippincott, 1975.

———. *One Life at a Time, Please.* New York: Holt, 1988.

———. *Slumgullion Stew.* New York: Dutton, 1984.

Abramson, Rudy. *Spanning the Century: The Life of W. Averell Harriman.* New York: Morrow, 1992.

Adams, Henry. *Democracy.* New York: Holt, 1880.

———. *The Education of Henry Adams.* New York: Modern Library, 1931/1918.

———. *History of the United States during the Administrations of Jefferson and Madison.* New York: Scribner's, 1889.

Agar, Herbert, and Allen Tate, eds. *Who Owns America?* Boston: Houghton Mifflin, 1936.

Allen, Gay Wilson. *Waldo Emerson.* New York: Viking, 1981.

"America: Still a Melting Pot?" *Newsweek.* August 9, 1993.

257

"Amos Pinchot Tries to Commit Suicide." *New York Times,* August 7, 1942, p. 1.

"Amos R. E. Pinchot Dies Here at 70." *New York Times,* February 19, 1944, p. 13.

"Amos Richard Eno Pinchot." *The National Cyclopedia of American Biography* 32 (New York: James T. White, 1945).

Anderson, Maxwell. *Both Your Houses.* New York: Samuel French, 1933.

———. *Knickerbocker Holiday.* Washington, D.C.: Anderson House, 1938.

———. *Valley Forge.* Washington, D.C.: Anderson House, 1934.

"As American as Apple Pie, Dim Sum or Burritos." *New York Times,* May 31, 1992, p. E2.

"As Ethnic Wars Multiply, U.S. Strives for a Policy." *New York Times,* February 7, 1993, p. 1.

Ashby, LeRoy. *The Spearless Leader: Senator Borah and the Progressive Movement in the 1920s.* Urbana: University of Illinois, 1972.

Associated Press. "Most Americans Disapprove Haiti Invasion, Poll Says." June 23, 1994.

Avery, Laurence G., ed. *Dramatist in America: Letters of Maxwell Anderson, 1912–1958.* Chapel Hill: University of North Carolina, 1977.

Bagdikian, Ben. *Media Monopoly.* Boston: Beacon, 1983.

Bandow, Doug. "Korea: The Case for Disengagement." *Cato Policy Analysis,* December 8, 1987.

Barnes, Fred. "War Footing." *The New Republic,* March 16, 1992.

Beer, Thomas. *Hanna.* New York: Knopf: 1929.

Behlmer, Rudy. *Inside Warner Bros.* New York: Viking, 1985.

Beisner, Robert L. "1898 and 1968: The Anti-Imperialists and the Doves." *Political Science Quarterly* 85 (June 1970).

Bell, Millicent. *Marquand.* Boston: Little, Brown, 1979.

Bellamy, Edward. *Looking Backward, 2000–1887.* New York: Random House, 1951/1887.

Berry, Wendell. *Collected Poems*. San Francisco: North Point, 1985.

———. *A Continuous Harmony*. New York: Harcourt Brace Jovanovich, 1975/1972.

———. *Home Economics*. San Francisco: North Point, 1987.

———. "Out of Your Car, Off Your Horse." *The Atlantic Monthly,* February 1991.

———. *Remembering*. San Francisco: North Point, 1988.

———. *The Unsettling of America*. San Francisco: Sierra Club, 1977.

———. *What Are People For?* San Francisco: North Point, 1990.

Berlin, Isaiah. "Edmund Wilson among the 'Despicable English.' " *The Yale Review,* Winter 1987.

Blackorby, Edward. *Prairie Rebel: The Public Life of William Lemke*. Lincoln: University of Nebraska Press, 1963.

Blumenthal, Sidney. "Tomorrow Belongs to Me." *The New Republic,* January 6 and 13, 1992.

Bolt, Ernest C., Jr. *Ballots before Bullets: The War Referendum Approach to Peace in America 1914–41*. Charlottesville: University Press of Virginia, 1977.

"Borah Says People May Take Rule over War If Nation Joins in the 'Hysterical' Arms Race." *New York Times,* December 4, 1938, p. 1.

Boyle, Peter G. "The Roots of Isolationism: A Case Study." *Journal of American Studies* 6 (April 1972).

Braeman, John. "Seven Progressives." *Business History Review* 35 (Winter 1961).

Brewer, Helen Maxwell. "Amos Richards Eno Pinchot." *Dictionary of American Biography,* Suppl. 3 (New York: Scribner's, 1973).

Bromfield, Louis. *A New Pattern for a Tired World*. New York: Harper, 1954.

Brooks, George S., and Walter B. Lister. *Spread Eagle*. New York: Scribner's, 1927.

Brooks, Van Wyck. *The Flowering of New England.* New York: Dutton, 1936.

———. *New England: Indian Summer.* New York: Dutton, 1940.

Brough, James. *Princess Alice.* Boston: Little, Brown, 1975.

Brown, Edmund G., Jr. "Free Trade's Huge Costs." *New York Times,* May 2, 1993.

Brown, John Mason. *The Worlds of Robert E. Sherwood.* New York: Harper & Row, 1962.

Brownstein, Ronald. *The Power and the Glitter.* New York: Pantheon, 1990.

Bryan, William Jennings. *The First Battle.* Chicago: W. B. Conkey, 1896.

Buchanan, Patrick J. "America First—and Second, and Third." *The National Interest,* Spring 1990.

———. "American Melting Pot Is Not Melting." Syndicated column, June 8, 1993.

———. "Bush Was Right to Stand Up to Israeli Lobby." Syndicated column, September 18, 1991.

———. "Call Gorbachev's Bluff." *Cato Policy Report,* March–April 1989.

———. "The Election Is about Who We Are." *Vital Speeches,* September 15, 1992.

———. "Embargoes Hurt Kids, Weak, Elderly." Syndicated column, May 26, 1994.

———. "Is Rockefeller Laughing Last?" Syndicated column, May 4, 1991.

———. "It's Only the Truth that Hurts, Abe." Syndicated column, September 19, 1990.

———. "NAFTA Surrenders U.S. Sovereignty." Syndicated column, August 22, 1993.

———. *Right from the Beginning.* Boston: Little, Brown, 1988.

———. "Who Approved U.S. Bombing Serbs?" Syndicated column, February 16, 1994.

Burroughs, William S. *Junky.* New York: Penguin, 1977/1953.

"Calls to Restrict Immigration Come from Many Quarters." *New York Times,* December 13, 1992, p. E5.

Cane, Melville H., and Harry E. Maule, eds. *The Man from Main Street.* New York: Random House, 1953.

Carlson, Allan C. "Remarks to the Presidential Commission on the Assignment of Women in the Armed Forces." Evanston, Ill., July 13, 1992.

Carpenter, Ted Galen. "The Dissenters: American Isolationists and Foreign Policy, 1945–1954." Ph.D. dissertation, University of Texas, 1980.

———. "From Republic to Empire: The Constitution and the Evolution of U.S. Foreign Policy." *Cato Policy Report,* September/October 1987.

———, ed. *NATO at 40.* Washington, D.C.: Cato Institute, 1990.

Chadwin, Mark Lincoln. *The Hawks of World War II.* Chapel Hill: University of North Carolina Press, 1968.

Chamberlain, John. *Farewell to Reform.* New York: John Day, 1932.

Charters, Ann. *Kerouac: A Biography.* London: Deutsch, 1974.

Cherny, Robert W. *A Righteous Cause: The Life of William Jennings Bryan.* Boston: Little, Brown, 1985.

Chesterton, G. K. *The Napoleon of Notting Hill.* Mineola, N.Y.: Dover, 1991/1904.

Clark, Tom. *Jack Kerouac.* New York: Harcourt Brace Jovanovich, 1984.

"Clinton Asked Senator's Help on Draft, His Aides Confirm." *New York Times,* September 19, 1992, p. 1.

Cockburn, Alexander, and Andrew Kopkind. "Interview with Jerry Brown." *The Nation,* April 20, 1992.

Coevolution Quarterly, "Earl Butz versus Wendell Berry." *Ten Years of Coevolution Quarterly.* San Francisco: North Point, 1986.

Coffin, Tristam. *Senator Fulbright: Portrait of a Public Philosopher.* New York: Dutton, 1966.

Cole, Wayne S. *America First: The Battle against Intervention, 1940–41*. Madison: University of Wisconsin Press, 1953.

———. "America First and the South, 1940–1941." *Journal of Southern History* 22 (February 1956).

———. "And Then There Were None!" In *Behind the Throne*, Thomas J. McCormick and Walter La Feber, eds. Madison: University of Wisconsin Press, 1993.

———. *Charles A. Lindbergh and the Battle against American Intervention in World War II*. New York: Harcourt Brace Jovanovich, 1974.

———. *Roosevelt and the Isolationists*. Lincoln: University of Nebraska Press, 1983.

———. *Senator Gerald P. Nye and American Foreign Relations*. Minneapolis: University of Minnesota Press, 1962.

———. "United States Isolationism in the 1990s?" *International Journal* 48 (Winter 1992–93).

Coles, Robert. *Dorothy Day: A Radical Devotion*. Reading, Mass.: Addison-Wesley, 1987.

Colman, Elizabeth Wheeler. *Mrs. Wheeler Goes to Washington*. Hartland, Wis.: Elizabeth Wheeler Colman, 1989.

Cook, Blanche Wiesen. *The Declassified Eisenhower*. New York: Doubleday, 1981.

Cooper, James Fenimore. *The American Democrat*. New York: Funk & Wagnalls, 1969/1838.

Cooper, Stephen. *The Politics of Ernest Hemingway*. Ann Arbor: UMI Research, 1987.

Craig, Douglas B. *After Wilson*. Chapel Hill: University of North Carolina Press, 1992.

Croly, Herbert. *The Promise of American Life*. Cambridge, Mass.: Harvard University Press, 1965/1909.

"Cuckoo's Nest." *The New Republic,* November 16, 1992.

"The Cry of the Dead." *Newsweek,* May 10, 1993.

Daniels, Jonathan. *The Time between the Wars*. Garden City, N.Y.: Doubleday, 1966.

Darwent, Brian, ed. *The New Saroyan Reader.* San Francisco: Creative Arts, 1984.

Davidson, Donald. *Attack on Leviathan.* Chapel Hill: University of North Carolina Press, 1938.

———. *Still Rebels, Still Yankees.* Baton Rouge: Louisiana State University Press, 1957.

Dayton, Katharine, and George S. Kaufman. *First Lady.* New York: Random House, 1935.

De Forest, John W. "The Great American Novel." *The Nation,* January 9, 1868.

———. *Miss Ravenel's Conversion.* New York: Holt, Rinehart and Winston, 1965/1867.

Derleth, August. *Three Literary Men.* New York: Candlelight, 1963.

Dickason, David H. "Benjamin Orange Flower, Patron of the Realists." *American Literature* 14 (1942): 148–56.

Doan, Edward N. *The La Follettes and the Wisconsin Idea.* New York: Rinehart, 1947.

Doenecke, Justus D. "The Anti-Interventionist Tradition: Leadership and Perceptions." *The Literature of Liberty,* Summer 1981.

———. *In Danger Undaunted: The Anti-Interventionist Movement of 1940–1941 As Revealed in the Papers of the America First Committee.* Stanford: Hoover Institution, 1990.

———. *The Literature of Isolationism: A Guide to Non-Interventionist Scholarship, 1930–1972.* Colorado Springs: Ralph Myles, 1972.

———. "The Literature of Isolationism, 1972–1983: A Bibliographical Guide." *Journal of Libertarian Studies* 7 (Spring 1983).

———. "The Lone Eagle." *Libertarian Forum,* March 1972.

———. *Not to the Swift.* Lewisburg, Pa.: Bucknell University Press, 1979.

"Dole and Mondale Clash over Inflation and U.S. Foreign Policy." *New York Times,* October 16, 1976.

Donald, David Herbert. *Look Homeward: A Life of Thomas Wolfe*. Boston: Little, Brown, 1987.

Dooley, D. J. *The Art of Sinclair Lewis*. Lincoln: University of Nebraska Press, 1967.

Dos Passos, John. *The Grand Design*. Boston: Houghton Mifflin, 1949.

Dreiser, Theodore. *America Is Worth Saving*. New York: Modern Age, 1941.

"The Duke of Louisiana." *Time*, November 4, 1991.

"Duke's Followers Lean to Buchanan." *New York Times*, March 8, 1992.

Dumbauld, Edward, ed. *The Political Writings of Thomas Jefferson*. Indianapolis: Bobbs-Merrill, 1955.

Edel, Leon. *Henry James 1895-1901: The Treacherous Years*. Philadelphia: Lippincott, 1969.

Ekirch, Arthur A., Jr. *The Decline of American Liberalism*. New York: Atheneum, 1976/1955.

Emerson, Ralph Waldo. "Politics." In *Emerson's Works*, vol. 2. Boston: Houghton Mifflin, 1883.

"Exchange." *The Nation*, April 26, 1986.

"Exchange." *The Nation*, May 3, 1986.

Feinman, Ronald L. *Twilight of Progressivism*. Baltimore: Johns Hopkins University Press, 1981.

Felsenthal, Carol. *Alice Roosevelt Longworth*. New York: Putnam's, 1988.

Ferguson, Otis. "They're Down! They're Up!" *The New Republic*, May 10, 1939.

———. "Three for the Show." *The New Republic*, October 18, 1939.

Findley, Paul. *They Dare to Speak Out*. Chicago: Lawrence Hill, 1984.

Fine, Nathan. *Labor and Farmer Parties in the United States, 1828-1928*. Berkeley: Center for Socialist History, 1984/1928.

Fleming, Thomas. "America First." *Chronicles*, December 1991.

———. "Banana Republicans." *Chronicles*, January 1990.

Fleming, Thomas. "Leveraged Buyout." *Chronicles,* June 1992.

———. "The New Fusionism." *Chronicles,* May 1991.

———. "New World Disorder." *Chronicles,* July 1992.

———. "Peace on Earth among Men of Good Will." *Chronicles,* February 1990.

———. *The Politics of Human Nature.* New Brunswick, N.J.: Transaction, 1988.

———. "Surviving in the New World Order." *Chronicles,* April 1991.

Fletcher, John Gould. *Arkansas.* Fayetteville: University of Arkansas Press, 1989/1947.

Flynn, John T. *As We Go Marching.* New York: Free Life, 1973/1944.

———. *Country Squire in the White House.* New York: Doubleday, 1940.

———. "Fifty Million Americans in Search of a Party." *The American Mercury,* February 1955.

———. *The Road Ahead.* New York: Devin-Adair, 1949.

"Flynn Says Films Bar Peace Side." *New York Times,,* September 12, 1941, p. 24.

Fonda, Peter, Dennis Hopper, and Terry Southern. *"Easy Rider."* New York: Signet, 1969.

Foshee, Andrew. "The Political Economy of the Southern Agrarian Tradition." *Modern Age,* Spring 1983.

Francis, Samuel. *Beautiful Losers.* Columbia: University of Missouri Press, 1993.

———. "The Buchanan Revolution." *Chronicles,* July 1992.

———. "Principalities and Powers." *Chronicles,* December 1991.

———. "Stupid and Proud." *Chronicles,* September 1993.

Fulbright, J. William. *The Arrogance of Power.* New York: Random House, 1966.

———. *Crippled Giant.* New York: Random House, 1972.

———. *Old Myths and New Realities.* New York: Random House, 1964.

Fulbright, J. William. *Prospects for the West*. Cambridge, Mass.: Harvard University Press, 1963.

Fulbright, J. William, and Seth P. Tillman. *The Price of Empire* New York: Pantheon, 1989.

Furness, Clifton Joseph. "Walt Whitman's Politics." *The American Mercury*, 1929, pp. 459–66.

Fussell, Paul. *Wartime*. New York: Oxford, 1989.

Garland, Hamlin. *Afternoon Neighbors*. New York: Macmillan, 1934.

———. *Companions on the Trail*. New York: Macmillan, 1931.

———. *Crumbling Idols*. Chicago: Stone & Kimball, 1894.

———. *A Daughter of the Middle Border*. New York: Macmillan, 1921.

———. *Main-Travelled Roads*. Boston: Arena, 1891.

———. *A Member of the Third House*. Chicago: F. J. Schulte, 1892.

———. *My Friendly Contemporaries*. New York: Macmillan, 1932.

———. *Other Main-Travelled Roads*. New York: Harper, 1910.

———. *Roadside Meetings*. New York: Macmillan, 1930.

———. *Rose of Dutcher's Coolly*. Chicago: Stone & Kimball, 1895.

———. *A Son of the Middle Border*. New York: Macmillan, 1917.

———. *A Spoil of Office*. Boston: Arena, 1892.

Garraty, John A. *Right-Hand Man*. New York: Harper, 1957.

George, Henry. *Progress and Poverty*. New York: Schalkenbach Foundation, 1981/1880.

Gibson, William M. "Mark Twain and Howells: Anti-Imperialists." *New England Quarterly* 20 (1947).

Gifford, Barry, and Lawrence Lee. *Jack's Book*. New York: St. Martin's Press, 1978.

———. *Saroyan*. New York: Harper & Row, 1984.

Gifford, Bill, and James Ridgeway. "The Griz Gets His." *Village Voice*, July 25, 1989.

Gilbert, Felix. *To the Farewell Address.* Princeton: Princeton University Press, 1961.

Ginsberg, Allen. *Collected Poems: 1949–1980.* New York: Harper & Row, 1985.

Ginsberg, Allen, and Neal Cassady. *As Ever: The Collected Correspondence of Allen Ginsberg and Neal Cassady,* edited by Barry Gifford. Berkeley: Creative Arts, 1977.

Glass, Charles. "Gore, Poddy and Midge." *The Spectator,* September 20, 1986.

Goodwyn, Lawrence. *Democratic Promise.* New York: Oxford, 1976.

"Gore Vidal: The *Progressive* Interview." *The Progressive,* September 1986.

Gottfried, Paul. *The Conservative Movement.* New York: Twayne, 1993.

———. "Toward a New Fusionism." *Policy Review,* Fall 1987.

Graham, Otis L. *An Encore to Reform: The Old Progressives and the New Deal.* New York: Oxford, 1967.

Green, David. *The Language of Politics in America.* Ithaca: Cornell University Press, 1987.

Greider, William. *Who Will Tell the People.* New York: Simon and Schuster, 1992.

Griffith, Robert. "Old Progressives and the Cold War." *Journal of American History* 66 (September 1979).

Gwertzman, Bernard M., and Haynes Johnson. *Fulbright the Dissenter.* Garden City, N.Y.: Doubleday, 1968.

Hall, Brian. "Blue Helmets, Empty Guns." *New York Times Magazine,* January 2, 1994.

Hamilton, Ian. *Robert Lowell: A Biography.* New York: Random House, 1982.

———. *Writers in Hollywood 1915–1951.* New York: Harper & Row, 1990.

Hard, William. "In Bad All Around." *The Nation,* December 3, 1924.

Harrington, Fred Harvey. "Literary Aspects of American Anti-

Imperialism 1898–1902." *New England Quarterly,* December 1937.

Harrison, Barbara Grizzuti. "Pure Gore." *Los Angeles Times Magazine,* January 28, 1990.

Hatfield, Senator Mark O. "Bringing Political Power Back Home: The Case for Neighborhood Government." *Ripon Quarterly* 19 (1974).

Havard, William C., and Walter Sullivan. *A Band of Prophets.* Baton Rouge: Louisiana State University Press, 1982.

Hawthorne, Nathaniel. *The Blithedale Romance.* New York: Standard Book, 1931/1852.

Herron, Ima Honaker. *The Small Town in American Literature.* Durham: Duke University Press, 1939.

Hesseltine, William B. *Third-Party Movements in the United States.* Princeton: Van Nostrand, 1962.

Hicks, John D. *The Populist Revolt.* Minneapolis: University of Minnesota Press, 1931.

Higham, Charles. *Kate.* New York: Norton, 1975.

Hilburn, Robert. "Rockers Rally 'Round the Flag." *Los Angeles Times Calendar,* June 30, 1985.

Hill, Eldon Cleon. "A Biographical Study of Hamlin Garland from 1860 to 1895." Ph.D. dissertation, Ohio State University, 1940.

Hill, Richard. "Kerouac at the End of the Road." *New York Times Book Review,* May 29, 1988.

Hinckle, Warren. "J. William Fulbright: A Profile in Courage." *Ramparts,* June 1966.

Hoagland, Edward. "Edward Abbey: Standing Tough in the Desert." *New York Times Book Review,* May 7, 1989.

Hofstadter, Richard. *The Age of Reform.* New York: Knopf, 1955.

———. *The Paranoid Style in American Politics.* New York: Knopf, 1966.

———. *The Progressive Historians.* New York: Knopf, 1968.

Horemans, Rudi, ed. *Beat Indeed!* Antwerp: EXA, 1985.

Howe, Edgar W. *The Story of a Country Town.* New York: Dodd, Mead, 1927/1882.

Howland, Harold. *Theodore Roosevelt and His Times.* New Haven: Yale University Press, 1921.

"Hull Again Hits War Referendum." *New York Times,* January 9, 1938, p. 24.

Hurston, Zora Neale. "A Negro Voter Sizes Up Taft." *Saturday Evening Post,* December 8, 1951.

Huxley, Aldous. *Brave New World.* New York: Harper & Row, 1969/1932.

Ickes, Harold. *The Autobiography of a Curmudgeon.* New York: Reynal & Hitchcock, 1943.

———. "Who Killed the Progressive Party?" *American Historical Review,* January 1941.

"Interview with Wendell Berry." *Safe Food News,* Winter 1994.

"Invite Movie Witnesses." *New York Times,* August 18, 1941.

Jacoby, Russell. *The Last Intellectuals.* New York: Basic, 1987.

James, Henry. "Pandora." In *The Novels and Tales of Henry James,* vol. 18. New York: Scribner's, 1909.

"James Hetfield." *Rolling Stone,* April 15, 1993.

Jeffers, Robinson. *Collected Poetry of Robinson Jeffers,* edited by Tim Hunt. Stanford: Stanford University Press, 1988.

———. *The Double Axe,* foreword by William Everson. New York: Liveright, 1977/1948.

———. *Rock and Hawk,* edited by Robert Hass. New York: Random House, 1987.

Jefferson, Thomas. *Jefferson: Writings.* New York: Library of America, 1984.

Johnson, Claudius O. *Borah of Idaho.* New York: Longmans, Green: 1936.

Judis, John. "White House Vigilante." *The New Republic,* January 26, 1987.

Kaplan, Justin. *Walt Whitman: A Life.* New York: Simon and Schuster, 1980.

Kernell, Samuel, and Samuel L. Popkin, eds. *Chief of Staff:*

25 Years of Managing the Presidency. Berkeley and Los Angeles: University of California Press, 1986.

Kerouac, Jack. "Belief and Technique for Modern Prose." *Evergreen Review* 2, no. 8 (1959).

————. *On the Road.* New York: Viking, 1957.

————. "The Origins of the Beat Generation." *Playboy,* June 1959.

————. *Visions of Cody.* New York: McGraw-Hill, 1972.

————. *Visions of Gerard.* New York: Farrar, Straus & Giroux, 1963.

Knight, Arthur and Kit, eds. *The Beat Vision.* New York: Paragon, 1987.

Koblas, John. *Sinclair Lewis: Home At Last.* Bloomington, Minn.: Voyageur, 1981.

Korda, Michael. *Charmed Lives.* New York: Random House, 1979.

Krock, Arthur. "In the Nation." *New York Times,* December 14, 1937, p. 26.

La Follette, Belle Case and Fola. *Robert M. La Follette.* 2 vols. New York: Macmillan, 1953.

La Follette, Robert M. *A Personal Narrative of Political Experience.* Madison: Blied, 1911.

Lasch, Christopher. *The True and Only Heaven.* New York: Norton, 1991.

Lawson, R. Alan. *The Failure of Independent Liberalism.* New York: Putnam's, 1971.

Lazare, Daniel. "Pat Buchanan Keeps the Faith." *Present Tense,* January–February 1990.

Le Guin, Ursula. *The Language of the Night.* New York: Putman, 1978.

Lewis, Sinclair. *Arrowsmith.* New York: Harcourt, Brace, 1925.

————. *Babbitt.* New York: Harcourt, Brace, 1922.

————. *Cass Timberlane.* New York: Random House, 1945.

————. *Dodsworth.* New York: Harcourt, Brace, 1929.

————. *Elmer Gantry.* New York: Harcourt, Brace, 1927.

————. *Gideon Planish.* New York: Random House, 1946.

Lewis, Sinclair. *It Can't Happen Here*. Garden City, N.Y.: Doubleday, Doran, 1935.

———. *Kingsblood Royal*. New York: Random House, 1947.

———. *Main Street*. New York: Harcourt, Brace, 1920.

———. "Main Street's Been Paved." *The Nation,* September 10, 1924.

———. *The Man Who Knew Coolidge*. New York: Harcourt, Brace, 1928.

———. *The Prodigal Parents*. Garden City, N.Y.: Doubleday, Doran, 1938.

Liberty Poems: Inspired by the Crisis of 1898–1900. Boston: James H. West, 1900.

"Lillian Gish Quits America First Group." *New York Times,* September 2, 1941.

Lindsay, Vachel. *Collected Poems*. New York: Macmillan, 1925.

Long, Huey. *My First Days in the White House*. Harrisburg, Pa.: Telegraph Press, 1935.

Longstaff, S. A. "*Partisan Review* and the Second World War." *Salmagundi* 43 (Winter 1979).

Longworth, Alice Roosevelt. *Crowded Hours*. New York: Scribner's, 1933.

———. "What's the Matter with Bob Taft?" *Saturday Evening Post,* May 4, 1940.

Loomis, Mildred J. *Alternative Americas*. New York: Universe, 1982.

Ludlow, Louis. "Vision of Jefferson." *Vital Speeches,* May 15, 1940.

"The Ludlow Resolution." *New York Times,* December 16, 1937, p. 26.

Lutton, Wayne. "Edward Abbey, R.I.P." *Chronicles,* June 1990.

Lytle, Andrew. "They Took Their Stand: The Agrarian View after Fifty Years." *Modern Age,* Spring 1980.

McCarthy, Eugene J. *The Limits of Power*. New York: Holt, Rinehart and Winston, 1967.

McCarthy, Eugene J. *Up 'Til Now*. New York: Harcourt Brace Jovanovich, 1987.

McClaughry, John. "Announcement of Candidacy for the United States Senate." Mimeograph, May 13, 1982.

———. "Decentralizing Vermont." Institute for Liberty and Community, August 9, 1975.

———. "The Future of Private Property and Its Distribution." *Ripon Quarterly,* Fall 1974.

———. "A Political Message from Senator John McClaughry." Printed material, March 1992.

———. "Populism for the '80s Gaining Momentum." *Human Events,* April 16, 1983.

McClaughry, John, and Frank Bryan. *The Vermont Papers.* Colchester, Vt.: Chelsea Green, 1989.

McCoy, Donald R. *Angry Voices: Left-of-Center Politics in the New Deal.* Lawrence: University of Kansas Press, 1950.

McCullough, David. *Truman.* New York: Simon and Schuster, 1992.

McCullough, Joseph B. *Hamlin Garland.* Boston: Twayne, 1978.

Macdonald, Dwight. *Discriminations.* New York: Da Capo, 1985/1974.

———. *Memoirs of a Revolutionist.* New York: Farrar, Straus and Cudahy, 1957.

MacLeish, Archibald. "The Irresponsibles." *The Nation,* May 18, 1940.

McMath, Robert C., Jr. *Populist Vanguard: A History of the Southern Farmers' Alliance.* New York: Norton, 1975.

Madsen, Axel. *William Wyler.* New York: Crowell, 1973.

Mailer, Norman. "An Instrument for the City." In *Existential Errands.* Boston: Little, Brown, 1972.

Maney, Patrick J. *Young Bob La Follette.* Columbia: University of Missouri Press, 1978.

Marquand, John P. *B.F.'s Daughter.* Boston: Little, Brown, 1946.

———. *So Little Time.* Boston: Little, Brown, 1943.

Masters, Edgar Lee. *The Enduring River,* introduction by Herbert
K. Russell. Carbondale: Southern Illinois University Press, 1991.
———. *Lincoln, The Man.* New York: Dodd, Mead, 1931.
———. "Stephen A. Douglas." *The American Mercury,* January
1931.
Masters, Hardin Wallace. *Edgar Lee Masters.* Madison, N.J.:
Farleigh Dickinson, 1978.
Matthau, Carol. *Among the Porcupines.* New York: Turtle Bay,
1992.
Mencken, H. L. *A Carnival of Buncombe.* Chicago: University
of Chicago Press, 1984/1956.
———. *A Mencken Chrestomathy.* New York: Knopf, 1949.
———. *My Life As Author and Editor.* New York: Knopf, 1992.
Miller, Merle. "One Man's Long Journey." *New York Times
Magazine,* January 7, 1973.
Milton, Joyce. *Loss of Eden: A Biography of Charles and Anne
Morrow Lindbergh.* New York: HarperColins, 1993.
Morison, Elting E., ed. *The Letters of Theodore Roosevelt,* vols.
7 and 8. Cambridge, Mass.: Harvard University Press, 1954.
"Movies Feed Propaganda, Nye Charges at Inquiry." *New York
Times,* September 10, 1941, p. 1.
Mowry, George E. *The California Progressives.* Berkeley and
Los Angeles: University of California Press, 1951.
———. *Theodore Roosevelt and the Progressive Movement.* New
York: Hill & Wang, 1946.
"The New Isolationism: An Interview with Murray Rothbard
and Leonard Liggio." *Reason,* February 1973.
Nisbet, Robert A. *Conservatism: Dream and Reality.* Minnea-
polis: University of Minnesota Press, 1986.
———. *The Present Age.* New York: Harper & Row, 1988.
Noonan, Peggy. *What I Saw at the Revolution.* New York:
Random House, 1990.
Norris, Frank. "Novelists of the Future." In *Collected Works,*
vol. 7. Garden City, N.Y.: Doubleday, Doran, 1928.
———. *The Octopus.* New York: Viking, 1986/1901.

Norris, Kathleen. *Noon: An Autobiographical Sketch.* Garden City, N.J.: Country Life, 1924.

Nye, Gerald P. "Testimony before Senate Committee on Cause for Propaganda Investigation." *Congressional Record,* October 6, 1941.

Nye, Gerald P. "War Propaganda." *Vital Speeches,* September 15, 1941.

Oglesby, Carl, and Richard Schaull. *Containment and Change.* New York: Macmillan, 1967.

Olerich, Henry. *A Cityless and Countryless World.* Holstein, Iowa: Gilmore & Olerich, 1893.

Olin, Spencer C. *California's Prodigal Sons.* Berkeley and Los Angeles: University of California Press, 1968.

Pareles, Jon. "The Blue Messiahs Raise a Ruckus." *New York Times,* September 24, 1986.

———. "Country Boys Plow the Past for Songs." *New York Times,* September 4, 1988.

Paris, Barry. *Louise Brooks.* New York: Knopf, 1989.

Parrington, Vernon. *Main Currents in American Thought.* New York: Harcourt, Brace, 1930.

"Pat Buchanan: The *Liberty* Interview." *Liberty,* March 1992.

"Pat Buchanan's Small World." *New York Times,* editorial, January 13, 1992.

"Patriotic Gore." *The New Republic,* April 28, 1986.

Patterson, James T. *Congressional Conservatism and the New Deal.* Lexington: University of Kentucky Press, 1967.

———. *Mr. Republican: A Biography of Robert A. Taft.* Boston: Houghton Mifflin, 1972.

Pinchot, Amos R. E. "Captain Hoover: Afloat in a Sieve." *The Nation,* March 23, 1932.

———. "A Fair Deal for the Public." *The Forum,* February 1924.

———. "The Flag and the Dollar." *The Forum,* September 1927.

Pinchot, Amos R. E. *History of the Progressive Party 1912–1916,* edited by Helene Maxwell Hooker. New York: New York University Press, 1958.

———. "Hoover and the 'Big Lift.' " *The Nation,* December 26, 1928.

———. "Hoover and Power." *The Nation,* August 5–12, 1931.

———. "The Liberal Position." *North American Review,* December 1937.

———. "Relief: 1931 Style." *The Nation,* December 16, 1931.

———. "Two Revolts against Oligarchy." *McClures,* September 1910.

———. "We Meet Mr. Hoover." *The Nation,* January 14, 1931.

———. "What Shall Germany Pay?" *The Forum,* April 1921.

"Pinchot's War on Perkins." *The Literary Digest,* June 20, 1914.

Pizer, Donald. *Hamlin Garland's Early Work and Career.* Berkeley and Los Angeles: University of California Press, 1960.

Pizer, Donald, ed. *Hamlin Garland's Diaries.* San Marino: Huntington Library, 1968.

Podhoretz, Norman. "A Monument to Jack Kerouac?" *Washington Post,* January 8, 1986.

"President Perot?" *Time,* May 25, 1992.

Pringle, Henry F. *Theodore Roosevelt.* New York: Harcourt, Brace, 1931.

Radosh, Ronald. *Prophets on the Right.* New York: Simon and Schuster, 1975.

Radosh, Ronald, and Murray N. Rothbard, eds. *A New History of Leviathan.* New York: Dutton, 1972.

Raimondo, Justin. "Bring Back the Bricker Amendment." *Free Market,* September 1992.

Ravenal, Earl C. *Defining Defense.* Washington, D.C.: Cato Institute, 1984.

Reagan, Ronald. *An American Life.* New York: Simon & Schuster, 1990.

Real, Jere. "Gore Vidal, Roman Senator." *Inquiry,* May 17, 1982.

Remini, Robert. *Henry Clay: Statesman for the Union.* New York: Norton, 1991.

Remnick, David. "Our Nation Turns Its Lonely Eyes to H. Ross Perot." *The Washington Post Magazine,* April 12, 1987.

Ribuffo, Leo P. *The Old Christian Right: The Protestant Right from the Great Depression to the Cold War.* Philadelphia: Temple University Press, 1983.

Risjord, Norman K. *Old Republicans: Southern Conservatism in the Age of Jefferson.* New York: Columbia University Press, 1965.

"Ross Perot's Formula for Totalitarian Rule." *In These Times,* June 24–July 7, 1992.

Rothbard, Murray N. "Confessions of a Right-Wing Liberal." *Ramparts,* June 15, 1968.

———. "A Foreign Policy for the Post-Cold War World." *Chronicles,* May 1990.

Rothbard, Murray N. "The Foreign Policy of the Old Right." *Journal of Libertarian Studies,* Winter 1978.

———. "A Strategy for the Right." *Rothbard-Rockwell Report,* March 1992.

———. "The Transformation of the American Right." *Continuum,* Summer 1964.

Rothbard, Murray N., and Karl Hess, eds. *The Libertarian Forum.* New York: Arno, 1972.

Rudolph, Frederick. "The American Liberty League, 1934–1940." *American Historical Review,* October 1950.

Safire, William. "Buchanan's Campaign." *New York Times,* December 16, 1991.

———. "When an Aide Dies Violently." *New York Times,* August 2, 1993.

Salvatore, Nick. *Eugene V. Debs: Citizen and Socialist.* Urbana: University of Illinois Press, 1982.

Saroyan, William. *The Adventures of Wesley Jackson.* New York: Harcourt, Brace, 1946.

Schacht, John N., ed. *Three Faces of Midwestern Isolationism.*

Iowa City: Center for the Study of the Recent History of the United States, 1981.

Schlesinger, Arthur. "Desperate Times." *New York Review of Books,* November 24, 1983.

Schmidt, Hans. *Maverick Marine.* Lexington: University Press of Kentucky, 1987.

Schorer, Mark. *Sinclair Lewis: An American Life.* New York: McGraw-Hill, 1961.

Schwartz, Nancy Lynn. *The Hollywood Writers' War.* New York: Knopf, 1982.

Shain, Russell Earl. *An Analysis of Motion Pictures about War Released by the American Film Industry 1930-1970.* New York: Arno, 1976.

Shapiro, H. R. *Democracy in America.* New York: Manhattan Communications, 1986.

Sherwood, Robert. *Abe Lincoln in Illinois.* New York: Scribner's, 1937.

———. *Idiot's Delight.* New York: Scribner's, 1936.

Shivers, Alfred S. *The Life of Maxwell Anderson.* New York: Stein and Day, 1983.

"Should the People Declare War?" *New York Times,* December 19, 1937, iv, p. 8.

Shuman, R. Baird. *Robert E. Sherwood.* Boston: Twayne, 1964.

Sipchen, Bob. "Abbey: Rage on the Range." *Washington Post,* January 5, 1988.

———. "Author Edward Abbey Is Remembered." Rochester, N.Y., *Democrat & Chronicle,* May 23, 1989.

"The Situation in American Writing." *Partisan Review,* Summer–Fall, 1939.

Stanton, Doug. "Jack and Diane are Dead." *Esquire,* March 1992.

Steinbeck, John. *The Grapes of Wrath.* New York: Viking, 1939.

Stephenson, William. *A Man Called Intrepid.* New York: Harcourt, Brace, 1976.

Stone, I. F. "Fulbright of Arkansas." *New York Review of Books,* December 29, 1966–January 12, 1967–January 26, 1967.

Stone, Ralph. *The Irreconcilables.* Lexington: University Press of Kentucky, 1970.

Sumner, William Graham. "The Conquest of the United States by Spain." In *On Liberty, Society, and Politics: The Essential Essays of William Graham Sumner.* Indianapolis: Liberty Fund, 1992/1898.

Swindell, Larry. *The Last Hero: A Biography of Gary Cooper.* Garden City, N.Y.: Doubleday, 1980.

Tannenbaum, Rob. "Steve Earle: Country Boy Rocks the Big City." *Rolling Stone,* September 11, 1986.

Taylor, John. *Arator.* Indianapolis: Liberty Classics, 1977/1818.

Teague, Michael. *Mrs. L: Conversations with Alice Roosevelt Longworth.* Garden City, N.Y.: Doubleday, 1981.

Teichmann, Howard. *Alice.* Englewood Cliffs, N.J.: Prentice-Hall, 1979.

Thompson, Dorothy. "The Man and Boy from Sauk Centre." *The Atlantic,* November 1960.

Thoreau, Henry David. *Walden.* New York: Signet, 1960/1854.

"To the Editor." *New York Times,* December 22, 1937, p. 14.

Tuccille, Jerome. "From Libertine to Libertarian." *Libertarian Forum,* January 15, 1970.

Twain, Mark. *A Connecticut Yankee in King Arthur's Court.* New York: Dodd, Mead, 1960/1889.

Twelve Southerners. *I'll Take My Stand.* Baton Rouge: Louisiana State University Press, 1977/1930.

Tweraser, Kurt. *Changing Patterns of Political Beliefs: The Foreign Policy Operational Codes of J. William Fulbright, 1943–1967.* London: Sage, 1974.

"Unpleasant Business." *National Review,* June 16, 1989.

Updike, John. *Buchanan Dying.* New York: Knopf, 1974.

"The Vidal Exemption." *National Review,* June 6, 1986.

Vidal, Gore. *At Home.* New York: Random House, 1988.

———. *Burr.* New York: Random House, 1973.

Vidal, Gore. *The City and the Pillar.* New York: Dutton, 1948.

———. *1876.* New York: Random House, 1976.

———. *Empire.* New York: Random House, 1987.

———. *Hollywood.* New York: Random House, 1990.

———. *Homage to Daniel Shays.* New York: Random House, 1972.

———. *Lincoln.* New York: Random House, 1984.

———. *Matters of Fact and Fiction.* New York: Random House, 1977.

———. *Screening History.* Cambridge, Mass.: Harvard University Press, 1992.

———. *The Second American Revolution.* New York: Random House, 1982.

———. *United States.* New York: Random House, 1993.

———. *Washington, D.C.* Boston: Little, Brown, 1967.

Vidal, Gore, and Robert J. Stanton, eds. *Views from a Window: Conversations with Gore Vidal.* Secaucus, N.J.: Lyle Stuart, 1980.

Villard, Oswald Garrison. "Issues and Men." *The Nation,* June 22–June 29, 1940.

Vinson, John Chalmers. *William E. Borah and the Outlawry of War.* Athens: University of Georgia Press, 1957.

von Hoffman, Nicholas. *Make-Believe Presidents.* New York: Pantheon, 1978.

"War Propaganda Is Denied by Hays." *New York Times,* September 1, 1941, p. 17.

"War Referendum Is Defeated in the House as Roosevelt Scores It." *New York Times,* January 11, 1938, p. 1.

"War Referendum Revived in Senate." *New York Times,* March 1, 1939, p. 1.

"War Referendum Up in House Today." *New York Times,* January 10, 1938, p. 1.

Warren, Donald. "Ross Perot and Middle-American Radicalism." *Chronicles,* April 1993.

Washington, George. "Washington's Farewell Address." In *Documents of American History,* vol. 24. New York: Meredith, 1946/1796.

Weinberger, Caspar W. "The Uses of Military Power." *Defense* 85 (January 1985).

Weiss, Marc. "He's a Hillbilly and Proud of It." *Los Angeles Herald,* March 17, 1986.

Wheeler, Burton K. *Yankee from the West.* New York: Doubleday, 1962.

"Where Are the Pre-War Radicals?" *Survey* 55 (February 1, 1926).

Whitaker, Robert W. *The New Right Papers.* New York: St. Martin's Press, 1982.

White, William Allen. *The Autobiography of William Allen White.* New York: Macmillan, 1946.

Whitman, Walt. "Democratic Vistas." In *Whitman: Poetry and Prose.* New York: Library of America, 1982/1871.

———. *Leaves of Grass.* New York: Doubleday, Doran, 1928/1855.

"Why Is Buchanan So Angry?" *Newsweek,* January 27, 1992.

Wilkins, Robert P. "Middle Western Isolationism: A Re-Examination." *North Dakota Quarterly* 25 (Summer 1957).

Williams, T. Harry. *Huey Long.* New York: Knopf, 1969.

Williams, William Appleman. *America Confronts a Revolutionary World: 1776–1976.* New York: Morrow, 1976.

———. *The Contours of American History.* Chicago: Quadrangle, 1966/1961.

———. *Empire As a Way of Life.* New York: Oxford, 1980.

———. *Some Presidents: From Wilson to Nixon.* New York: Vintage, 1972.

Williamson, Chilton. "Striking Back at the Empire." *Arizona Republic,* February 23, 1992.

Wills, Garry. *Confessions of a Conservative.* New York: Doubleday, 1979.

Wilson, Clyde. "The Future of American Nationalism." *Chronicles.* November 1990.

Wilson, Edmund. *The Cold War and the Income Tax.* New York: Farrar, Straus, 1964.

———. *Patriotic Gore.* New York: Oxford, 1962.

Wilson, Joan Hoff. *Herbert Hoover: Forgotten Progressive.* Boston: Little, Brown, 1975.

Wood, Grant. "Revolt against the City." In Dennis James, *Grant Wood.* New York: Viking, 1975/1935.

Woodward, C. Vann. *Tom Watson: Agrarian Rebel.* New York: Oxford, 1972/1938.

Wrenn, John H. and Margaret. *Edgar Lee Masters.* Boston: Twayne, 1983.

"You Can't Go Home." *The Economist,* September 28, 1991.

"Young Bill Clinton Didn't Impress Fulbright." *New York Times,* January 22, 1993 .

Zweig, Paul. *Walt Whitman: The Making of the Poet.* New York: Basic, 1984.

Index